WATER'S EDGE

WOMEN WHO PUSH THE LIMITS IN ROWING, KAYAKING & CANOEING

LINDA LEWIS

THE SEAL PRESS

Cover photos: Cathy Hearn (kayaker) and 1984 Women's Olympic Eight (rowing), copyright © Brian Hill 1992. All rights reserved.

Design by Clare Conrad.

Library of Congress Cataloging-in Publication Data
Lewis, Linda, 1948–
    Water's edge : women who pushed the limits in rowing, kayaking & canoeing / by Linda Lewis.
        p.   cm.
    ISBN 1-878067-18-4 (pbk.)
    1. Women rowers—United States—Biography.   2. Women canoeists—United States—Biography.   I. Title.
GV790.9.L48   1992
797.1'23'0922—dc20
[B]
                                                                              92-4361
                                                                              CIP

Printed in the United States of America.
First printing, June 1992
10 9 8 7 6 5 4 3 2 1

Foreign Distribution:
In Canada: Raincoast Book Distribution, Vancouver, B.C.
In the U.K. and Europe: Airlift Book Company, London.

Acknowledgments

I owe special thanks to a number of people for their contributions to this book. First of all, Mary-Carter Creech deserves mention for sacrificing part of her birthday celebration so that the idea of doing such a book could begin to form. I want to thank her, too, along with Jane Hadley, for dragging me to my first rowing experience at six o'clock on a cold February morning.

All of the athletes who agreed to be interviewed were generous with their time and extremely thoughtful and articulate about the activities in which they are so engaged. Their obvious passion for their sports was inspirational. The material from these athletes was so rich that I regret not being able to profile every one of them. Thanks to Sherri Cassuto, Holly Hatton, Nancy Storrs, Peggy McCarthy and Elizabeth Hayman for providing particular insight into the athletes whom I did profile.

Both the U.S. Rowing Association and the U.S. Canoe and Kayak Team provided invaluable support, supplying facts and tracking down photographs. Photographers M.L. Thomas, Susan Stein and Craig Bohnert were generous with their images. Wanda Downing from Anita DeFrantz's office was especially helpful in delivering photographs.

I would not have known where to begin without the guidance of Sara Lopez, who is one of rowing's most effective advocates. She had compiled her own archives, filled with fascinating material about women in the sport. She freely turned these over to me and then dug up more information whenever I needed it.

George Scheer was kind enough to apply his more than fifty years' experience in the book business to a reading of my first draft. His suggestions were invaluable. Faith Conlon of Seal Press has been everything an editor should be—exacting, fair and brilliant. In her hands, my manuscript became a much leaner, more focused, more athletic piece of work. Thanks, too, to Seal's Holly Morris for her meticulous copyediting and Clare Conrad for her design.

I want to thank my parents, Herman and Barbara Lewis, for their support; Walker Richer & Quinn, Inc., for giving me steady work; and the women of the Conibear Rowing Club, for their example and their companionship.

Finally, I want to express my gratitude to Bonnie Harris for her encouragement, patience, tireless reading, helpful suggestions and, above all, for giving me a home.

Seattle, Washington
December, 1991

For Bonnie

CONTENTS

WATER'S EDGE

ROWING

First, there is the poetry of rowing, which women have known since the late nineteenth century. The motion of the stroke is grace itself, a fluid gesture that propels the delicate shell inexorably forward. The sun is wedging itself into the pale sky. A mist rises off the still water. The shell barely intrudes. Eight rowers slide forward on their moving seats, drop their oars as one into the water, catch the momentum and pass it on, release the water and listen for its rush beneath the boat. They repeat this gesture endlessly, captive to its rhythm. Quickly, the water smoothes over any trace of their presence. And the rowers themselves forget their separateness.

But then there is the pain of rowing, which women were not encouraged to know until the 1970s. Second only to cross-country skiing in the demands that it puts on an athlete, competitive rowing was for more than a century only a masculine endeavor. Ideally, the rower in a race passes out on the stroke that sends the boat across the finish line. Such a complete expenditure of effort for something so extravagant as sport has never been considered feminine. But in the 1970s, women began to be heard when they said, "To hell with what you think is feminine. I'm going to be the best athlete I can." They began to see how hard they could push themselves and how fast they could make boats go. They welcomed the pain because it signalled the edge of their limits. The longer they could coexist with the pain, the stronger they were getting. Sometimes, they stayed with the pain so long that it ceased being a boundary and became instead a door, flung wide to immortality.

3

To know both the poetry and the pain of rowing, women have had to fight—first just to be allowed to have their own races, then to be given facilities and coaching equal to those their male counterparts were receiving. When Ernestine Bayer wanted to race in the 1930s, she had to start a club and a movement in defiance of one of the most tradition-bound amateur athletic fraternities in the United States. By the time her efforts paid off, she was too old to race at the level she had envisioned. Even her daughter was too old. But the next generation of women embraced her work and turned it into gold at the 1984 Olympics. And other individual women—like Anita DeFrantz and Kris Karlson—have recorded remarkable political and athletic achievements in rowing since Bayer first put her oar into the water.

Consequently, countless women now know the passion of rowing, from the self-mastery and control of single sculling to the communion of the eight. They know the groove that rowing wears in the soul where nothing else can ever fit.

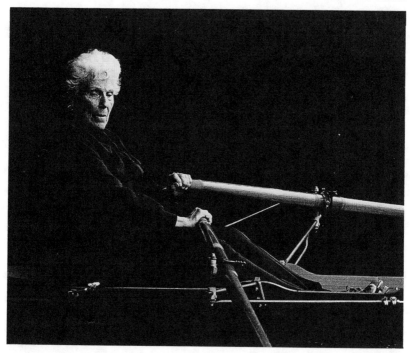

Ernestine Bayer is the matriarch of women's rowing. Her efforts to establish a competitive program for women in the U.S. began in 1938, when she founded the Philadelphia Girls Rowing Club. Now in her eighties, Bayer still competes in at least two regattas a year.

Ernestine Bayer

~

EARLY ON A BRISK December morning in 1984, nine women took a borrowed shell from Philadelphia's Vesper Boat Club for a short row on the Schuylkill River. The women had all been inducted into rowing's hall of fame the night before in an emotion-filled ceremony. The chill of the morning air and the mist rising from the still waters of the river provided a delicious contrast with the heat and excitement of the previous evening. The moment just before the row began was particularly sharp and poignant for the woman sitting in the number two seat of the shell. This woman did not look like the others in the boat. She was smaller and considerably older, by about fifty years. The other eight women—the coxswain and seven rowers—were Olympic gold medalists, having swept with power and precision to that honor just four months earlier. The white-haired woman had never rowed in an Olympic event or even in any kind of elite national competition. Yet, the eight gold medalists felt that they owed what they had accomplished in rowing to her. They had impulsively invited her to row with them the night before when they were all celebrating how far women had come in a sport that was closed to them for so long. The eight Olympic gold medalists had used all the words they knew to thank this white-haired woman for insisting, nearly fifty years earlier, on women's right to row competitively. Now they wanted her to feel with her body what a force she had unleashed.

The Olympic eight wanted to perform exquisitely, to show the woman in the number two seat the level of athletic accomplishment that she had made possible. There was some hesitation, though, out of deference to the woman's age. The eight wondered how much of a display of speed and strength they could put on without pushing her too hard. After all, they were in their twenties and thirties, the best rowers in the world. She was seventy-five and primarily a recreational rower. If they took the stroke rate up too high, would they turn what was meant to be a triumph into a disaster?

As the coxswain considered what cadence to call after the warm-up, the woman in the number two seat yelled out: "Let's do a start and a ten."

She was asking to feel the boat's explosiveness off the starting line. A start is five rapid strokes designed to get sixty feet of shell and 1,500 pounds of bodies moving. The ten strokes after the start are full power strokes at the high rate set in motion by the start.

The coxswain stopped the boat and got the rowers ready for a start. All eight moved forward on their sliding seats, planted their blades in the water and breathed deeply, preparing for the quick burst that would get the boat going. The coxswain gave the traditional French starting sequence: *"Etes vous prêts?"* (*Are you ready?*) Every body was at the same angle, knees bent, back forward, arms extended, compressed, poised to release maximum power.

"Partez." (*Go.*)

All eight oars pulled as one. The shell heaved through the water as the rowers rammed their legs down and pulled through on the oars to pry the boat forward. All eight brought the oars out of the water together and slid forward on their seats together to begin the next stroke. After the tenth power stroke, the coxswain told the rowers to *"weigh enough"* (*stop*) and let the boat glide.

For a moment there was only the rush of water and the

sound of hard breathing. All nine women floated in a cocoon of suspended time. Then from the number two seat again came the call: "Let's take a start and a ten."

The other women in the boat came fully awake. They understood immediately what the tone of that request implied. The honored guest in the number two seat was saying to them, "Come on, you gold medalists, show me how it *really* feels." She was challenging them to row as hard and as fast as they could. That first start and ten had not been at full pressure. The Olympians had held something back. They had been quick and graceful but had not turned on the explosive power. The woman in the number two seat had kept her part of the bargain, staying right with them. Now she wanted to see what more they all could do.

The second five-stroke start and ten high on that December morning was charged. All eight rowers moved up their slides into the starting position determined to hold nothing back. They buried their blades in the water and shook the tension out of their shoulders. They were coiled and ready to explode when the starting command came. *"Partez."* The boat flew, slicing through the placid waters of the Schuylkill. With every stroke, the rowers translated their muscle into motion. They took every stroke as one flawless unit, achieving a power that transcended their individual efforts and lifted the boat over the water. When the rowers stopped and feathered their oars so the boat could glide, Ernestine Bayer, in the number two seat, wept.

✦ ✦ ✦

Ernestine Bayer is rowing's matriarch. Her efforts to establish a competitive rowing program for women led directly to the high point of women's rowing in the United States—the eight's winning of the gold medal in the 1984 Olympics. Her continuing involvement in the sport is an inspiration. She is in her eighties, and she still competes in certain regattas. People point and exclaim when they spot that cap of white hair and that sharp, intense profile out on the water, gracefully rowing her single to the starting line.

Ernestine Bayer began working for women's right to row in 1938 when she founded the Philadelphia Girls Rowing Club (PGRC), which marked the beginning of the modern women's competitive rowing movement. From the PGRC's boathouse on the Schuylkill River, she taught hundreds of young women how to row in the forties, fifties and sixties. She rowed in the first women's race on the Schuylkill in 1938. In 1967, she took the first American women's eight to compete in Europe, where they proved they had the skills to go up against international crews. And she served on the first U.S. Women's Olympic Rowing Committee, which sent rowers to the Montreal games in 1976.

Ernestine Bayer now lives with her husband and daughter in Stratham, New Hampshire, in a spacious house on nine acres along the Squamscott River. She likes to imagine rowing from the dock in her back yard all the way to France. Such an adventure is possible, for the Squamscott flows into Great Bay, which leads to the Atlantic. Rowing has taken Ernestine Bayer to Europe already, but that was the plodding, plotting organizational side of the sport, not the pure, undiluted movement that she has sought all her life. All that Ernestine Bayer ever wanted to do was to race a rowing shell against other women. But to perform that simple act, she had to create an entire structure. She had to start from less than zero, faced with a firmly entrenched bias against women's participation in the sport. To get what she wanted, she had to sit in stuffy meeting rooms instead of in her single on her beloved Schuylkill River. She had to learn how to make astute political moves instead of concentrating on the timing of her oars' entry into the water. She never considered herself very good at politics. It was not her "dish of tea," as she puts it. Yet she managed to become proficient enough on the organizational side of rowing to stage the kind of races that she craved. The sad irony is that by the time women's events in regattas became accepted, Ernestine Bayer was too old to compete at an elite level.

✦ ✦ ✦

Ernestine Bayer was born Ernestine Stepbacher on March 25, 1909, in Philadelphia. Her parents had both been in the theater before retiring to open a candy business and to raise a family. Ernestine's brother Augustus was born eighteen months before she was. Her mother, who had used the stage name Lillian Verona and had played alongside W.C. Fields and Lillian Russell, constantly told young Ernestine that she could not do the things young Augustus did. Ernestine Bayer later recalled:

"I remember that for one birthday, my brother got a pony ride. I can still see him sitting on that pony. I wanted a ride, too. 'That's not for girls to do,' my mother said. I remember that. When my brother had a tricycle, I wanted one. My mother said, 'That's not for girls.' When he had a racing bike, I wanted a two-wheeler. My mother said, 'That's not for girls.'"

Rather than discouraging Ernestine, her mother's refrain worked as a challenge. "I remember my brother had a car. I was sixteen. I decided I was going to get in it and drive it around the neighborhood. I made it with no mishaps."

Ernestine was a fair student, but she excelled in gym class. In other classes, she was always looking out the window, longing for the bell that would release her to the outdoors. Her preference was to be in constant motion. Neither her mother nor her schooling encouraged that. When Ernestine graduated from high school, she went to work in a bank. She satisfied her need for motion by swimming during her leisure hours. One of her swimming pals was a woman whose family had a summer place near the Stepbachers' summer place at the Jersey shore. When this woman couldn't keep her swimming date with Ernestine one day in Philadelphia, she sent her brother instead. So Ernestine got acquainted with Ernest Bayer, a tall, lanky fellow who also worked in a bank in Philadelphia. But, more importantly, he was a rower. His rowing club was the Pennsylvania Barge Club on the Schuylkill River. He was an exceptionally good rower, and was being groomed for the 1928 Olympics.

In January of 1928, Ernestine Stepbacher married Ernest Bayer. They had to keep their marriage a secret until after the 1928 Olympic Games. Ernest Bayer had made the team, and his coach believed that sex sapped an athlete's strength. Nevertheless, Ernest's boat, a four without coxswain, won a silver medal in Amsterdam that year.

After the Olympics, Ernestine and Ernest could be seen together. They worked the same hours, nine to four, in different banks and met every day after work to walk together to Boathouse Row, where Ernest met his teammates at the Pennsylvania Barge Club for practice. Ernestine would sit on the porch and watch. One day, after ten years of sitting and watching Ernest and his fellow club members row, she asked him why women didn't row. He answered with a slight variation on her mother's refrain. "Women don't row," he said. That was all Ernestine Bayer needed to begin a lifelong devotion to seeing that women did row. That and the fact that her mother had been deathly afraid of water.

✦ ✦ ✦

On the day in 1938 that Ernestine Bayer's husband told her women didn't row, he was not entirely correct. Women were rowing at the time and had been for more than fifty years. They were not rowing in Philadelphia, which was then the center of the rowing universe for American men and had been for a hundred years. And they were not racing, which is the *raison d'etre* of the sport.

Organized rowing for women began in this country at Wellesley College in 1875. College founder Henry Durant encouraged the women at Wellesley to row on Lake Waban, a pretty little lake in the center of the three-hundred-acre campus. He considered the activity useful for developing the proper posture that was so important for the late nineteenth-century woman. Durant purchased three rowboats in which five pairs of rowers could sit side by side, each woman pulling her own oar.

The rowers occasionally ferried college guests across the lake from one building to another and entertained as they did so. Henry Wadsworth Longfellow was one of the Wellesley visitors transported this way. One of the boats was named *Evangeline* in honor of his October 1875 visit. The women who rowed him between buildings were chosen for their singing ability. As the rowing program developed, singing became much more important than rowing. In 1886, a pageant called Float Night made its first appearance, soon becoming an annual Wellesley tradition. Crews from each class would work all year writing songs, making costumes and designing floats. Then on a spring night, in front of hundreds of spectators who had taken the train out from Boston to stand along Lake Waban's shore, after the brass band played and before the fireworks went off, the rowers would demonstrate their form and their singing ability.

Float Night was at its most glorious by 1920 when a committee announced the theme in the fall so that crews would have plenty of time to prepare their floats. The students submitted their plans, and the committee chose nine for execution. College carpenters and electricians helped with the sets, each of which fit across two canoes. Each canoe had two paddlers, but the attention was not on the women doing the work of moving the canoes; it was on the women in costume aboard each float. These women waved to the spectators on shore as an announcer narrated the story that inspired their floats. The varsity crew that year, as every year, was called upon to display perfect rowing form to the spectators before the floats made their appearance.

Before Float Night began evolving into something to which the rowing motion was entirely incidental, a woman named Lucille Eaton Hill had instituted a crew program that insisted on discipline and devoted itself to the development of form. Gym Hill, as she was known, arrived at Wellesley in 1882 to be the first director of the Department of Physical Training. She believed in athletics for women as a means to health and beauty.

And she believed in rowing as a means of "developing the muscles of the girl symmetrically and teaching her bodily freedom and self-reliance." Gym Hill regularly invited crew and coaches from Harvard and Yale to Wellesley for advice, and she traveled to pick up pointers on technique. She brought in four eight-oared shells with sliding seats, just like those used at Harvard and Yale. The women of Wellesley were allowed to wear Turkish trousers under their long skirts and to remove their skirts once they were in the boat so that they could move more freely on the slides.

Gym Hill issued regulations for her crews: No sweets, iced beverages, caffeinated drinks or eating between meals. A minimum of eight hours of sleep a night. A cold plunge or sponge bath upon arising. Absolutely no hot baths. And no bathing after exercise, except in the unlikely event of perspiration. The women of Wellesley were taught to row for skill and grace rather than for the speed that their male counterparts sought. Gym Hill had a passion for form and a disdain for what she considered the evils of men's athletic programs. She was an extremely influential figure in the development of women's athletic programs in the United States around the turn of the century. She was editor of *Athletics and Outdoor Sports for Women*, a book published in 1903. In the introduction, she wrote: "Our ever present ideal should be Health and Beauty; and during this early stage of our experience in athletics our watchword should be 'Moderation.'"

Gym Hill was wary of competition unless it fostered the greatest good for the greatest number. One of the evils of men's athletic programs, in her opinion, was the development of a few talented athletes at the expense of everyone else. She also thought that racing led to professionalism and was generally unsocial, expensive and a cause of "unnecessary nerve fatigue." Her views dovetailed with society's perception of women as pure, fragile creatures who should not be permitted to assert themselves physically. The competition that Gym Hill allowed at Wellesley was on the basis of excellence in rowing form and was limited to intramural events.

Gym Hill left Wellesley in 1909 but remained a major influence in women's collegiate athletics. At a 1920 meeting of the Conference of College Directors of Physical Education, her view that women should not be involved in intercollegiate competitive sports prevailed. Wellesley crews did not even race against each other until later in the 1920s. They competed, but the competition was based on form. Sometime in the twenties, the scoring method in the intramural events was expanded to include form during a race. Then it was possible for a crew to finish first in a race but lose the competition because of low marks for technique. Vestiges of Gym Hill's passion for form lingered at Wellesley until 1964, when judging for technique disappeared altogether from the intramural scoring system, and Wellesley rowers began to win races the way men's crews did— by crossing the finish line first. In 1966, Wellesley participated in its first intercollegiate crew event, a challenge that came from the women of the Massachusetts Institute of Technology. In 1970, an official intercollegiate rowing program for women was established, and Wellesley was a participant.

On the West Coast, organized rowing for women got its start in 1892 when four teenagers formed a club around their explorations of San Diego Bay. The girls—Zulette Lamb and the three Polhamus sisters, Lena, Agnes and Caroline—named their club with the initials of their first names: ZLAC. They started rowing in a four-oared dinghy borrowed from a meat-packing company.

Lena Polhamus soon emerged as the leader of this group. She ordered an eight-oared rowing barge, priced at $1,000, in 1895 when the club had thirty-five cents in its treasury. The group had grown to ten by then, and the members got busy putting on skits and plays, holding dances and cooking dinners to raise money. The launching of the new barge was a spectacle, with nearly 1,000 people out of the town's 18,000 total turning out to watch the women row the new boat and hear a poem written for the event and a brief history of ZLAC.

Lena became captain and coach of the rowers. Eventually, she was named commodore, the designation that ZLAC decided to give its leader and one that the club retired when Lena did. She reigned over the club for forty years. For formal occasions, she would wear a military costume with buttons up the front, a tight upstanding collar and various Navy-like insignia. Crew members would wear full skirts, middies, black silk ties and dinner-plate hats.

ZLAC members rowed for exercise and adventure. They kept careful records of the number of rows made each year. Lena recorded forty-nine rows in 1915. She also described in the club records a "morning call on some man-o'-war, drinking high tea on board an English ship, or—drifting—singing—to the accompaniment of violin and guitar."

ZLAC members did some racing against each other, but the club was primarily social. Women met there for lunch and tea. They gave parties. They organized fundraising activities. ZLAC was able to buy property on the north shore of Mission Bay and build a clubhouse there in 1932. Deb DeAngelis, whose mother and grandmother had both belonged to ZLAC, joined in the 1960s at the age of fifteen, the earliest age at which a young woman could become a ZLAC. She described the event this way: "I was inducted at a tea where I had to prove I had the social skills to be a lady."

DeAngelis, who grew up hearing ZLAC lore, noted that despite the growing popularity of women's rowing clubs—by the turn of the century there were more than twenty in addition to ZLAC on San Diego Bay—the activity itself was restricted to "maiden ladies." "You had to stop rowing when you got married because it might damage your reproductive organs." Once married and forced to retire from rowing, a woman could nevertheless remain an active social member of ZLAC. She could use the club for lunch, teas and other events. She could participate in skits and fundraising activities. She could attend all club functions—bridge parties, fashion shows, rummage sales, dances. But she could not row.

DeAngelis rowed with ZLAC through the club's first competitive season in the mid-1960s. She was a member of the first competitive crew, which formed in response to a challenge from a women's crew from the Lake Merritt Rowing Club in Oakland, California. ZLAC practiced only on Saturdays for races against Lake Merritt. "Lake Merritt would trounce us. They would practice every day."

DeAngelis moved on to more serious competitive programs in the 1970s. In 1971, she was in the first women's crew program at Santa Barbara College and rowed competitively in a four. After college, she moved to Long Beach, which was the training center for sculling. She went to her first national competition in 1973, rowing a single. She made the national team in 1975. No matter what her achievements in rowing, they were always reported on the society pages.

✦ ✦ ✦

Deb DeAngelis characterized the ZLAC approach as the social side of rowing and the Wellesley approach as the figure skating side. These were the two models that prevailed in 1938, when Ernestine Bayer decided that she wanted to row. She was not aware of either of these models. She knew only what her husband Ernest had told her: Women did not row. Once, she had pressed him to elaborate on the fact that women did not row. Their exchange went like this:

Ernestine: "I would like to row. Why don't women row?"

Ernest: "Women don't row."

Ernestine: "Why not?"

Ernest: "Women don't row. Besides, they don't have a place to row."

Ernestine Bayer then had a definite obstacle that she could overcome. If she found a place for women to row, then women could row. She began to scheme about getting that place. Her scheming took on an urgency and a new dimension the day she saw a woman actually rowing on the Schuylkill River. She saw Lovey Kohut rowing a single past Boathouse Row, a small group of buildings along the east side of the river just above the Fairmount Dam, which, when it was constructed in 1822, created a perfect, three-mile-long pool for rowing. These structures, built in the mid-1800s, house some of the oldest and most famous rowing clubs in the country. In 1938, the membership of the Boathouse Row clubs was exclusively male and not about to change. After seeing Lovey, Ernestine approached Ernest with more questions:

Ernestine: "Who was that woman out there rowing today?"

Ernest: "Oh, that's the girlfriend of Tommy Farrell, and that's his boat. She takes it out once in awhile."

Ernestine: "If she can row, why can't I?"

Ernest: "That's different. She's the girlfriend."

It didn't take Ernestine long to figure out her strategy: She would organize a group of rowers' girlfriends and find a place they could use as a boathouse. At Fidelity Trust Company, where she worked, Ernestine sat around the corner from Gladys Hauser, who was going out with a member of the Fairmount Rowing Club (another Boathouse Row institution) and who knew other women in the same situation. She approached Gladys with her idea and asked her for introductions to other women connected to rowers. Gladys rounded up everyone she could from the Fairmount group. Ernestine recruited Lovey Kohut. And the fourteen women who met to form their own rowing organization decided to call themselves the Philadelphia Girls Rowing Club. Ernestine, who was twenty-eight at the time and ten years older than any other woman in the group, was elected president. Lovey Kohut, who was the only one who knew how to row, was elected captain.

PGRC set up its boathouse in what had been a skating club in one of the buildings along Boathouse Row. Ernestine had spotted the building, learned that an officer in her bank was a member of the skating club and gotten him to introduce her to the club's president. Soon PGRC had a home, complete with showers and lockers, for forty dollars a month. Ernestine Bayer had a place to row. Now she needed to learn how to row.

In May of 1938 her husband Ernest put her in a boat for the first time. The boat was a gig, a wide-bottomed rowboat. Ernest made sure that Ernestine had a grip on the two oars. Then he pushed her away from the dock along Boathouse Row and into the middle of the Schuylkill River. Ernestine has not forgotten that first row: "I rowed in circles. The harder I tried, the worse I got. All the boys on their porches stood there and laughed their fool heads off. I got madder and madder. It made me more determined than ever to row well."

All the boys on all the porches along Boathouse Row, laughing at a woman trying to row for the first time, had no inkling that some day women would row as well and as seriously as they did. When the boys joined the rowing clubs along the Schuylkill River, they entered an exclusively male domain that was likely the most tradition-bound athletic fraternity anywhere in the country. The clubs had their start in the early 1850s, and by 1858, the Schuylkill Navy was founded by nine of the clubs to supervise and regulate amateur rowing competition on the river. It was the oldest controlling body for amateur sport in the United States. The reputation of rowing as a gentlemen's sport was briefly threatened in the late 1800s by the rise of professional oarsmen and the unsavory business of rowing for money, but that menace had passed by the 1890s, when spectators turned their attention to baseball and horse racing. The men in the clubs along Boathouse Row never suspected that the next threat to their domain would come from the women they loved. The appearance of the PGRC sent shock waves through the dark, musty clubhouses along the row. Ernestine watched the aftershocks: "There were men that my husband knew that wouldn't speak to us. The commodore [of the Schuylkill Navy] was furious. One oarsman took my husband aside and warned him that if he permitted me to row, I would get tuberculosis.

And then, of course, there were those who said that many of the girls were just down there for the boys."

Soon there were defections from the fraternity. Ernest Bayer offered to coach any women determined to try rowing. Tom Curran, who had rowed in the 1930 world champion eight, also offered to coach. Fred Plaisted, who had been a professional rower, gave the PGRC two old boats. Ernestine Bayer's second row was in a training barge borrowed from the University of Pennsylvania. Sixteen women—eight on each side—sat in the barge and rowed while Ernest Bayer walked up and down the aisle in between them, stopping by each woman to give instruction.

By July 1938, the women of PGRC felt they were ready to race. They borrowed three racing doubles and organized their own event as part of a traditional Fourth of July regatta on the Schuylkill. Jeanette Waetjen and Ernestine Bayer rowed in one double. Lovey Kohut and Stella Sokolowski rowed in another. Ruth Adams and Betty Flavin were in the third. The race was half a mile.

Ernestine: "We went up to that line not knowing what was going to happen. I was fearful of Lovey. She weighed 170 pounds. We were lightweights—I rowed at 128 and Jeanette at 118. They caught crabs [misplaced strokes that slow or even stop the boat] and we didn't. Of all the races I've been in, that's the one I remember best. And I'm glad I won."

That first sweet taste of victory only whetted Ernestine Bayer's appetite. Within six months, she had bought a used single scull. For years, from May until October, she rowed that single for an hour every day after work. After she developed a serious interest in the sport, she and Ernest ate dinner out every night.

✦ ✦ ✦

Once they began racing, PGRC rowers became a fixture on the regatta scene. They were the only women in what had been, before their arrival, all-male regattas. The men who organized the regattas gave the PGRC rowers a racing slot, and gradually the male rowers in Philadelphia got used to seeing women on the race course three or four times a summer.

Because there were no other women's clubs to compete against, PGRC rowers had only themselves to beat. This lack of competition remained a source of frustration for Ernestine Bayer. She served as a coach for PGRC, introducing scores of young women to the sport and trying to develop serious competitors for herself. Not many women had the passion for the sport that she did and the discipline to practice as much as she did. Adding to her frustration was the club's policy to "split up the power" in races—those PGRC rowers considered the best were not permitted to row together. Ernestine had strenuously objected to that decision. Racing in her single was not satisfying either: "Stella was never able to beat me in the single, and it rankled. Lovey beat me once and she wouldn't race me after. I didn't have anyone to row against for years."

Yet she persisted, practicing diligently every day, loving the rhythmical motion and the setting: "I can remember one evening in June, rowing back in the single. The sun was on the water. It looked like the sun was pulling the water up. The Schuylkill looked beautiful. All I thought was, 'What a way to die. What a wonderful way to die.'"

In 1945, Ernestine Bayer's pursuit of significant rowing competition was interrupted by the birth of her daughter, Ernestina (later known as Tina). Ernestine stopped rowing when she was pregnant and then spent the first two years of Tina's life as a social member of PGRC. She held Tina's first birthday party at the club. When she was ready to pick up her oars again, she took Tina with her every day to the boathouse, where either another PGRC member or Ernest watched the toddler while Ernestine rowed. When she grew up, Tina would look back on her early childhood and claim that she spent "more time in the coaching launch than the gas can did. Mom would want to row. She would give me to Dad in the launch."

Back to practicing every afternoon and racing several times each summer against members of her own club, Ernestine alternated between determination to be the best that she could be and despair over the lack of women against whom she could test her skills. Then, in 1956, PGRC got its first chance at outside competition—an invitation to Lakeland, Florida, to race against a women's eight that had formed at Florida Southern University. Ernestine was forty-seven and had been rowing for eighteen years. She wanted desperately to see how she measured up against someone besides the members of PGRC. She began to train hard, arriving at the boathouse at five every morning. Ernest stayed home and got Tina ready for school.

Some of the younger members of the club were not convinced that their boat should have a forty-seven-year-old in the number six seat, where the coach Tom Curran had put Ernestine. She recalled: "One of the girls in the eight went to Tom Curran and said, 'She's too old to row.' Tom said, 'She's the best one in the boat.' If somebody else had come along and could row that six seat better than I, I would have deferred to her."

In what Ernestine Bayer has come to call "the first intersectional eight-oared race for women crews," an unofficial event arranged by the participants, PGRC lost by about a foot to Florida Southern. Ernestine had an explanation: "We had trained for half a mile, but the race was 1,000 meters."

Ernestine had several other opportunities to see how she rowed against other women. In the 1960s, more women's teams were forming and challenging the original racing team, PGRC. Nine years after the race against Florida Southern, Ernestine Bayer competed in one last regatta before she reluctantly turned racing over to a younger generation. In 1965, when an eight from Lake Merritt Rowing Club, the Oakland, California, club that had been racing some against ZLAC in San Diego, traveled to Philadelphia to challenge PGRC, Ernestine, at age fifty-six, rowed in the number four seat. The outcome of that race was not what mattered to her. That race against Lake Merritt was significant to Ernestine because sitting in front of her in the eight was her daughter, Tina. The challenge of getting Tina interested in rowing had been one of Ernestine's preoccupations. Once her daughter was hooked on the sport and nearly as desperate for competition as her mother had been, Ernestine could devote herself to coaching and to the efforts that would be her legacy—expanding the arena for women's rowing.

✦ ✦ ✦

Tina Bayer had managed to avoid being a rower for twenty years before her mother finally hit upon the trick that would get her into a boat. Tina had wanted nothing to do with rowing. By the time she was old enough to choose her sport, if she had to have one (which her mother insisted she did), she had been forced to spend more hours on Boathouse Row than most rowers. She wanted to be away from the place. She chose swimming as her sport, and she took it seriously. She practiced five days a week, trained with weights and developed into an excellent swimmer.

But Ernestine looked at Tina and thought about what a wonderful rower she would be. By the time she was twenty, she was five feet, nine inches tall and broad-shouldered. She would have a lovely, long stroke. Ernestine sighed when she thought about what she herself could have done with that height and how much farther a stroke would have taken her had she been closer to six feet than to five feet tall, as she actually was.

Ernestine knew that her daughter was like her in many ways. She thought about what would motivate her to try something. Ernestine's biggest motivator was the word "no." "I'm the type that if you tell me something can't be done, I'll try my best to do it." She thought that Tina might be similarly goaded.

In 1965, Ernestine invited the new head coach of PGRC to dinner. His name was Ted Nash, and he was an Olympic oarsman. She told Nash about her dilemma with Tina, and he agreed to become a co-conspirator in the effort to get the young woman to try rowing. At the dinner table, when the talk was—what else?—rowing, Nash casually remarked to the Bayers: "Now look at your daughter. She's not big enough to be in one of my boats." The next week Tina asked Ernestine to teach her how to row.

As her mother had suspected, Tina was a natural rower. Soon, she was practicing in a double with Nancy Farrell, Lovey Kohut Farrell's daughter. Then the two young women began rowing in an eight. Unlike their mothers, Tina Bayer and Nancy Farrell had outside competition from the start of their rowing careers. In the early 1960s, women started rowing out of Vesper Boat Club, PGRC's neighbor on boathouse row. The Vesper women were serious about the sport and raced to win. Early races between Vesper and the PGRC were fierce. Joanne Wright Iverson, who had joined PGRC in 1959, was shocked by the Vesper attitude in her first race: "They went off the line like a bat out of hell, like they were really trying. My girl attitude said, 'Hey, that's not fair.' But then I thought I could try, too. I learned how to try harder than I ever thought I could try. That one incident threw a switch in me. I learned to put forth an effort that I never knew I could put forth. Rowing teaches you that you're stronger than anyone ever told you."

If Tina Bayer was heir to Ernestine Bayer's rowing skills, Joanne Iverson was heir to Ernestine Bayer's rowing fervor. That first race made a believer out of Iverson: "It's difficult to describe the urge people have to do this sport. It's like being in love. You're crazy for it." While Iverson rowed with Tina Bayer, she teamed up with Ernestine Bayer to move the sport toward more opportunities for women. Both of them had in mind an Olympic event for women. They attacked their goal from different directions: Ernestine Bayer pushed her daughter and the PGRC women to be at their best and to seek out tougher and tougher competition. Joanne Iverson helped organize events at which the best rowers could compete.

In 1962, Iverson contributed a column to a publication of the National Association of Amateur Oarsmen (NAAO), the all-male body that governed rowing in the United States. The Schuylkill Navy had evolved into the NAAO as rowing spread across the country and eventually became an Olympic sport in 1896. (The first Olympic regatta was in 1900; the 1896 rowing events were cancelled because of bad weather.) In her column, Iverson predicted that women, too, would soon have Olympic rowing events and that American women would be serious contenders when the Olympics opened up to them. Most of the men who read Iverson's column scoffed, for they assumed that American women were not serious about rowing. After all, American women had barely begun to form enough teams to race against each other. (In the early 1960s, only a dozen or so women's rowing programs existed either at clubs or in colleges, and competition for these crews was mainly intra-squad.) European women seemed to take the sport more seriously. There had been an annual European Championship Regatta for women since 1954. That regatta was open to women from all over the world, but American women had never entered. American women would be embarrassed if they tried to row against the strong international women's teams, like the Soviets or the East Germans.

While they scoffed at the notion of women's rowing, most American men were not about to do anything to encourage women to embrace the sport. The widespread attitude among male rowers, when women wanted access to coaches, racing shells and regattas, was evident from the catch phrase: "Get the broads out of the boathouse." Most men of the 1950s and early 1960s did not want to share their facilities with women. Most male rowers of that era were disgusted by the idea of women's attempting what they considered the most rigorous of sports, one that demanded muscle and sweat, two decidedly unladylike attributes.

However, at least two American male rowers of that era

were mavericks. When they read Iverson's article, they contacted her to see what they could do to help get women's rowing moving toward a place in the Olympic program. These two men—Ed Lickiss and Ted Nash—were coaching women in 1962. Lickiss was coach at the Lake Merritt Rowing Club. His efforts on rowing's behalf were legendary in the Bay Area, where he encouraged everyone, regardless of gender or ability, to take up the sport. His Lake Merritt women's group was made up primarily of high-school girls. Nash was coaching a group of forty-five women who belonged to the Lake Washington Rowing Club in Seattle, Washington. Nash had gone to the Seattle area to train for the 1960 Olympic team. He began coaching women because his wife rowed and wanted competition. He had encountered resistance to his efforts on women's behalf from other men involved in the sport. In one instance, when Nash was on an airplane, flying to compete in the 1960 Rome Olympics, the chairman of the Olympic Rowing Committee came up to him and demanded, "Nash, what's this crap about women's rowing?"

The year after Iverson's article appeared, she met with Lickiss, Nash and Peter Lippett, a coxswain for the Lake Merritt Rowing Club, in Mitch's Piano Bar in Oakland. This small group decided to form a national rowing organization for women. The purpose of the organization would be to encourage the development of women's rowing programs and to push for international competition. The four founders called their new organization the National Women's Rowing Association (NWRA). They registered the organization with the NAAO as the official governing body for women's rowing in the United States. A separate rowing organization for women was necessary because the NAAO seemed intent on ignoring or, in some cases, impeding women's efforts to row. According to Iverson, "We had to beg to get women's races in some regattas."

The NWRA would remain a separate women's rowing organization until 1986 when the membership voted to dissolve the organization and leave the governance of rowing to one body, the United States Rowing Association, which included both men and women.

Under the new NWRA, women's rowing began to focus on competition. The NWRA organized the first national championships for women in 1966. The regatta, held in Seattle, consisted of thirteen different events. Eight clubs from around the country participated—Lake Washington, Lake Merritt, PGRC, Green Lake (from Seattle), Oregon State University, University of California at Berkeley, Mills College and Seattle Tennis Club. The Lake Washington Rowing Club won seven of the thirteen events. PGRC won the first national elite eight-oared title. Tina Bayer was in that eight, as was Nancy Farrell.

The next year, the NWRA's national championships were in Oakland. Again, the PGRC eight won. Ernestine Bayer thought that was the boat—Tina's boat—that ought to go to Vichy, France, for the European championships. The head of the NAAO said absolutely not—the American women were just not up to the caliber of the European women. His no seemed like the last word because American women would not be admitted to the European championships without the sanction of the only U.S. governing body recognized internationally, the NAAO.

Iverson and other members of the NWRA began writing letters and making phone calls, urging the men in the NAAO to support American women in international competition. Polite in her urgings, Iverson nevertheless perceived the powers running the NAAO as old fogies: "Their attitude was, 'Isn't it cute.' We were perceived as being weak. They thought there was no way we could compete against those European women."

Ernestine Bayer knew that all the letters and phone calls in the world would not move the NAAO. She wondered how she was going to get around the men's organization. She got her answer at an international all-male regatta in St. Catharines, Ontario, in 1967. Ernestine Bayer arranged for the PGRC national

championship eight to row in an exhibition race at the St. Catharines regatta. The women would sprint against an eight made
up of men who were former national champions and Olympians. It would be fun for everyone. Ernest Bayer was one of the
rowers in the men's boat. Thomi Keller, the head of the Federation Internationale des Societes D'Aviron (FISA), the organization that is rowing's international governing body, was also in
the boat. To everyone's astonishment, the PGRC eight won the
sprint. Keller immediately gave the women's crew a formal invitation to the European championships. The NAAO's opinion
no longer mattered.

Ernestine Bayer was elated. She immediately began making
plans for the trip to France. She paused briefly when she learned
that not all of the young women rowing in PGRC's eight were
as enthusiastic as she was about going to Europe to row against
international competition. They had been listening to the men's
comments about how good the Europeans were and how funny
it was that American women thought they could row. National
champions for the second time, the PGRC eight did not want
to compete in Europe if they had no chance of winning. And
most of them thought they had no chance.

Ernestine Bayer knew that the women would not win in Europe, but she also knew that they could make a respectable
showing. She pleaded with them to go: "Someone had to be
first. I knew they couldn't win, but I wanted to have a breakthrough for other women."

While she worked on their attitudes, Ernestine arranged for
financing for the trip. She borrowed $7,000 from Horace Dav-
enport, the founder of the National Rowing Foundation, promising him that the members of the eight would make monthly
installments to pay him back. ("Each girl paid off her share
within a year.") Then she supervised their training. The members of the PGRC national championship eight began to work
harder than they ever had before. Every day they spent hours on
the Schuylkill River, doing drills that would increase their

speed. On the day that the eight rowed out for one final practice before leaving for the European championships, the boys on Boathouse Row came out on their porches to watch. This was a new generation of boys from the one that had laughed as Ernestine Bayer rowed in a circle in 1938. These boys on the Boathouse Row porches applauded as the 1967 PGRC eight swept by.

✦ ✦ ✦

Today, Ernestine Bayer continues to accumulate memories about the sport of rowing, and she probably will until the day she dies. She competes in at least two regattas a year. Each time she appears at the Head of the Charles, a three-mile-long race held every fall on Boston's Charles River, she sets a record for being the oldest woman in the master's rowing category, which is for rowers twenty-seven and older. She keeps clippings of her rowing exploits in a couple of file folders and big manila envelopes. Those from the early days of PGRC are crumbling and yellowed. Some day, when she has time, she says, she might put together a scrapbook.

She and Ernest and Tina moved away from Philadelphia in 1971 because Tina wanted to leave. The rising crime rate disturbed her, especially since she went on early morning training runs in the middle of the city. Tina had continued to row after the breakthrough trip to the European championships in 1967, where her eight turned in a respectable performance, making the finals and finishing sixth. In 1969, Tina became the first American woman to enter an international singles competition.

For Ernestine, leaving the close-knit rowing community in Philadelphia was more wrenching than she had imagined it would be: "When we moved to New England, I was very lonely. It was the first time I had ever felt sorry for myself." She had bought a double because Tina and Ernest both had said they would row with her in New England. But they didn't. She traded the double for a single and tried going out by herself: "I didn't like it at all. It was lonely."

Then she heard about a rowing shell designed for rough water. This was the Alden ocean shell, a wider, steadier design than the sleek racing single she had been rowing. She bought one in 1972. She liked it so much that she founded a club, the Alden Ocean Shell Association. Whenever a dealer sold a shell, Ernestine Bayer would get the buyer's name and address. Soon the first recreational rowing organization in the U.S. had more than 800 members nationwide. And before long the Alden Ocean Shell Association was a member of the NAAO. Ernestine Bayer met the usual resistance from the NAAO. "They didn't want recreational rowers, only racers. I said we would eventually race." The Alden Ocean Shell Association now has regular regattas and its own class in the Head of the Charles.

While she was organizing the Alden Ocean Shell Association, Ernestine was also helping start a women's rowing program at the University of New Hampshire. That effort was a Bayer family affair, with both Tina and Ernest also pitching in. In 1973, the University of New Hampshire sent its first women's eight to compete in the Head of the Charles. To fill out the crew, both Tina and Ernestine took seats in that eight. The spectators at the regatta looked twice when they saw a college crew row by with a sixty-four-year-old woman in the number four seat.

One of the young women who benefitted from the Bayers' attention at the start of the New Hampshire program was Liz Hills O'Leary, who is now head of the women's crew program at Harvard. "The Bayers are the original American rowing family," O'Leary says. "They have done incredible things for women's rowing." The Bayers picked O'Leary out as having a natural talent for rowing while she was at New Hampshire. They loaned her a single and gave her individual coaching. "You can do it. You can be great," Ernestine told her.

In 1975, Ernestine was named to the first U.S. Women's Olympic Rowing Committee. Her work and the efforts of the

NWRA had paid off. The U.S. would be sending a women's team to the 1976 Olympics, where women's rowing events would be included for the first time. Ernestine encouraged O'Leary to try to make the Olympic team. O'Leary fulfilled the promise that the Bayers had seen in her and went to Montreal to row in the 1976 Olympics. After she retired as an athlete, she was the first woman to be named head coach of the U.S. women's sculling team.

"Ernie [Ernestine] had to fight that uphill battle getting women into the sport when women weren't wanted," O'Leary says. "I was lucky that I stepped in when she had done most of the work."

When Ernestine Bayer resigned as secretary of the Alden Ocean Shell Association in 1988, she gave up her last official duties on behalf of rowing. A case of pneumonia was the impetus behind her resignation. Until the pneumonia, she had been remarkably healthy all her life. She says that she sometimes regrets all the rowing she missed because she was so busy creating a structure that would support women who wanted to row competitively.

Had Ernestine Bayer been born fifty years later, she could have stepped into a ready-made rowing program as a youngster and gone as far with the sport as her talent and will would have taken her. As it is, she takes satisfaction from knowing that young women now have the opportunities she longed for because of efforts she made. And she still has the pleasure of rowing itself, the hypnotic rhythm of it, the constant motion her body craves: "I like to keep my body moving. What better way than to be in a boat on the water that you love. It's a beautiful sport. You don't have to have quickness and power. But rhythm you have to have. You can row as easy as you want to. You can row along and look around. I don't know why everybody doesn't row."

Every spring, as soon as the ice melts from the Squamscott and flows in chunks out to sea, she is on the river in her single three times a week. She has a regular partner, a forty-year-old man who can keep up with her. She trains for her two favorite regattas, the Alden nationals and the Head of the Charles. She cannot imagine her life without rowing. One recent year, when *Life* magazine planned to do a feature story on her appearance at the Head of the Charles, she flipped her single before she got to the starting line. Race officials fished her out of the water and, over her protests, took her to shore so that she could put on some warm, dry clothes. They were concerned about hypothermia, and they persuaded her to sit the regatta out. Consequently, *Life's* photographer did not get her photographs, and the magazine cancelled the story. Ernestine was initially upset at the missed opportunity for a tribute to her career and nationwide exposure for the sport of rowing, but she felt better when she heard the proposed title of the feature. It was to have been called "The Last Hurrah."

"I don't know why they wanted to call it that," she says. "I plan to continue rowing." And so she certainly will.

Anita DeFrantz, pictured here (center) after the 1976 Montreal Olympics race in which she and her crew in the eight won a bronze medal, became one of the most passionate defenders of the Olympic ideal during President Jimmy Carter's boycott of the Games in 1980. In 1986, DeFrantz became the first black woman elected to the International Olympic Committee, where she is a strong voice for increased participation by women in the Games.

Anita DeFrantz

WHY WOULD A WOMAN want to discover how fast she could row a racing shell or, for that matter, how well she could do in any sport? Anita DeFrantz, one of the most influential women in amateur athletics today, thinks the answer lies in a feeling that lasts only a moment but promises immortality. The feeling comes after hours of training and discipline, of struggling to learn and develop a skill. Suddenly mind, body and the circumstances of the contest fuse into one incandescent moment of perfect execution. At that moment, the athlete feels like a god. A woman who has experienced such a moment knows that she can do anything.

DeFrantz has experienced such a moment, and ridden it to Olympian achievements. She was an Olympic bronze medalist in 1976. In 1980, she was the only U.S. athlete to receive an Olympic medal. In 1984, she was "one of the superstars of the L.A. Olympics," according to the Games' chief organizer Peter Ueberroth. She is a woman who can do almost anything. And she has placed her considerable capabilities in the service of groups that have traditionally been denied access to the shining moment that athletic competition allowed her to possess. White males regard such moments as their birthright. Women, the disabled and the poor generally don't have the chance of using sports to discover the perfection within themselves.

As president of the Amateur Athletic Foundation (AAF) in

Los Angeles, DeFrantz administers ninety-nine million dollars of the surplus from the 1984 Los Angeles Olympics. The money funds sports programs for the young people of Southern California, with special attention to girls, the poor and the disabled. DeFrantz's office is in a red brick, Corinthian-pillared mansion, the Britt House, built in 1910. Across a courtyard garden, which blooms with Southern Californian luxuriance, is a recently built sports resource center that houses the most complete sports library in North America.

Working with an eighteen-member board that includes L.A. luminaries from business, show business, sports and politics, DeFrantz has developed a program that is aimed at giving ghetto kids a chance to shoot baskets instead of rival gang members and encouraging girls to throw down their pompons and pick up baseball bats. She is establishing community sports clubs in the poorest, most desperate neighborhoods. These clubs, which are run by people who live in the community, give kids coaching, uniforms and a chance to participate in organized competition. DeFrantz's idea is that the clubs will become centers that hold communities together and build positive traditions where none existed.

DeFrantz drives around L.A.'s neighborhoods in a black Buick Park Avenue, looking to make things happen. "We go out and see nothing happening so we ask if anyone is interested in seeing something happening," she says. "There are always individuals who care. We just have to ask if they want to give time to this effort." She would like to see every existing sports facility in the region in use twenty-four hours a day, schools open to communities after the administrators and teachers go home, parking lots converted to basketball courts or soccer fields when the commuters are gone.

At nearly six feet tall, DeFrantz is an imposing crusader for sports opportunities. Trained as a lawyer, she frames her arguments eloquently and without gaps. She has a rich laugh and an easy manner with children, who are her priority.

"It's heinous the way we treat children in sports in this country," she says. "Sports should be an opportunity to learn and to succeed. When you've succeeded in sports, you can succeed in other parts of your life."

It is the potential for personal development that DeFrantz emphasizes when she talks about the importance of sports. She has no illusions about sports changing the world. "I'm not one to believe that sports will change the social fabric," she says. "I believe that sports mirror the social fabric." But she also believes that a positive experience in athletics can change the way a person perceives herself and her prospects.

◆ ◆ ◆

Anita DeFrantz's passion for creating sports opportunities stems partly from the fact that she herself was denied the chance to develop as an athlete when she was growing up. She was born in Philadelphia in 1952 and grew up in Indianapolis. Girls were not encouraged to be athletes in the 1950s; nevertheless, Anita DeFrantz's father wanted her to become a great swimmer. His dream for his only daughter (he also had three sons) was that she be the first African-American to win an Olympic gold medal in swimming. But African-Americans were excluded from the only swimming pools open all year in Indianapolis. Anita joined a swim team whose pool was open for only three months in the summer. She was not inspired: "Three months a year did not a swimmer make. If I had had the coaching and the year-round opportunities, maybe I would have gotten the fire."

A bright young woman from an accomplished family—her mother was an education professor, her father a community organizer, her grandfather a leader in the YMCA movement—DeFrantz pursued other interests. It wasn't until she was nineteen that she found the sport in which she could develop her athletic potential. The sport was rowing.

In 1970, she was a freshman at Connecticut College in New London when she saw her first racing shell. The long, sleek look of the boat intrigued her, and she decided to find out more about it. The crew coach was delighted by her interest. At five-eleven, she was the perfect size to be a sweep rower. Soon Anita DeFrantz was hooked on rowing in team boats: "I was captured by rowing because it's an outdoor sport, and I love being near the water. Plus, it's an egalitarian sport. Everybody in the boat is equally important. There are no stars. The fate of the boat is tied together. It's the ultimate team sport."

Rowing may be egalitarian within each boat, but when Anita DeFrantz took up the sport it was anything but open to people who were any race except white and any gender except male. Fortunately for the sport, Anita DeFrantz developed a passion for it during a time when its exclusivity was being challenged by a group of remarkably tenacious women. Eventually, she became one of the leaders of that group.

◆ ◆ ◆

Anita DeFrantz discovered rowing when several forces were converging to break the grip that white males had on the sport. These were political forces, and the 1970s were highly charged with political actions among women athletes at colleges and clubs around the country. As the decade started, women were rowing, but their involvement in the sport was in spite of their male counterparts.

Carol Brown was a freshman at Princeton in 1971, when the women's rowing team was newly organized and using hand-me-down boats from the men. Lake Carnegie and its boathouse were off-limits to women after seven each morning. "We were not to be seen by the men's team or the coaches." Brown was hungry enough for competition to endure such indignities. She had gone to high school in Illinois, which had a state law against competitive activities for school girls.

Jeanne Friedman was a freshman at Boston University in 1971, when the women's crew had the six a.m. shift on the water and the men's old equipment. The women held marathon rows to raise money, setting up a tank in front of the student union and rowing around the clock. They had to provide their own funding if they wanted to participate in the sport.

In 1970, Jan Harville was a freshman at the University of Washington, where the stories about the early hours and the cast-off equipment were the same: "We would have to be off the dock by five-thirty because maybe some guys would mosey on down and see us there, and it sure wasn't too cool to have women walking around the boathouse."

To these women rowers and others like them who were trying to establish themselves as athletes, the 1970s delivered a promise. It was called Title IX, and it was an amendment to the Omnibus Education Act of 1972. Title IX declared: "No person in the United States shall on the basis of sex be excluded from participation in, be denied the benefits of, or be subjected to discrimination under any education program or activity receiving federal financial assistance."

Title IX applied to all academic disciplines, but the slowest acceptance and most visible battles came in college sports. Title IX did not bring automatic parity with men but it did give women a weapon. The women's crew at Yale made imaginative use of that weapon in the spring of 1976 to protest their second-class status as rowers. Frustrated and angry at having to wait on the crew bus while the male rowers showered and dressed after practice, the women schemed to draw attention to this inequity. They wanted their own showers and their own locker room in the boathouse, which was a half-hour from the campus, so that they did not have to sit on the bus, feeling their sweat turn cold and knowing that their male teammates were standing under hot showers. They asked their captain Chris Ernst to make an appointment with the director of physical education and to invite the local stringer for *The New York Times* and a photographer to the meeting. Then nineteen members of the women's crew put on their new Yale sweats—blue with white letters— and kept the appointment. When they were all assembled in front of Yale's director of physical education, the nineteen women rowers took off their new sweats. The photographer snapped pictures of their bare backs with "Title IX" written across them. The director of physical education got a good look at their bare chests with "Title IX" written across them. The message was, according to Ernst, "We are here. This is what we look like." The next day the story was on the first page of the second section of the *Times*. The photo was in the Yale campus newspaper. And, in Ernst's words, "The university was incredibly embarrassed." Yale built an addition to the boathouse the next spring, giving the women their own facilities. The university also hired a new women's athletic director who knew all about Title IX.

As other women on other campuses across the country filed Title IX complaints or took Title IX actions, sports began to open up to them. Ten years after Title IX was written, 15,000 women were attending colleges on athletic scholarships. More and more women were getting the chance to be real athletes and to learn the lessons that American society uses athletics to teach, lessons about achievement and success through self-discipline, lessons about independence and a strong sense of identity, lessons about teamwork and developing skills.

The women in the 1970s were learning all those lessons simultaneously on and off the race course as they struggled to establish both their right to compete and the skills to be competitive in their chosen sports. Most of them had no idea about the kind of work that went into being a top-level athlete when they first got to college. At Connecticut College, Anita DeFrantz initially thought that she could be competitive as a rower by just going out and rowing and having fun. She had enough natural talent to get by on this philosophy until her senior year, when she was dropped from the varsity ranks to the junior varsity level. Then she began to reconsider her approach to the sport. Her coach told her that she had the potential to be an Olympic rower. She would need, however, to work hard. DeFrantz remembered her father's dream for her and the segregated society that had thwarted it. In 1974, she saw no barriers to what could be her own Olympic dream except those that she might erect herself. She was beginning to get the fire and to develop a philosophy around it. As she would tell the *New York Times* six years later: "When you send an Olympic team, you're saying, 'These are our best.' That's the only time this country says that to black people."

◆ ◆ ◆

In 1974, Anita DeFrantz enrolled in law school at the University of Pennsylvania and joined Vesper Boat Club on the Schuylkill River in Philadelphia. She began to lift weights and run hills to build her strength and endurance. There were other women at Vesper who were as serious as DeFrantz was about shaping their bodies to fit their goals of becoming Olympic athletes. This group varied in number, from six to as many as twenty. They had their own locker room at Vesper and access to boats. But some of the men at the club were reluctant to accept these women as their peers. They tried nailing the women's locker room shut as an indication of their displeasure. According to DeFrantz, "We were dealing with a lot of tradition, and when you're dealing with tradition that usually means someone is excluded."

Jack Kelly, who was the star at Vesper, thought that the chance for the club to attach its name to Olympic medals was more important than preserving it as a male domain. It was the elevation of women's rowing to Olympic status that forced the men in the American rowing world to take it seriously. The Olympic movement has its own rules and traditions that supersede even those of the oldest amateur athletic governing body in the United States. When the International Olympic Committee (IOC) made the decision in 1972 to add women's rowing events to the next Olympics (scheduled for 1976 in Montreal), that meant women would be getting money for equipment and travel. Their performance would reflect on the entire U.S.A. team. Their medals would count just as much as anyone else's when the national tallies were made.

The chance to be the best in the world, with an Olympic gold medal to prove it, brought a number of young women into rowing in the 1970s. The inclusion of rowing in the Olympics had as great an impact on the development of the sport as did Title IX. In 1972, fewer than 500 women were rowing in the entire U.S. Ten years later, the National Women's Rowing Association (NWRA) had 125 member organizations representing thousands of women.

The NWRA made the most of all the opportunities that were opening up for women. Gail Pierson Cromwell was president of the organization in 1972 when the Olympic decision was made. As soon as she heard the news about the IOC's vote, she resolved that the National Association of American Oarsmen (NAAO)—one of the last organizations to support the inclusion of women's rowing in the Olympics—was not going to have any chance to undermine women's participation now that the Olympic decision had gone in their favor. She called the United States Olympic Committee (USOC) and persuaded that group to sanction a women's Olympic rowing committee separate from the men's. Then after two quick consultations with her NWRA membership, she hand-picked her committee.

With the organizational battles settled, at least temporarily, it was the athletes' turn in the arena. In 1973, for the first time, the U.S. sent a full women's team to the European championships, which were in Moscow. The team performed respectably but took home no medals. Another full women's team went to the world championships the next year, with the same results. In 1975, there were enough talented women rowers in the country that the Olympic Women's Rowing Committee decided to use a camp system, similar to the one that the men used, to select the national team. Based on their performance in certain regattas and on certain strength and endurance tests, women from around the country were invited to a camp to race against each other for seats in the boats that would go to the world championships. Anita DeFrantz was one of the athletes invited to the camp. A number of other women who had trained with her at Vesper were also invited. Vesper was one of the powers in women's rowing in 1975. The University of Wisconsin was another.

DeFrantz's performance at selection camp earned her a place on the national team. All of the women who made the team that year were, in the words of one rower, "people who knew how to close their eyes and grit their teeth and really put it all on the line." DeFrantz was put into a four for the world championships. The priority boat that year, however, was the eight. This meant that the highest expectations were riding with the rowers chosen for the eight. But even the highest expectations that year were not much. No one in the United States thought that the women had seen enough high-caliber competition to do anything spectacular at the world championships. Getting into the finals would be sufficient.

In that 1975 eight, which was dubbed the "Red Rose Crew" because the team manager had put roses in all the foot-stretchers before one race, was a group of rowers ranging in height from Carie Graves at six-one in the stroke seat to Chris Ernst at five-four in the bow. Gail Cromwell, at thirty-five, was the oldest in the boat. Graves described her crew as a "motley-looking group." She was aware of the low expectation level. But she also knew that every member of that crew had gotten where she was by exceeding the expectations of those around her: "We were all really tough. We had to fight for any little piece of thing we got. Those were some formidable women in that boat."

Cromwell was interviewed for a *Sports Illustrated* profile that ran right before the world championships. She talked about her own passion for excellence as being an anomaly in American society: "Women have never been taught to put their hearts and souls into anything, except a family maybe. It's only total dedication that will win anything."

The world championships were in Nottingham, England, in 1975. The American women's eight, in a race that shocked the rowing world, edged out the Romanians and finished second to the East German boat. Graves said afterwards, "Of course, we thought we should have done well anyway. There was no reason why we shouldn't have."

That silver medal finish at the world championships in 1975 gave a boost to the entire U.S. women's team and made competition for the 1976 national team, the one that would be going to the first women's Olympic rowing events, fierce. Once again, the women' committee decided to hold selection camp. Anita DeFrantz had been training to get to the Olympics for the past two years. "It was a goal I had set. I took the steps I needed to get there." She made the 1976 team, and she won a place in the eight, which was once again the priority boat. She rowed in the number seven seat.

Just being at the Olympics among other athletes was a thrill for DeFrantz: "Living in a community of 10,000 successful people is extraordinary. The variety that packages of success come in is also extraordinary."

The silver medal in 1975 had raised expectations for the women's performance. There were those, however, who considered that medal a fluke. The athletes wanted to prove otherwise. At the Montreal Games, the 1976 eight rowed to a third place finish, behind the East Germans and the Soviets. This performance established American women as a presence on the international rowing scene. For the rowers themselves, the bronze medal was a seductive treasure. It made an Olympic gold medal seem within reach. The first time that the bronze medal eight raced together was on the starting line at the Olympic Games. If their first effort was worth bronze, then wouldn't four years of hard work and dedication get gold? Anita DeFrantz thought so. She began to train for the Moscow Games in 1980.

✦ ✦ ✦

The competition that Anita DeFrantz faced in 1980 was not
what she had prepared for in her training program. "I was competing against the president of the United States, and it was a
hellish year." It was the year that the U.S. Olympic team stayed
home from the Games as part of President Jimmy Carter's response to the Soviet invasion of Afghanistan. DeFrantz was
training in Princeton when she heard Carter propose boycotting
the Olympic Games. She was at a friend's birthday party in January of 1980 and saw the president on television talking about
the Soviet invasion that had happened the month before. She
stared at the television set in disbelief as she heard him say he
was not in favor of sending the team to Moscow for the summer
Games. Her incredulity quickly turned to outrage.

The U.S. Olympic women's rowing team had not yet been
selected for the 1980 Games and would not be until May. The
women who were aiming for the team were pushing themselves
through long, difficult winter workouts—running stadium
steps, lifting weights, cranking on the rowing machine called
the ergometer, sloshing through puddles and snow. Some days
the one thing that kept these women going was the hope of
making the Olympic team.

Jeanne Flanagan, who was in the group training with
DeFrantz in Princeton, heard the announcement of the proposed Olympic boycott when her clock radio went off at 5:25
a.m. Her routine was to get up every day at that time so that
she could be at the boathouse ten minutes later for her morning
workout. She and her pair partner, Cathy Thaxton, lived together and shared a daily routine. After the morning workout,
they each went to their jobs. Then they met after work for the
evening workout. "Then we went home, threw a casserole in
the oven and went to bed."

The day Flanagan heard the announcement, part of the
morning workout was running stadium steps: "It was eighteen
degrees. We were running stadiums. All I really wanted was to

have Jimmy Carter standing there watching me run stadiums and tell me personally that I couldn't go to the Olympics. That was all I lived for."

Carol Bower, another rower with the Olympic dream pushing her, had a day similar to Flanagan's when she heard the boycott announcement: She had gotten up in the morning, worked out, gone to school, gone to work and gone to work out again. That night she was too tired to make dinner. She made toast. "Here I am eating this mangy piece of toast, and Carter's on TV telling me that maybe I couldn't go to the Olympics."

The athletes continued to train, hoping that Carter's boycott plans would evaporate. Anita DeFrantz added lobbying to her workout regimen. She left Princeton every weekend to go to Washington, D.C., to plead the athletes' case. DeFrantz testified before the Senate Foreign Relations Committee, appeared on network television and was interviewed in newspapers. "I tried to make people understand the Olympic movement and what it was about. The Olympic Games are a sporting event where athletes are testing themselves, their courage and their integrity on the field of play. The Olympic movement is a tie with the entire world that spans millennia. It's a celebration of human excellence. It has a specific site and a specific time, but it belongs to the entire world, not to that site or those people. It's not a toy."

DeFrantz emerged as the most eloquent defender of the Olympic ideal in the United States. The founder of the modern Olympics, Baron Pierre de Coubertin, did not live to see his torch carried so capably by a woman. He had fought to keep women out of the Games, saying in 1912 when the Olympics had the first official women's events: "Women have but one task—that of crowning the winner with garlands." He had begun the modern Games in 1896 and had patterned them after the ancient Greek games, which were built around the concept of a sacred truce. All warring halted during the month-long games. The modern Games sought the equivalent of this truce, if only as an ideal. They were to demonstrate international fellowship and communication, with the symbol of the intertwining rings representing five continents linked in sport, peace and friendship. DeFrantz fought for that ideal. Her conviction was that the Games exist above political realities.

In her battle against Carter's boycott proposal, DeFrantz received nearly unanimous support from the women who had been or who hoped to be her teammates on the U.S. rowing squad. In 1980, she was twenty-eight and one of the older rowers on the team. She also had been rowing longer than most of the other women. Her seniority and her imposing presence made her a natural leader. She possessed a charisma that had most of the other rowers in awe. According to one of her teammates, "She seemed more together and mature than the rest of us. She was very articulate and had a grasp of what was happening to her." DeFrantz had also functioned as a mentor for many of the younger women, supporting their efforts to make the team, rather than viewing them as a threat to her seat in the boat. She was a gifted teacher and readily shared her skills. She was quick to identify another rower's strengths and to encourage her to build on those strengths.

The women who wanted to row on the Olympic team were the group of athletes most visible in protesting the boycott. They all may not have shared DeFrantz's larger ideals about the sanctity of the Olympics, but they all felt the government had no business telling them they could not compete. As Carol Brown said, "We had been fighting to be allowed to participate in the sport, so we weren't afraid to be vocal. We paid a high price to get where we were, and we felt very strongly that this was an opportunity that should not be denied."

Hunger for some recognition outside the rowing world also played a part in the rowers' vigorous campaign to go to Moscow. The sport is not one that receives a great deal of attention during the years in between Olympics, yet the athletes must train just as hard for the international competition that occurs during those years. According to rower Jan Harville, "Going to the Olympics is a big deal. Mom and Dad can kind of brag, 'Oh my daughter's on the Olympic team.' That means something to their friends. And it means something to our society. 'You're on the Olympic team.' That's a big symbol of something everybody agrees on and everybody's in favor of and everybody knows what it means."

President Carter had a better public relations machine than the women's rowing contingent. By March, the boycott looked as if it would happen. Public opinion was running seventy percent in Carter's favor. According to rower Jan Palchikoff, "The public sentiment was, 'What a bunch of crybaby athletes. They're not going to win product endorsements because they cannot win medals.'"

Following DeFrantz's lead, the rowers wrote letters to politicians and to editors. They gave newspaper interviews. They looked for ways that they could compete if Carter persisted in his boycott notion. Their best hope was that the USOC would defy Carter's wishes. DeFrantz was the athletes' elected representative to the USOC's executive board. She believed strongly that the USOC should live up to its charter, which gave it responsibility for sending the best team from the U.S. to the Olympics. She concentrated most of her efforts on persuading the USOC to do what she considered the only right thing.

The USOC vote on whether to send a team to Moscow came in April of 1980. Vice President Walter Mondale attended the meeting of the USOC House of Delegates and said that a boycott was crucial to the nation's security. The subtext of his speech contained both threats and bribes. Sports organizations might be in danger of losing their tax-exempt status and corporations might be persuaded to withdraw financial support of the USOC if the vote went one way. If the boycott were to be supported, federal funds would make up an eight-million-dollar shortfall on the USOC's books and put sixteen-million dollars toward the 1984 Games.

DeFrantz spoke after the vice president did. "We define our liberty by testing it," she said. "This is such a test."

The USOC's House of Delegates voted 1,604 to 797 to support the Carter Administration's boycott.

DeFrantz was not finished fighting. She had received her law degree from the University of Pennsylvania in 1977. After the vote, she filed a law suit against the USOC to try to force it to live up to its charter and send a team to Moscow. While she was pursuing this avenue of protest, she had to try out for the 1980 team. The NAAO had decided to select a team, as had most of the national governing bodies for the other Olympic sports.

DeFrantz did not perform well enough at selection camp to make the eight that year. She did get a seat in one of the fours. Her efforts against the boycott affected her performance as an athlete, although she never said as much. Her teammates, however, noticed her absence at training sessions. What most of them did not know about was the extent of the abuse she was taking from the American public. Her stand on behalf of the athletes stirred up all kinds of hostilities. DeFrantz was an obvious target. She received hate mail daily, but she told very few people. "I got more hate mail than I needed. Why share it?" A few years after the boycott, she showed Holly Hatton, who was the coxswain for the 1980 eight, a box full of the letters she had received. Hatton was shocked: "It was scary, the intensity of the hatred. There were hundreds of letters from people calling her a Nazi. She lived with all that, yet she followed it through all the way."

Carol Bower, who was selected for the 1980 eight, thinks she took DeFrantz's seat in that boat. "Anita was the one who was really using her energy to battle this thing. I was putting all my energy into just making the team. In leading us, she essentially gave up her position as the strong rower on the team."

The 1980 team went to Europe to compete in several regattas that year. Right up until the opening ceremonies for the

Games in Moscow, the women's team was trying to find a way to participate in the Olympics. Many of the women were listed as plaintiffs in DeFrantz's lawsuit, and they held out some hope for its success. A group approached the president of the international rowing federation to explore competing under the IOC flag without representing the U.S., without even being eligible for medals. "We wanted to go and we wanted to race and we didn't care whether anyone recognized us or whether we were an official part of the Olympics and could win a medal," according to Carol Brown. "It was the whole idea that as an individual and as athletes we had made a commitment to something, and we were never going to get our chance to test ourselves."

The rowers took their protest of Carter's boycott to Europe with them. When they raced, they wore shirts that had the team name on the front and on the back: "Jimmy Carter's Threat to National Security." They also wore black armbands. In the two European regattas in which they rowed that season, the women performed so well that it broke their hearts. In Lucerne, at the first international regatta of the 1980 season, the U.S. women's eight actually won a race against the East Germans, who were considered the best in the world. That historic victory made the team even more desperate to have the chance to compete in Moscow.

In July *DeFrantz v. USOC* was dismissed, on the grounds that the plaintiffs had no legal standing. The women's team was still in Europe when news of that decision reached them. They had also been refused the chance to compete under the IOC flag and been told if they tried to travel to Moscow, their passports would be revoked. The feeling of betrayal spread among all the members of the team. According to Carol Brown, "We had taken some pride in the fact that we did things differently in this country. We starved our athletes and forced them to beg and borrow to make it, on the grounds that we didn't want them to be beholden to the government. It was like a slap in the face that even though we didn't take their money, they could still control us. It was a real disillusionment."

The last race for the 1980 women's team was in Amsterdam. The East Germans were not there, and neither were the Russians. The Canadian team and the West Germans were the main competition for the U.S. eight. It was a blustery day with rain coming down hard. Halfway through the 1,000-meter race, the U.S. boat had a clear lead. All the women in that boat knew they were good at what they did. They might have been the best in the world on a given day. They had once hoped that day would coincide with their event in the Olympic Games. One by one, as they opened their lead, the women in the eight began to cry. According to Brown, "We were crying so hard by the time we got to the finish line that we could hardly row. We didn't want it to end. Each of us was off in our own world, thinking about what this meant and what we'd been through. We were all very bitter at the time."

The 1980 U.S. women's Olympic rowing team staged its last public protest against the boycott on July 30, during a reception for the entire U.S. Olympic team in Washington, D.C. The USOC had invited all the athletes to D.C. to honor them with shows, parties and special medals. On July 30, all the athletes were bussed to the White House for a presidential reception. They had the opportunity to shake Jimmy Carter's hand and pose for photographs with him. The women's rowing team was not ready to put differences aside. Holly Hatton had a friend of hers print buttons that read: "The only reason I'm here is to be sure this never happens again." Many of the women wore their racing shirts with the slam against Carter on the backs. All but three of the forty women on the team refused to pose in the rowing team's picture with Carter and refused to shake his hand. Their boycott of his public relations effort was noticeable, since rowing's Olympic contingent is the second largest after track and field's.

Other athletes from other sports went along with the photo opportunity. They had abandoned the fight against the boycott long before. The women rowers, a few of the men rowers and the field hockey players were the only athletes willing to fight for their right to compete. The other athletes, while they grumbled privately, said nothing in public. DeFrantz was disappointed by most of the U.S. Olympic team: "I learned that a lot of athletes, unlike us rowers, really believe in doing what the head coach says. When the head coach of the U.S. says don't go, they don't."

For her unflinching support of the Olympic ideal, DeFrantz was awarded the Bronze Medal of the Olympic Order. She was only the second American athlete to be so honored by the IOC. She likes to say, "I was the only American to be awarded a medal in 1980."

The U.S. boycott of the 1980 Olympics had no effect on the Russian presence in Afghanistan. With each year that passed, the rowers who had missed their Olympic chance noticed that the Russian army was still in Afghanistan. In 1988, when the Russians finally pulled out, the women on the 1980 U.S. Olympic rowing team called each other and said, bitterly, "It worked. The boycott worked."

◆ ◆ ◆

Anita DeFrantz retired from competitive rowing after 1980. The next year Peter Ueberroth invited her to join his organizing team for the 1984 Los Angeles Olympic Games. She was the liaison between the Games and the African nationals who were threatening to boycott to protest the participation of Zola Budd, the South African runner granted British citizenship so that she could compete. DeFrantz persuaded forty of the forty-three National Olympic Committees from Africa to participate. While the Games were on, she was chief administrator of the Olympic Village.

On October 17, 1986, DeFrantz was appointed to the International Olympic Committee, the fifth woman and the first black woman to serve on that ninety-two member body. She was thirty-four. The rules say that she can be a voting member of the IOC until she is seventy-five, giving her forty years in sport's most powerful institution.

When she talks to kids about setting goals, she often asks them what they plan to be doing in 2027, the year she'll be retiring from the IOC. Her goals with the IOC are to make sure that the Olympic Games continue and to work so that women have increasing opportunities to compete.

DeFrantz became president of the Amateur Athletic Foundation (AAF) in Los Angeles in June of 1987. She never sought a career in sports administration, but opportunities kept opening for her there, and she made the most of them.

Her definition of sport is:

"You use your mind to control your body through dimensions of time and space. There is no such thing as a dumb jock.

"Sport is a personal experience. It's the one area where you can set a goal and rely on yourself to achieve it. If you want to run a mile in seven minutes, it's up to you to go out and do that. That's so different from the rest of society."

One of her continuing crusades at the AAF is to improve the quality of coaching kids receive. "The coach-athlete relationship is probably the most powerful relationship there is. You are using both your body and your mind. Yet very few coaches in this country have been trained to coach. They are given a whistle and a clipboard, and that's it. If we had better trained coaches, kids would get what sports have to offer—the chance to learn skills, the chance to succeed." AAF programs are teaching people how to coach and setting coaching standards. DeFrantz would like to see something like a ministry of sport in this country to apply coaching standards nationwide and to take a more systematic approach to offering the benefits of sport to everyone.

Her own participation in sport has not ended. She still rows, going out in a double at least once a week with Jan Palchikoff, a teammate from the 1980 national rowing squad.

Others from that 1980 women's rowing team get together every
fall in Boston to race an eight in the Head of the Charles, the
three-mile regatta. They call themselves the 1980 Club. When
they gather in Boston, they reminisce about 1980 and what it
might have been. They are one of the few crews to stage this
kind of reunion. Because of their battle against the boycott,
they have an extra dimension to the bond that is common
among crews. And they still have the dream of being the best in
the world. As DeFrantz says, "A dream untested is forever a
dream." They race in Boston against current national team and
college crews. And although they are in their thirties and doing
too many other things to train for an annual regatta, they regularly beat most of the younger crews. DeFrantz has not yet participated in one of these rowing reunions, but she is not surprised that her teammates continue to perform well. "We don't
fully understand the power of the mind in sport."

When she was competing, DeFrantz's favorite boat was the
pair. This is a two-oared shell, as opposed to the double, which
has four oars. Many consider the pair the most difficult boat to
row. Rowers in a pair have to match perfectly. If one bobbles
slightly, the other knows it immediately. As DeFrantz puts it,
"It's the boat with the least options. You have to rely totally on
your partner." One day in 1990, she had the chance to row a
pair with an Australian woman who won a bronze medal in
1984. These two medalists climbed into the boat, grabbed their
oar handles and moved perfectly together. DeFrantz had that
feeling once again, and she greeted it with a rich Olympian
laugh. "We were gods."

Celebrating their gold medal victory in the 1984 Los Angeles Olympics are the members of the U.S. women's eight: (from left) Shyril O'Steen, Holly Metcalf, Carol Bower, Carrie Graves, Jeanne Flanagan, Kristi Norelius, Kris Thorsness, Kathy Keeler and Betsy Beard. The gold medal came after a long struggle for recognition of women's rowing programs in the U.S.

The 1984 Eight

~

At THE STARTING LINE on Lake Casitas outside Santa Barbara, California, seven crews worked to align their eight-oared shells for the beginning of their event in the 1984 Los Angeles Olympics. A gusty August wind buffeted the narrow, sixty-foot-long carbon fiber boats in their lanes. Officials on small platforms in each of the lanes held the sterns of the boats while coxswains shouted instructions to their crews to move the boats into position and hold them there long enough for the start.

In lane number five, coxswain Betsy Beard was working with her crew to get the U.S. eight aligned. This was the boat that would in four months be named to the rowing hall of fame. This was the crew that would invite rowing's matriarch Ernestine Bayer out for a celebratory row the morning after she, too, had been inducted into the hall of fame. This was the world-champion-caliber boat that the women of the United States had finally produced after years of struggling to be acknowledged as serious athletes and given the opportunity to compete.

But no one in the 1984 eight was imagining the honors that awaited the boat at the other side of the finish line. Everyone was concentrating on the task at hand and trying to summon all that was best in her to row as fast as possible down the 1,000-meter Olympic course.

Focusing on the race was difficult. The hype of the Olympics was distracting. These athletes were accustomed to pursuing their sport in obscurity. Suddenly, because they were at the Olympics, the rest of the world seemed to be interested in why they would want to spend their lives getting up before dawn to sit backwards in a boat and endure great pain to try to make that boat move fast across the water. Because they were in the eight—the show boat of rowing—these were the most hyped of all the women rowers at the Olympics. This U.S. women's Olympic eight was favored to win, a position that no U.S. women's boat had ever before occupied in international rowing competition. This eight was now the only hope that the host country's rowing program had for a women's gold medal. The race among the best eights in the world was the final women's rowing event of the 1984 Olympics. The Romanian women had won every other women's rowing event thus far.

Watching the eights fight the wind to get into position for the start was thirty-one-year-old Carol Brown, who had been on the only two previous U.S. women's Olympic rowing teams. She had wanted more than anything in the world to be in the eight that was now at the starting line on Lake Casitas. But she was on the shore, nearly as nervous as the women in the boat, knowing how hard they had worked to get to that starting line. Brown understood only too well the single-mindedness required to pursue a place on an Olympic team. She knew the price of all-out effort. The price was shutting out everything in life other than training, eating, sleeping and the job required to finance the obsession.

After the 1980 boycott had frustrated her goal of testing herself against the world's best, Brown had searched her soul to decide whether she should continue rowing. One question she had to answer was whether she was afraid to stop. Sport can be so pure and its rewards so straightforward and so direct that athletes are reluctant to give themselves over to the ambiguities of everyday life. Another question had to do with her willingness to put her personal life on hold for another four years. The man she was dating wanted to get married. She knew that if she decided to row for another four years, she might lose him. If she aimed for the Olympics, marriage was out of the question. She could not risk any additional challenges or stresses in her life. She could not let anything extra in.

The question that ultimately persuaded Brown to let the pursuit of an Olympic gold medal control her life for a third time was: *How important is it to me to be able to say that I didn't make any compromises and that I did the best I could do?* And the answer was: *Nothing is more important.* Rowing would be her top priority, the arena where she tested her ability to pursue excellence without compromise. Everything else in her life would have to wait.

What Brown had not counted on, when she was wrestling with these questions, was the vulnerability of her body. In February, three months before the 1984 Olympic team would be selected, Brown was lifting weights and felt something go in her back. Doctors diagnosed a herniated disk. Rest was the immediate remedy. There was a permanent weakness and no cure. Brown was incredulous. She had never been injured in her rowing career. She had, in fact, come to believe that her body was a machine and that any limitations on its capabilities came from her mind. Improving her rowing had become a mind-over-body exercise, with the only questions being: *How hard can I push myself? How much pain can I take?* When her back gave out, she had to accept the idea of physical limits.

She was in traction for ten days and then barely able to sit up. She could not row or lift weights, but she decided that she could swim. As soon as she felt her back had healed enough, she got into a boat. She had been rowing again for four weeks when she arrived at selection camp, the place where the national team eight is formed through a brutal process called seat racing. Rowers who have been teammates, who are often best friends and who may be teammates again race against each other for seats in the boats that will represent the United States in international competition.

Brown arrived at selection camp in Princeton, New Jersey, wearing a support corset and taking muscle relaxers. She said that her back was fine. Her self-confidence, however, had been shaken. In addition to the normal pressures of seat racing, she had the added stress of wondering whether the stroke that she was wanting to put all of her body into would be the one that sent her back out again. That worry undermined her performance and kept her out of the eight. She did make the 1984 Olympic team as a spare, one of the people who would be called upon to get into a boat if, for some reason, one of the regulars were unable to row. And now she watched from the shore as the U.S. women's Olympic eight lined up to race for the gold medal.

Betsy Beard, the coxswain, was nervous and slightly distracted as she directed individual rowers to take strokes to straighten the boat in the lane. The coxswain sits in the stern of the boat and is the only person facing forward. She is the eyes and the brain of the boat. The rowers are the muscle and guts.

This was not only Beard's first Olympics; it was also her first year coxing a national heavyweight crew. She had been a surprise choice to be the one sitting in the coxswain's seat in the eight at the Olympics. Her competitor for the job had been the national team eight's coxswain for four years in a row. Many of the rowers who were chosen for the 1984 eight were veterans of the national team and had been satisfied with the previous coxswain. Beard was an unknown. There had been grumbling when she was selected.

Beard loved the eight—the exhilaration of the ride, the surge of power when all eight rowers dug their blades into the water and put all of their strength into moving the boat forward. She also loved the challenge of dealing with eight different personalities, trying to figure out the best way to get the most from each of them.

She had proven herself as coxswain of the eight in June at a regatta in Lucerne, Switzerland. The boat had set a course re-

cord and beaten the East Germans twice. That spectacular performance had bolstered everyone in the boat. They had suspected they were fast. After Lucerne, they knew. The rest of the
rowing world knew, too, that the U.S. women had a fast boat,
perhaps the fastest in the world that year. At the Olympics, the
eight had a good chance of winning the first gold medal for the
U.S. women's rowing program in any world championship. Beginning in 1981, the U.S. women's eight had finished second
to the Soviets for three years in a row at the world championships. Those three silver medals were the highlights of the relatively new U.S. women's rowing program.

Beard had been a coxswain since she was a ninth-grader at a
boarding school in Delaware. Originally, she had liked the idea
of just sitting in the back of a boat and fulfilling her sports re-
quirement for each term. Soon, however, she began to think of
herself as a coxswain, as the liaison between the coach and the
crew, as a person who could steer a straight line down the course
and implement the tactics that might make a difference in a
race. She had been a coxswain in college, for two years at Washington College in Maryland for the men's crew and then for two
years at the University of Washington in Seattle for the
women's crew. At the University of Washington, she had
worked with Bob Ernst, who was the coach of this 1984 U.S.
women's Olympic eight. Beard's rapport with Ernst was one
reason she was in the coxswain's seat of the Olympic eight. Another reason was her skill. She knew how to call a good race. She
had won the confidence of her crew, a group whose inclination
is to regard the coxswain as dead weight to haul down the race
course.

Beard: "You've got to be really confident of yourself and
what you're doing, but you also have to convey a kind of humil-
ity. You have to understand that the athletes are working very
hard, and you're not doing the same kind of physical work."

To the spectator, Olympic-level rowing might not look like
hard work. In fact, the best crews make it look effortless. Few

other sports, however, require such superb conditioning and place such demand on every part of the athlete's body. The rower's legs are just as important as her upper body in supplying the power that drives the boat through the water.

As the rowers in the 1984 U.S. Olympic eight moved into position for a start, they slid their seats (which are on tracks) forward, bent their knees and stretched their arms out over them. Their oar blades were squared and buried in the water. They were in what is called the catch position, the beginning of the rowing stroke. When the starting command came, each rower would begin uncoiling her body to pull the oar through the water. She would use all of her weight and strength, pushing off first from the shoes that are attached to a bar called a footstretcher, slamming her legs down to begin her drive, hanging on the oar and then opening her body gradually until the tilt of her back gave her room to pull the oar in and around. During the finish of the stroke, she would push down on the handle to get the oar out of the water and then turn the handle so that the blade was flat and parallel to the water's surface. This feathering motion would help the blade clear the water and resist the wind as the rower moved forward on her seat to prepare for the next catch.

Beard had worked with her crew on making the entire stroke one fluid motion that all eight rowers performed in perfect unison. They practiced and drilled and rowed together until all eight dropped their oars into the water at the same instant, and all eight brought their oars out of the water at the same instant. They feathered at the same instant and kept their blades at the same height as they moved, as one, up the slide.

Beard had kept journals of each practice, noting what each rower was doing and the variety of responses to what she was suggesting that they do. She had tape recorded herself to know exactly how she sounded. She had worked with the crew off the water, too, going with them to their weight lifting sessions and timing their circuits through different strength and conditioning exercises. The man she was dating, John Stillings, was also a coxswain at the Olympics. His boat was the men's four. She and Stillings would sit together in the living room and cox races against each other. He had helped her learn to be more competitive.

What she had not counted on was the pressure of being favored to win the gold medal at the 1984 Olympics. She knew that anything short of a first place finish would be regarded as a defeat for her boat. The Soviets and the East Germans were not at the Olympics, having boycotted the Los Angeles Games in response to the U.S. boycott of the Moscow Games in 1980. Beard worried that the crew might be over-confident of a victory. She had tried to read the mood of the boat, but that was nearly impossible. The eight was made up of so many different personalities that keying in on one emotion, which the coxswain often tried to do to motivate the boat, was hopeless.

Most of the rowers were national team veterans, having stayed in the sport after 1980 in order to have the Olympic competition that had been denied them. Sitting right in front of Beard and facing her in the number eight seat was Kathy Keeler, who had been on the 1980 team. Keeler had begun her rowing career at Wesleyan College in Connecticut and had coached at Smith after she graduated and while she trained for the national team. She was known as a volatile perfectionist, who tended to get angry over incidentals. She hated to lose. Keeler had only one focus, which was to win a gold medal at the 1984 Olympics. Anything that jiggled that focus infuriated her.

In the number eight seat, Keeler was the stroke of the boat. Her job was to set a pace that the rest of the boat followed. She had to be strong to control what the rest of the boat was doing, and she had to be able to reach within herself to take the stroke rate up or increase the power when the boat needed to move ahead.

Keeler: "The stroke has to have a certain rhythm, has to set a pace that demands people follow. It's a leadership position. People have to trust you. People have to like the way it feels to row behind a good stroke."

The rest of the people in the eight did like rowing behind Keeler. They described her as a thoroughbred, temperamental but an extraordinary competitor. They could count on her to put forth whatever kind of effort winning the race required and to communicate the quality of that effort all the way to the bow of the boat. When she changed the stroke rate, the whole boat felt the change instantly and knew what she wanted. They knew that she would accept from them nothing less than the complete effort that she herself was giving.

In practice, however, Keeler was less inspired. Beard thought that she gave 120 percent in a race and about 85 percent in practice. Since they are the only two people in the boat who sit face to face and since they have to work together to lead the rest of the boat, the stroke and the coxswain talk back and forth about how the practice is going. Occasionally, Beard would be bothered by Keeler's negative comments. Beard was more upbeat by nature. She had decided, when she was chosen as the coxswain of the 1984 eight, that her approach would be more cheerleader than dictator. She did not think the veterans in the boat would tolerate her ordering them around. Keeler's scowling face right in hers, however, often distracted her from her efforts to maintain a positive, encouraging stance.

When she needed some reinforcement during practice, Beard looked around Keeler to Kris Thorsness in the number seven seat. Thorsness was cheerful during practice. She was known to her teammates as Spike, because of her hairstyle. She listened to loud, wild rock 'n' roll and described herself as the "weirdo from Wisconsin." She had made her first national team in 1982, after rowing for four years at the University of Wisconsin.

Thorsness loved the daily grind of training. Her brother, who rowed, had encouraged her to try the sport because he thought she had the pigheadedness necessary for success. Once she got into a boat at Wisconsin, she was hooked. She and a friend would regularly show up an hour early for practice. What she liked most about rowing was the repetition. "You're doing an incredibly repetitive motion thousands of times. There's a beauty to it and a grace. There's an attention to minute details that requires an obsessive personality. For those of us who are obsessive, rowing is ideal."

She also liked to work hard and see the boat going faster. She liked feeling strong and powerful. "You can't be a rower without being strong. The kind of training you do is crazy, year-round, thankless, tireless training, running hills and stadium stairs until your legs are shaking so hard you can't keep going. It was a real step for women to think of themselves as athletes and to take pride in their strength and their muscle mass. Rowing is a step outside the boundaries for the women who become involved in it. Women are taught to be demure and quiet and to defer to men and take direction from men and to define ourselves according to a male standard of what's beautiful. Women who row are in a sport run by women that values strength, assertiveness, aggressiveness."

Thorsness loved talking to the media at the Olympics about rowing and about the eight's gold medal chances. Many of the other rowers in the eight took pride in their obscurity and saw no need to tolerate the press. They were impatient with uninformed questions and a misunderstanding of what they did. Thorsness did her best to make up for their inhospitable treatment of the press.

In the number seven seat, Thorsness's job was to weld herself to Keeler, to match her down to the smallest detail. Thorsness was the leader of the starboard side of the boat. She had to catch Keeler's rhythm perfectly and pass it back. The two had been training and racing in a pair before the selection of the national team that year. They won the pairs trials, which is a set of races that is one way of determining who goes to selection camp where the final boatings are decided. Anyone making the finals at pairs trials automatically gets an invitation to selection camp. Thorsness was intimately familiar with Keeler's style of rowing and with her temperament.

Sitting behind Thorsness, in the number six seat, was Kristi Norelius, a quiet, mild-mannered woman who would push herself to the limit to win a race. Beard trusted her more than anyone else in the boat: "Kristi was always there for you. She never said a word in the boat, but you knew she was willing to pay the ultimate price to win the race."

Norelius had begun her rowing career in 1975 at Washington State University. Her brother Mark was an Olympic rower on the 1976 team. When she was growing up in Seattle, she would stand outside in the wind and rain watching her brother race and thinking that rowing was a ridiculous sport. Nevertheless, when she got to college, she decided the rowers looked like a fun group and she joined. Tall and gangly (six-one and 145 pounds), she was uncoordinated and reluctant to take the sport seriously. She did her workout runs in desert boots because she had no running shoes, and she raced in blue jeans. Yet rowing felt like home to her. "Having this big body, I never felt like I fit anywhere. Finally, I had a place where this big body could be put to use, and you're sort of admired for putting it to use. You can have some pride in your body."

After two years at WSU, Norelius went to Long Beach, California, to learn how to scull. The group there, centered around Joan Lind, was highly competitive and serious. Norelius stayed four months and learned how much she did not know about rowing. Then she moved to Seattle and got involved with a group of women whom Bob Ernst was coaching. They all rowed singles and did 500-meter racing pieces in practice. Norelius consistently finished a minute behind everyone else. She called herself the "doormat" of the group. Carol Brown and Jan Harville, who were experienced rowers and members of the national team, saw potential in Norelius and encouraged her to stick with rowing. Norelius: "They were wonderful to me, very supportive, always giving me pats on the back. I think they knew that once things clicked for me, I would take off." She made the 1980 team as a spare and then rowed in the '81, '82 and '83 silver medal eights.

Beard considered Norelius's position in the number six seat pivotal to the crew's performance. In her mind, the six seat dictated the amount of momentum on every stroke. She knew Norelius was quick enough to keep the momentum going.

The six seat is the first seat in what rowers call the "engine room." The four seats in the middle of the boat—numbers six, five, four and three—supply the power. The rowers in those seats are generally the biggest and strongest in the boat.

Norelius viewed her job as linking the stern pair—Keeler and Thorsness—to the rest of the boat. She had to attach herself to the stroke's blade and send that rhythm back. She tried to be almost ahead of the stroke so that not a millisecond would be lost at the catch.

Doing this job for the other side of the boat was Jeanne Flanagan in the number five seat. A talented athlete, she had been on every national team but one since 1979. After the 1980 Olympic boycott, she was seriously depressed about being washed up at twenty-four, with nothing left in her life to do. So she went to graduate school, studying exercise physiology at the University of Massachusetts.

Flanagan knew all the scientific reasons why her body was so efficient at making a boat go fast. She knew that the capacity to take in oxygen is key to success as a rower, and that the normal person can take in three liters of oxygen per minute while a world-class rower can take in six. She knew when to push her body during workouts so that her limits would keep moving beyond her reach. Rowing a 1,000-meter race is similar physiologically to running a mile. She modeled her workouts after milers', changing the emphasis on muscle groups.

For all she had learned about physiology, Flanagan knew

that success at her level of competition depended more upon mental conditioning than physical. In fact, she considered the sport eighty percent mental at the world-class level. Flanagan: "You have to be able to use imagery, to translate the perfect rowing stroke to your muscles. You have to know how to concentrate and focus and be able to lock in on demand. You have to be ready to race on race day."

Flanagan, whom Beard viewed as a quiet, very strong force in the boat, considered herself ready to race. She might have been in better physical condition in 1980, but in 1984 she was more prepared mentally.

Sitting behind Flanagan, in the number four seat, was Carie Graves, the most experienced rower in the boat. She had been on the 1975 team that surprised the rowing world by winning a silver medal in Nottingham and on both the 1976 and 1980 Olympic teams. By 1984, she obviously wanted to move on to other things in her life. She was burned out and still angry about the 1980 boycott. She had tried to retire from the sport after 1976. Then, at age twenty-four, she had been named head coach at Radcliffe, the first woman coach of a major women's program. The job was a disaster for her.

Graves: "There was a lot of pressure on me, and I didn't know what I was doing. I was picked because I was a woman and because of my athletic credentials. I found out later that the athletes used to call me Old Ironface. I figured the best thing I could do was keep my mouth shut and be an authority figure. My philosophy was: *Row hard; it's easy.* A lot of women dropped out."

Because she felt she had no control over what was happening in her job, she started working out again, where no one but she had any effect on the outcome. In 1978, she was back on the national team.

When she had discovered rowing at the University of Wisconsin in 1973, Graves felt she had found her niche. Like Norelius, she had finally found a place where her height (six-one) was a source of envy. Like Thorsness, she loved the repetition of rowing. She loved the intensity of putting all of her mind and body into each stroke.

In a 1979 article in *The Oarsmen*, the official publication of the National Association of Athletic Oarsmen, she explored the reasons why she loved rowing: "What I really enjoy and what I really love about rowing is just cranking on it. I just love it, just being able to totally absorb myself in something physically and mentally, and just go for it. It's more the blood and guts of rowing than anything esoteric or aesthetic."

When she was preparing for the 1976 Olympics at Montreal, Graves was doing forty-stroke pieces, which called for rowing as hard as she possibly could for all forty strokes, then resting and going all out for forty more strokes, and so on.

"In the middle of a forty it was this exploding, all-enveloping, just the most wonderful feeling I've ever had . . . I was just cranking on it for my life, just as hard as I could, and I just knew right then . . . maybe it lasted only twenty or thirty seconds, but the glow was with me for days . . . I knew that I was all-powerful, that I had complete control over everything I ever did in my life. . . . It was just awesome to feel like that. . . . This is really bizarre, because here I am a woman and I'm supposed to be this and that . . . but I remember thinking I am God. . . . I remember thinking, if I died this very second, I could give a shit, because I am God and I am immortal and I am incredibly happy at this moment."

In the 1984 eight, everyone felt Graves's presence. Beard felt her strength; Graves could definitely move the boat. Beard also felt her displeasure more than once. Sometimes the word "deranged" came to mind when Beard thought about Graves's intensity as a rower.

Among the younger rowers, Graves had a mystique. She had been at the top of the sport for so long and had so many accomplishments that she seemed invulnerable. Her confidence in her skill was contagious, and everyone knew she would never give up in a race. But in 1984 everyone saw another side of Carie Graves. They saw a woman who was questioning why she had postponed the rest of her life for eleven years and why she was so angry.

Carol Bower, sitting in the number three seat behind Graves, thought the whole team was burned out. The boat had been put together in June and gone to Lucerne. But then the eight did not have another race until the Olympics, the first day of August. They had workouts every day, twice a day, hard workouts, the kind that make being on the starting line in a race feel like a relief.

Bower had made her first national team in 1979, after having rowed at the University of California at Los Angeles. Her first national team was nearly her last because of a disastrous mistake she made at the World Rowing Championships in Bled, Yugoslavia. The U.S. boat was ahead of the East Germans and moving on the Soviets with 250 meters to go. The stroke rate was more than forty strokes a minute, and the crew was taking it up, making a strong bid to win the first gold medal in the history of U.S. women's rowing. Somehow—maybe it was the wind or the choppy water—as Bower moved up the slide to get ready for the next catch, her blade tapped the water. She could not recover before the catch. The blade went in, not square, but at a slight angle. It plunged into the water, sending the oar handle flying for Bower's throat and breaking the boat's momentum. She recovered quickly from this crab, but not before the East Germans had passed the U.S. boat and the Soviets had increased their lead.

Bower: "In the last part of a race like that, you can hardly think straight because all your blood is in your body. You can't get enough oxygen. I felt like committing suicide." She was sure she had cost the team its gold medal, even though no one else in the boat blamed her. They all regarded the crab as a team mistake. The coach, however, felt differently and swore Bower would never make the team again.

Bower watched the video of the race a couple of times. She saw the boat slow down and heard the crowd gasp. Then she put the mistake behind her and worked as hard as she knew how to improve her rowing. The coach could not overlook her performance at selection camp in 1980. She made the eight go fast.

In the number two seat, behind Bower, was Holly Metcalf, a quiet, introverted young woman who had been discouraged from even trying to make the national team. She had begun rowing her sophomore year at Mount Holyoke, which is not a rowing powerhouse. The woman who was stroking the boat at Mount Holyoke had felt tremendous power coming out of the bow of the boat, where Metcalf sat. She encouraged Metcalf to develop as a rower and to see how far she could go with the sport.

When Metcalf thought she was ready, she made a trip to Boston to test for the national team. That year, scores on a stationary bike would be one of the factors considered when the coaching staff issued invitations to selection camp. Metcalf climbed onto a bike to see how well she could do. She knew she was strong. Besides the stroke's encouragement, she had the support of her coach at Mount Holyoke. When she first turned out for rowing, he had asked everyone to go off and see how many stadium stairs she could run in five minutes. He had been astounded at the number Metcalf had been able to run.

She was sitting on the bike, waiting for the starting signal, when Kris Korzeniowski, the women's national team coach, approached her. He asked her where she rowed. "Mount Holyoke," she said. Then he asked her how tall she was. "Five-eight." He told her to get off the bicycle and go home. He did not want to waste time that could be used by a more promising prospect.

She got off the bike and went back to Mount Holyoke, where she worked with her coach to try to figure out an effective training program. The next spring she trained in Philadelphia at College Boat Club, which had places for people like her, rowers from small colleges who wanted to train and learn.

In 1981, she competed in pairs trials. She made the finals and had to be invited to selection camp. There, she focused on rowing as hard as she could. She knew that her technique was not great. She kept hitting herself as she brought her hands around at the finish of the stroke. That only made her row harder. Korzeniowski was yelling at her to get out of the boat and telling her she would never make the national team. She rowed even harder. Too strong to ignore, she made the team. She found another coach, who worked with her on technique. When she returned to camp the next year and got in a boat and rowed, Korzeniowski dropped to his knees, saying, "Metcalf, what happened? Thank God."

For Metcalf, as for others in the boat, rowing was home. She had been a huge kid—she wore a size eight-and-a-half woman's shoe in the third grade—who had to be in constant motion. Her home was not happy. Her alcoholic father had left when she was four, and her mother had been unable to give Holly the attention she craved.

Metcalf: "I needed a place where I could use the strengths that I had. I needed some feedback. I needed some structure. And I needed to share with other people. I needed to be with people who could give each other pieces of what they were good at."

In 1984, she was rowing harder than ever, trying to distract herself from her father's death the year before and wanting to give her family a lift by winning a gold medal. In the number two seat, her job was to support the stroke, to make sure her rhythm reached all the way to the bow. The year before, she had been the stroke of the eight. Beard had wondered how Metcalf would adjust to being moved so far toward the bow. But with Keeler at stroke and Metcalf, who had become technically superb, in the two seat, the boat was tied together. Practices might have been better had Metcalf been the stroke, Beard thought, but Keeler was definitely the more spirited racer.

Shyril O'Steen, in the bow, felt that she had been holding her hand in the air forever as the boats blew around on the Lake Casitas starting line. The bow person keeps her hand raised at the start until the coxswain tells her to put it down. The officials train a camera across the bow of each boat to record the start. If there are problems, they can look at that record to determine what happened and who was at fault.

Besides having the nerves to keep her hand in the air until the moment of the start, O'Steen had the strong technique and the lightness necessary in a bow person. Because the bow is the leading end of the boat, coaches look for a lighter, smaller person to sit there; that part of the boat then rides higher. They also want someone who can match exactly what the stroke, fifty feet away, is doing. If the bow seat falters, the effect on the boat is more pronounced.

O'Steen was tall (five-ten) but light (147 pounds). She had trouble keeping weight on and was about ten pounds lighter than anyone else in the boat. She had rowed at the University of Washington. She liked being on the water, and she liked the rhythm and perfection of the sport. When she started rowing, she had no upper body strength. In the weight room, she could not do a military press with the lightest weight on the bar. Gradually, she built her strength. She learned how to train efficiently and to push when her body was begging for rest. Bob Ernst, who had arrived at the University of Washington to coach the women's team in 1981, helped her. She followed his training program and saw results. The UW eight that year won every race, and she began to think that a 147-pound weakling like her had a chance to make the national team. She still wasn't doing well on the strength tests that the national team coaches use to evaluate people, so she wasn't invited to the 1981 selection camp. Through Ernst, she found a partner to train with for the pairs trials. They finished fourth and got an invitation to camp.

O'Steen thought that 1981 was the year everything came

together for her. She made the national team and rowed in the four, which was not the priority boat. The four surprised everyone by winning a bronze medal at the world championships. O'Steen, who had never considered herself a competitive person, was ready to devote at least the next three years of her life to racing at an international level. Before she got serious about rowing, O'Steen had considered competition a dirty word. She did not like measuring herself against other people. Yet, when she was training to make the team, she found herself targeting other women who rowed on the starboard side of the boat and pushing herself to work harder by thinking, *I've got to beat Jeanne* or *I've got to beat Kris.* She began to change her ideas about competition, preferring to regard it as a mutually enriching experience. Competitors push each other to improve; they are role models for each other. During long, hard workouts, the idea of another person rowing harder and improving faster keeps the athlete focused on her own efforts.

Because she had gone up against first-rate competition, O'Steen was now in the bow of the 1984 U.S. women's eight, waiting on the starting line at the Olympics. Once, when she was eleven, her father had told her that she could do anything she wanted to do, be anything she wanted to be. Why, if she really put her mind to it, she could go to the Olympics and win a gold medal, he said. He did not have a sport in mind for her; he was just trying to make the point that she should not put any limitations on herself. His words had made a big impression on young Shyril. The context had a lot to do with their impact. She and her father were driving from Seattle to Portland, and he was telling her that he and her mother were separating. She was afraid, confused and uncertain; and he was persuading her that she could reach any goal she might want to set for herself.

Beard liked having O'Steen in the bow. She helped stabilize the boat, and she could be relied on to row her hardest. Beard saw that all the boats were aligned for a start and calmly, through the microphone she was wearing, told O'Steen to drop her hand. All eight rowers were at the catch position, bodies coiled, blades buried in the water. The starting command came. *Etes vous prêts?*

Partez.

The race for the 1984 Olympic gold medal was finally under way.

◆ ◆ ◆

The U.S. boat, which had proved itself capable of blinding starts in Lucerne, beating the powerful East Germans off the line both days, faltered at the line on Lake Casitas. The rowers were moving at forty-eight strokes a minute but did not seem to be grabbing all the water they could. They were churning up the water, rather than digging in and pushing it away.

Beard blamed the poor start on nerves. This was their only race of the Olympics, since the eights had not been required to compete in heats. Without heats, the rowers had no way to test themselves against the field before the final. They hadn't raced since June. They had been practicing, but they had also been standing around watching other races. They had seen Romanian boats dominate the Olympics. In every women's race so far—in the four, in the double, in the pair, in the single and in the quad—the Romanians had won the gold medal.

In the final event of the Olympics, the Romanians were once again going for the gold. Beard looked over into lane two, and saw that the Romanian boat was slightly ahead. This was not a long race for the gold; it was only 1,000 meters and would be over in less than four minutes.

Beard was counting on the experience and desire in the boat to carry it across the finish line first. There had been a lot of talk during the summer about the clash of personalities in the eight, but Beard knew they had a strong bond in their passion for a gold medal. They were a highly individualistic and idiosyncratic group of women, all with well-developed egos that they somehow managed to subordinate to the goal of making the boat go fast. They had lived and trained together all summer, but they tended not to socialize off the water. Off the water, their differences were too great to overcome. On the water, they relied totally on each other, trusted each other without question and believed they would rather die than let the boat down. During some workouts, even if someone had been particularly peevish before getting into the boat or if one of the rowers had made a sarcastic remark to another, all eight would begin to row together, and as their smooth strokes gained power and the boat began to move faster, they could feel it rising above their differences, moving into the quest for excellence that each of them shared.

After the shaky start, Beard called for the boat to settle into its body-of-the-race cadence. The stroke rate went down to forty. The power that the U.S. women were accustomed to feeling at that rate didn't seem to be there. The customary smoothness was not there. The boat was rocking around. Every so often someone would bobble a stroke and the whole boat would wobble.

Coach Bob Ernst was watching through binoculars. He was not good at dealing with the pressures on race day. During workouts, he was the man in command, getting results through intimidation. Beard was afraid of him, as were some of the others in the boat. O'Steen liked his brusqueness because she knew exactly where he stood. She regarded coaches' relationship to athletes as unusual. "They're living vicariously through you. All of their success is based on what you do."

Those who had learned rowing from Ernst in Seattle tended to think more highly of his coaching skills than those who had not. Those who did not like his manner of coaching tolerated it because the boat was getting faster.

Ernst was perhaps more nervous than the rowers were at the prospect of the eights race at the Olympics. He felt the pressure of being the favorite as much as they did. He had tried to isolate the rowers from the hype of the Olympics, keeping them near Lake Casitas, away from the main Olympic Village in Los Angeles. He had tried to focus them on their workouts. On the day of the race, just before the women launched their eight to head toward the starting line, Ernst asked them to form a circle around him. He did not say a word; he just went from one woman to the next and hugged all nine of them. Norelius teared up during this ritual, and by the time she was in the boat out on the lake warming up, she was sobbing. She reviewed her whole rowing career and sobbed for the entire warm-up. She had barely regained her composure in time for the start of the race.

Approaching the mid-point of the race, the U.S. women's eight seemed anything but composed. The Romanians were ahead. Beard was beginning to think, *Oh, my God, we could lose this race.* The stroke rate was at a forty-one, and the crew was not sharp. Beard knew that the way the eight were rowing had to change drastically. She also knew that most people who start out rowing badly in a race usually end the race rowing worse. She did not want to communicate this knowledge to her crew. Instead, she wanted the eight rowers to know that they were going to win this race and that they needed to make their move in that direction.

The 500-meter mark was the point in the race where the depth in the boat and the hours of relentless practice should kick in. Practice sessions are generally more brutal than a race because they simulate one race after another until the rowers believe they are going to die of exhaustion. When they survive, they develop the idea that race day will be a waltz compared with practice.

Selection camp is another tool designed to make racing against international competition look like fun. At selection camp, the best rowers in the country race against each other to see which are the very best. Invitations to selection camp come after testing and competitions throughout the year. Rowers report their scores on ergometer pieces (they see how fast they can do 2,500 meters on a rowing machine) and on bench pulls (they lie prone on a bench and see how many times in six minutes they can pull a seventy-pound barbell to the bottom of the bench). Coaches evaluate performances at various regattas. And the finalists at the national pairs trials automatically qualify for camp. Two or three weeks long, selection camp is designed to put together the fastest boat. It is also designed to see who falls apart under pressure. Camp is definitely a test of mental toughness.

Seat racing starts a couple of days after camp does and lasts until a four and an eight are picked. Seat races are held twice a day. In seat racing, the coach puts together two crews and sends them on a race against each other. Then the coach switches a rower from each boat and races them again. The coach compares the times and sees which rower makes the fastest boat faster. Seat racing is not an exact science. Sometimes the races are too close to be definitive. Then the coach has to use subjective standards to select the mix of people that will cohere over a summer of training together into the most efficient, powerful racing unit.

In 1984, camp was held in May at Princeton's Lake Carnegie. Twenty-six women were at the camp, contending for seats in the sweep boats—the eight, the four and the pair. The different athletes had different strategies for coping with the pressures of camp. Jeanne Flanagan took the approach that she was among her peers and would reach for that little extra something that would give her a place in the boat. She rowed as hard as she could during every seat race and performed no postmortems. She chose to be unaware of how she or anyone else had done in any race. Ultimately, the coach's perception was all that counted, and she would discover her place when the final boatings were made. She had been to enough camps to know that the athletes who did not make the team were the ones who thought they should get special treatment and who did not take the time to study the more successful rowers to learn what it was they did to survive.

Carie Graves, who had been to more selection camps (eight) than anyone else there, knew that she had to remain calm and focused on the entire process, not just on her particular seat race. She hated seat racing, hated the feeling of being the one person in the boat whose performance was being judged, hated having to compete against her teammates, women she had known for years. Yet she knew that she had to be psyched up for the duration so that she could row as hard as she possibly could on every single piece.

Holly Metcalf approached seat racing like a musician accepting an impromptu invitation to perform with a group. She opened herself to other people's rhythms and tuned into their strengths. She knew that her worst performances came when she concentrated on herself. The key for her was to pick up on the best of what everyone else in the boat was doing.

Kathy Keeler, who had taken at least one year away from rowing on the national team because she did not want to go through selection camp, took the one-day-at-a-time approach. She never looked back at a performance, never worried about whether she had won or lost. She believed in the camp system for its ability to produce the fastest boat, but she disliked giving up her independence for the regimen of seat racing.

Shyril O'Steen knew that seat racing worked to her advantage. She didn't have a chance at the bench pulls or the ergometer tests. But she could win a seat race where strength wasn't the only factor. She viewed seat racing as a way to prove to the other rowers that she, with limited upper body strength, belonged in the top boat. During the two weeks of seat racing, she went into a cocoon, focusing only on her rowing and not thinking about the fact that she was competing against some of her best friends.

The coxswain had to seat race, too, but her selection was based on more subjective criteria than rowers'. The coxswain has to get along with the coach and be able to impart the coach's instructions to the crew. The coxswain also has to get along with the crew. Sometimes, the rowers in a boat vote on which coxswain they want.

Betsy Beard went to selection camp sure that she had no

chance to be coxswain of the eight. The best she could hope for was to be chosen for the four. There were four coxswains at camp and places for two of them on the Olympic team.

Beard went through most of the camp convinced she was the least likely coxswain to make the team. She was seat racing with the eights group, and not with the fours. She thought if she didn't race with the fours, the athletes wouldn't get to know her and wouldn't have any confidence in her abilities and she would not be picked for that boat.

Then on a Sunday morning, her phone rang. It was the coach, Bob Ernst. Her heart sank. This was the way people were notified that they had been cut. The coach would call and say not to bother putting on turnout gear for the next practice. Call back if you have questions. Otherwise, thanks and good-bye.

In this phone call, however, Ernst did not give her bad news. Instead, he seemed to want to chat. He asked her how she thought she was doing, whether she thought the athletes were responding to her, how she felt each one of them was doing. Then he said so long, see you at practice.

Beard had no idea what that phone call was about. She went to practice that afternoon, and Ernst told her she would be riding in the coaching launch with him. Once they were on the water, he told her that this would be the last time she saw the crew of the eight from the launch. From this practice on, she would be in the coxswain's seat. He had decided that she was going to be the coxswain of the Olympic eight.

As the news penetrated her consciousness, Beard didn't know whether to leap for joy or to cringe. She knew some of the crew would resist Ernst's choice of her because she was new to them and untested. Some of the members of the eight did protest Ernst's choice. They were upset that he had not even consulted with them. His selection of Beard came as a surprise to everyone, and not everyone liked surprises.

Kris Thorsness was one of those concerned over Beard's being the coxswain. After the races in Lucerne, Thorsness began to think that Ernst had made the right choice. She gave Beard credit for pulling the boat together in the Swiss regatta. Thorsness liked Beard's style, which communicated a willingness to work with the boat instead of merely shouting orders. She liked Beard's confidence and her competence.

Now at the 1984 Olympics, Thorsness was once again hearing that confidence in Beard's voice as she told the eight rowers that it was time to make a move. She did not communicate any doubt. In fact, she communicated absolute certainty that they would win. The Romanians were ahead, but the U.S. was going to overtake them. Thorsness thought: *Betsy's certain, then so am I. So let's go.*

It was as if the whole boat suddenly woke up. Kathy Keeler thought she heard everyone in the boat say, *Fuck this. Let's go.* She picked up the rate.

Shyril O'Steen thought, *Shit, we might lose this race.* And she suddenly felt the eight smooth out their strokes and get a better rhythm going. Carol Bower thought she would be damned if she was going to lose the Olympics in her home state. Then she felt the extra power that the boat usually delivered. Carie Graves bore down with disgust, thinking, *Oh, for God's sakes we're supposed to win this.*

Now it was just a matter of digging in and rowing for their lives. It was a matter of giving everything on every stroke and then giving more.

In the last part of a race, the rowers are in acute pain. Their legs burn. They gasp for air. They have felt this pain many times. Their training teaches them that they will survive pain and that they can push beyond it. Some develop tricks to cope with the pain.

Kristi Norelius tried to label the burning in her legs as a cozy warmth instead of raging fire. Calling pain something else took the sting out of it. She imagined that she was sitting in front of a fireplace and that her skin felt deliciously warm.

Thorsness felt as if she were encased in a private hell. Every cell was screaming at her to stop, yet she couldn't. She was not sure whether she would live or die. But she keyed into the coxswain's voice and made it the only thing she knew. Beard's voice was promising her life and, even better, promising victory.

The U.S. women's Olympic eight began to move on the Romanian eight. At the hundred-meter mark, the boats were even. Past the hundred-meter mark, the U.S. boat began to pull ahead. The momentum was visible. The U.S. crossed the finish line one second ahead of the Romanians.

Betsy Beard's first reaction was relief. Kathy Keeler's first reaction was disbelief. She did not think her boat had won. She kept asking Beard if she was sure about the finish. Beard said, yes, she was sure. Keeler vowed she would never again under any circumstances root for the underdog.

✦ ✦ ✦

After winning the gold medal at the 1984 Olympics, five of the rowers in the eight—Kathy Keeler, Kristi Norelius, Carie Graves, Carol Bower and Shyril O'Steen—retired from elite-level rowing competition. Jeanne Flanagan stayed on to make another national team in 1985 before she retired. Holly Metcalf took a break in 1985 but made the national teams in 1986 and 1987 before a bad back prevented her from making the Olympic team in 1988. She had surgery on her back and turned out for selection camp in 1988, but she was not as strong as she had been. "It was the most frustrating thing to have an athlete trapped inside a body that couldn't do what it used to be able to do."

Kris Thorsness also competed until her body gave out. She made the national teams in 1985, 1986 and 1987. By 1988, she had had three operations on her left shoulder, which she had dislocated in her zeal to become what she calls "an upper body animal." The patched shoulder gave out during seat racing at selection camp in 1988. She was a spare on the U.S. women's

Olympic team in Seoul that year, a spare who could not even move her left arm.

Betsy Beard stayed with the national team through 1988, coxing the eight every year until she retired. The closest she came to the 1984 finish was a silver medal at the world championships in 1987.

Five of the rowers in the 1984 Oympic gold medal eight went into coaching. Kathy Keeler spent a year away from the sport entirely before she began coaching elite scullers at the Boston Rowing Center. She has been a national team coach, too. She tells her athletes what she told herself as a competitor: "When you're in the thick of it and trying to go for a boat, attaining your goal is the thing. Nothing else matters. It's worth it to go for it no matter what."

Carie Graves dropped out of rowing completely for four years before she decided that she was finally able to return as a coach. She did not attend the hall of fame induction ceremony for the 1984 eight. That left a seat in the boat open for Ernestine Bayer. Graves tried to figure out what it was about rowing that made her so angry. Gradually, she came to think that it was her own intensity that had pushed her to the burn-out point. No one could sustain the kind of intensity she put into rowing. And she was incapable of rowing without that intensity. When she took a coaching job at Northeastern in Boston, she was no longer angry. She felt she had a contribution to make to the sport. She went into coaching for the second time with a more relaxed attitude from the days at Radcliffe when she was known as Old Ironface. She could joke and express her feelings. She could work at providing a framework in which young women can learn about their capabilities by pushing harder than they ever imagined possible.

Carol Bower became head coach of the women's program at the University of Pennsylvania. Jeanne Flanagan coaches at a club in Boston and gives lectures on the physiology of workouts, on nutrition, on weight training. She has developed a lecture series called *Dragon Slaying*, in which she teaches the mental toughening techniques that contributed to her success as an athlete. Holly Metcalf went into coaching at Radcliffe. She tries to stay in good enough shape herself to keep in touch with what she is asking the athletes to do. "The athletes respect you and trust you a lot more when you're close to rowing, when it's clear that you know what rowing feels like. They respond to coaches who have still in their bodies the feel of what's good."

Betsy Beard stayed in touch with rowing by becoming active in the political side of the sport. She became a member of the U.S. Women's Olympic Rowing Committee. She married the man against whom she used to cox races in the living room, and she works as a pharmacist in a Seattle hospital.

Those members of the 1984 eight who have left rowing altogether remember the intensity and purity of the sport and hold it up as a standard against which they measure what they are doing with the rest of their lives. Kristi Norelius got a masters degree in social work and a job in a residential treatment facility for emotionally disturbed children. Some days she wishes that those kids would respond to her efforts the way her performance in rowing responded. In rowing, she knew that if she worked hard, improvement was inevitable. "The work I do with these kids is very intangible. We can work our rear ends off and never get anywhere."

Shyril O'Steen, who went to the University of Chicago to get her Ph.D. in zoology, would like to be the best scientist in the world, but wonders how to measure achievement in that field. She knew how to be the best in rowing. "In rowing, to be the best you win races. It's that simple. In rowing you have rhythm and perfection. You feel yourself getting stronger. You have that endorphin rush, the feeling of the other people in the boat and the timing of being right in there. When it feels good, there's nothing like it. I keep trying to get that feeling again."

Kris Thorsness went to work as a lawyer in a large corporate firm in San Francisco. She compares her job with what she did as an athlete. "Being a lawyer is a lot like training. You have to have the same dedication and concentration and willingness to set long-term goals and to work with other people and to accept the fact that what is necessary and expected to succeed is a lot of hard work."

✦ ✦ ✦

Proud as they are of being Olympic gold medalists, to this day the members of the 1984 eight are not proud of the race that won the gold. They all say it was a bad race. Carie Graves is the most blunt about it: "It was kind of a letdown actually. The culmination of an eleven-year career, and it's a crappy race." Shyril O'Steen has a video of the race, but she rarely watches it. "I can hardly watch it. I get the shakes and I have to go to the bathroom." This distaste for the race itself, however, does not take anything away from the pride the women feel in their rowing careers. All of them made tremendous sacrifices, pushed their physical and mental limits and did their absolute best. Knowing this is sufficient in itself. Having a gold medal in recognition of their efforts is abundant good fortune.

The woman who perhaps felt the best about her performance on that August day in 1984 when the U.S. women's rowing team won its first Olympic gold medal was Carol Brown, who watched the race from the shore as the team spare. Brown was thrilled at her teammates' gold-medal finish. But she felt a deeper satisfaction, one that came from knowing she had not compromised her efforts to be the best. She had, in fact, come back from a devastating injury to try to make the team. And even though her efforts fell short of her goal of a seat in the eight, she knew she had done her best. "After the '84 Olympics, I could walk away from rowing honestly being able to say that I did everything that I could. The tangible result isn't always what's most important. The satisfaction of the effort is what's most important. That's what I knew I wanted to carry with me the rest of my life."

Kris Karlson, pictured here after winning the U.S. Women's lightweight single title in 1989, went on that year to win two gold medals at the world championships. She is only the second American in the history of rowing—and the first woman—to win gold medals in two different events at a world championship regatta.

Kris Karlson

~

What have I got to lose? Nobody knows me, and I don't know anybody.

Until 1988, anonymity was Kris Karlson's edge in rowing. She liked appearing at a regatta and surprising everyone by her performance. She loved hearing amazed whispers and seeing heads turn in her wake. Expecting to do the unexpected gave her the extra push she needed on the race course. When she showed up at the 1988 world championships in Milan, Italy, few people knew who the gangly, curly-haired, twenty-four-year-old self-taught sculler was. She quietly dropped her single into the water. Then she blew everyone away. When she crossed the finish line, she was the new world champion in lightweight women's single sculls.

The next year, when everyone knew she was a champion, she decided to become a legend. She entered two events at the world championships in Bled, Yugoslavia—women's lightweight single and women's lightweight double sculls. She had to fight to enter both races. The United States Rowing Association had been reluctant to grant the necessary permission. The racing committee thought the physical demands of entering two different events would be too great, and her performance in both races would suffer. She spent the summer proving that she had enough stamina to hold her own in two events. By the world championships, there was no way to refuse her desire to compete against the world's best in her single and turn right around and go out again against the world's best in a double. In Bled, she lived up to the billing she had given herself. Kris Karlson won the gold medal in both the single and the double. No American rower since the fabled John Kelly Sr. at the 1920 Olympics had won two gold medals at a world championship event. Karlson took her place alongside Kelly in the pantheon of extraordinary rowing feats.

John Kelly's daughter Grace is better known than he to the American public. Among rowers, however, John and his son John Jr. are the members of the Kelly family who count. They are the Kellys who made the United States a force in international rowing competition. *Grace Kelly* is the name of an eight-oared shell that belongs to the Vesper Boat Club on the Schuylkill River in Philadelphia. *Grace Kelly* was the shell that the 1984 women's Olympic gold medal eight borrowed for a row with Ernestine Bayer, another mythical figure in the rowing world. To have duplicated John Kelly's accomplishment sixty-nine years later insured forever Kris Karlson's loss of anonymity in the small but intensely interested rowing world.

After 1989, the renowned Kris Karlson began looking for other ways of doing the unexpected and thus motivating herself to perform at levels beyond her normal capabilities. She decided that her best course was to leave the world of women's lightweight rowing, in which competitors cannot weigh more than 130 pounds, and to join the world of women's heavyweight rowing, where bigger is usually better. In 1990, when she made this switch, she was no longer expected to win. In fact, people doubted that an uncoordinated, skinny woman whose family called her "Bean" could even compete against athletes weighing 170 pounds and up. Those people, however, had not counted on Kris Karlson's hunger or on her heart, two intangibles that she has in abundance and that she had to call on more and more as she pushed herself toward the ultimate challenge of her rowing career: to win a medal at the 1992 Olympics in Barcelona, Spain.

✦ ✦ ✦

In many ways, Kris Karlson is the quintessential single sculler. Self-reliant, goal-oriented and highly intelligent, Karlson is at home in the single, a solitary, challenging craft. The single sculler often trains alone and takes sole responsibility for getting her boat and herself halfway around the world to a regatta. Single sculling is the most difficult event in rowing, requiring a combination of balance and power. And it takes unparalleled mental effort.

A single scull is a twenty-seven-foot-long boat that looks too narrow for anyone to sit in. The hull is often only ten inches wide at the gunwales. The rower sits above the gunwales and uses her two oars to balance herself. Rowing a racing single has a high-wire-act element to it. If the rower catches the water wrong or does not balance her body and her oars just right as she moves back and forth on the sliding seat, the boat will roll and dump her into the water. When Kris Karlson first tried to get into a racing single the summer after her junior year in college, she flipped it. She didn't try to row one again until after she had graduated.

Besides the delicate balance of the boat, the rower of a single scull has to worry about steering. In a 2,000-meter race, she has to keep looking back over her shoulder to be sure she is aimed straight in her lane. Plus, she has to keep track of what the other racers are doing. And she has to row as hard and fast as she can.

The rowing stroke is the same in sculling as it is in sweep rowing—the catch, the leg drive, the finish and the recovery. The rower keeps her hands as close together as possible when the oars cross over each other. The left hand comes in just over the top of the right hand. After a workout or a race, the backs of scullers' right hands are often scratched and bloody.

In the United States, the emphasis in collegiate rowing programs is on sweep rowing and the big team boats. Rowers who try to make the transition from sweep rowing to sculling often have difficulty. Good sweep rowers have adequate technique but in their quest for power often fail to understand the subtleties of technique that sculling demands.

Kris Karlson got into rowing in the sweep program at Williams College in Williamstown, Massachusetts, where she had gone for pre-med studies. She had planned to study medicine since she was a junior in high school. She had never planned to be a rower. Her group in high school was, in her words, "the brains." Nobody in that group was interested in sports, and Karlson was not interested in deviating from the group's standards. She also had a physical problem with her hip, which is rotated in too far and affects the way she walks. With her uneven gait, she was never very comfortable in earth-bound sports. Running is painful for her. She is also not particularly coordinated. Karlson, who was born on November 16, 1963, the oldest of five children, was simply not involved in sports when she was growing up.

When she went to Williams College, Karlson was ready to try anything new: "College is brand new. Nobody knows you. You don't know anybody. At Williams, everybody was 'brains' so that wasn't anything special any more. If you don't do something else, you're pretty boring." She noticed flyers about rowing posted around the campus, and she decided to investigate. She was intrigued to discover that she could take up rowing at her advanced age without being at any disadvantage for starting late. At five-nine she was a good size for rowing. When she got into a boat for the first time—a fiberglass eight—she was fascinated by seeing the sun dance on the water through the thin hull. She signed up for the crew team.

Her sophomore year, Karlson's eight came in third at the Dad Vails, a venerable regatta on the Schuylkill River in Philadelphia. It was her first medal ever in a competitive sport. Elated, she thought she might be at the pinnacle of a brief but glorious athletic career. By the end of her senior year, she was ready to say good-bye to rowing. She had a frustrating final season. As a senior, she was the veteran of the squad and felt dragged down by the demands of the younger, less experienced rowers. The team's record was undistinguished. When Karlson put her oars away after the last regatta of her senior year, she was looking forward to a summer off to get her mind right for medical school in the fall. She had no intention of continuing to row.

◆ ◆ ◆

What Karlson had not counted on when she entered the world of rowing was the addictive nature of the sport in particular and of athletics in general. Having trained to compete at the college level, Karlson found that she could not just stop being a physical creature. The summer after she graduated from Williams, she worked on renovating a house and she bought a bicycle to ride for exercise and as a way of keeping her athletic focus.

In the fall of 1985, when she started medical school at the University of Connecticut in Simsbury, along the narrow, twisting Farmington River, she found herself irresistably drawn to rowing. At the welcoming picnic, she saw a young man who looked like a rower. Karlson, who is usually shy and standoffish, walked right up to him and started talking. His name was Stewart Anderson. He had been a sweep rower at Amherst, and he was coaching rowing at the Simsbury High School Boathouse, in addition to going to the university. He invited Karlson to the boathouse, and they started rowing together in a double, teaching each other how to scull.

She learned how to keep the boat balanced and was soon able to put some power into her stroke. The summer after her first year of medical school, she bought a used single and took it to New Hampshire, where her parents were building a house on a lake. After helping with construction each day, Karlson went out on the lake in her single. She even entered a couple of local races that summer and was satisfied with her performance.

In Simsbury during her second year of medical school,

Karlson coached junior varsity girls at Simsbury High School and practiced her own sculling. To measure how much she had learned in a year, she entered the Head of the Charles, the three-mile Boston regatta that is held every October. Rowers are lucky to get into the Head of the Charles; the demand for spots is so great that selection is by lottery. Karlson got into the race in the club single category. She finished in second place and was pleased with herself. In fact, she was ecstatic. Others were impressed by her finish, too. "Everyone kept asking me who taught me how to scull," she was quoted in *Sports Illustrated*. "What was fun is that nobody taught me."

After her performance at the Head of the Charles, several of Karlson's friends suggested that she go to trials for the national rowing team. She was intrigued by that idea, having been unsure about what rowing goal to pursue next. The challenges of medical school were all mapped out for her. But as a rower without the structure of a college or a club program, she had to come up with her own objectives. By this time, she relied on rowing to provide a counterbalance to the intensity of medical school. One was so physical and the other so mental. But both, to be satisfying to Karlson, had to have the momentum of purpose. She decided to aim for the national team in 1987, saying: "What have I got to lose? Nobody knows me and I don't know anybody."

✦ ✦ ✦

To train effectively, Karlson needed a partner who could row faster and challenge her to pick up her speed. But Simsbury was not the best place to find rowing partners. Serious rowers in the United States usually migrate to Boston, Philadelphia, Seattle or Long Beach, where the coaches and the well-established national team rowing programs are. Simsbury had a high school rowing program and not much else. One day, however, at the Simsbury High School Boathouse, Karlson met Paul Carabillo, a man in his late thirties who worked as a contract administrator for a large engineering firm. Carabillo had rowed in the 1960s for Trinity College and had been unable to shake the sport from his life. He was eager for a training partner who wanted to work hard. He and Karlson were well-matched in size—both about the same height, with Carabillo weighting ten or fifteen pounds more—as well as attitude. They began doing the national team workouts together.

At that time, rowers hoping to be on the national team followed a training program sent to them by Kris Korzeniowski, the national team coach. Periodically, they gathered for tests of their strength and endurance. If they were invited to the next round of tests, they went home to continue the workouts. Every national team hopeful was theoretically doing the same workouts over the fall and winter of 1986-87. During a typical week in January, the prescribed workout looked like this:

Monday—a body circuit for flexibility and then weight lifting. The body circuit consists of push ups, one-leg squats on each side, leg circles, bench jumps, pull ups, squat jumps with push ups, sit ups (feet elevated), jumpies, sit ups (sculling motion). The weight routine is different lifts—cleans, bench pulls, bench presses, squats—gone through four times, with each lift repeated three to six times in its turn.

Tuesday—a body circuit plus 120 minutes of steady state exercise, either rowing on the water or on an ergometer or running. The goal is to keep the heart rate at between 140 and 160.

Wednesday—a repeat of Monday.

Thursday—running hills in competition with other athletes. This means racing up a hill for four minutes and doing four such races.

Friday—a repeat of Monday.

Saturday—a repeat of Tuesday.

Sunday—120 minutes of specific rowing either in a tank, on the water or on an ergometer. Four minutes at eighteen strokes a minute, three minutes at twenty, two minutes at twenty-two, one minute at twenty-four. Repeat twelve times. Heart rate should be between 140 and 160.

Karlson and Carabillo quickly got into the routine of the workouts. Each day, they attacked the assigned exercises. They both got faster. Carabillo was amazed at Karlson's progress. Her confidence and desire impressed him so much that he loaned her his new racing single for her national team effort. She took it to Boston in the spring of 1987 to make her rowing debut on the national team scene. The event was Speed Order Trials. She was pleased at her times. "I turned some heads. I got noticed. I heard Kris Korzeniowski say, 'Who is that?'"

The next step to a place on the national team was singles trials in Princeton, New Jersey. The trials were on a Saturday and Sunday. The Tuesday and Wednesday before, for six hours each day, Karlson had the opportunity to measure her progress in the other half of her life—she took exams covering her first two years of medical school. She did well. For balance, then, she also did well at the singles trials in Princeton. She finished a second and a half behind the winner, Ann Martin.

After her impressive performance at singles trials, she was invited to doubles camp, where the national team double would be picked. She had taken the summer off from medical school to devote herself to rowing, and she was excited at the prospect of going to a camp where she would be competing against elite athletes from all over the country. Camp, however, was a disappointment. She saw almost immediately that she had no chance of being half of the national team double. C.B. Sands and Chris Ernst, who had won a gold medal at the world championships the year before, were still rowing together and were at camp. "We knew they would beat the pants off the rest of us. Why were we there when they were still together?" After three days at camp, she went home to continue training in her single.

In 1987, Karlson was on the U.S. teams that went to the World University Games and to the Pan Am Games. As a member of those teams, she was eligible for coaching help.

Having been self-taught at sculling until then, she was eager for some outside expertise and she chose John Marden of Boston as her first sculling coach.

Marden saw right away that Karlson had a few fundamental problems with her technique. She did not prepare her body early enough for the catch, and she dove at the catch. He showed her how to prepare her upper body and hold it fixed, how to take the catch with just the legs, just the slide. Marden also worked with her on finesse. He told her she was hammering her catches, missing water, clutching the handles and using her wrists.

Marden found Karlson to be extremely coachable. "Kris is an incredible athlete. She's very very focused and has a very mechanical mind. She's better able than any other athlete I've seen to conceptualize the technique and then practice until she's got it."

Three weeks after her first coaching session, in her first international competition at the 1987 World University Games in Zagreb, Yugoslavia, Karlson won a bronze medal. At the Pan Am Games that summer, she did not row; she was the team lightweight spare. Nevertheless, the summer had given her what she considered a promising start on the road to becoming a world-class competitor. When she went back to her third year of medical school at the University of Connecticut and back to training with Paul Carabillo on the placid Farmington River in Simsbury, she was more confident and more determined. When they had first started rowing together, Carabillo had consistently beaten Karlson. Now she was beginning to win the racing pieces they practiced in their workouts.

In 1988, Karlson was handed a goal toward which she could focus her efforts—making the national team as the lightweight women's single sculler. Ann Martin, who had rowed the lightweight women's single for the national team the year before, had decided to move into the heavyweight class so that she could try for the Olympics that year. (Lightweight rowing is not an Olympic event; every Olympic rower competes as a heavyweight.) Karlson was confident that she could win Martin's old spot. If she did, she would not go to the Olympics, but she would row in a world championship event.

She worked with Carabillo over the winter season and into the spring. Carabillo would row as hard as he could, and Karlson would row harder. They were both getting faster. At the singles trials in 1988, Karlson finished as she had predicted. She won. She beat an experienced group of scullers, including C.B. Sands, who had hoped to row the single for the team after her doubles partner Chris Ernst decided to take a break from the sport. Sands was not happy about losing in the single, but she found a new partner, Nina Streeter, for the double and together they made the national team. Their coach was John Marden, who also happened to be married to Sands. Marden was Karlson's coach, too, at her request.

Sands and Karlson, on the same team and with the same coach, were noticeably cool toward each other. There was the friction of having been competitors for the lightweight single spot. And there was a drastic difference in personalities. Sands is outgoing and talkative, completely at ease in social situations. She enjoys being the center of attention. Karlson is shy and uneasy around people she doesn't know well. She tolerates attention in moderate doses only. In the summer of 1988, Karlson was beginning to get more attention for her rowing than Sands, a development that made them both uneasy.

Karlson: "There was a baseline tension between C.B. and me. I don't know exactly why."

Sands: "We were enemies. She drove me crazy. We had no reason to be cordial to each other. She's really focused, really targeted. She's more uptight than I am."

In the summer of 1988, Karlson raced the single in Boston, Lucerne, Varesi and Milan. In the Lucerne regatta, she amazed Marden with her sprint to the finish. "It was an incredible sprint. She was sprinting at about a forty-three in a single, which I'd never seen before. She shocked the world."

Karlson shocked herself with that sprint. "I was never a sprinter. I would hang on in the last 500 meters and just survive. But this time, the Italian was ahead. I knew I was catching up with her. I was excited and I just kept getting higher and higher. I looked at my stroke coach [a timing device in the boat]. It said forty-two. I thought, 'Oh my God. What have I done?'"

Her rowing performance in the summer of 1988 pleased Karlson. The friction with Sands did not particularly bother her. The major irritant of that summer for her was the public's perception of rowing. When she was in the United States training, everyone assumed that she would be going to the Olympics. The focus for most amateur athletes that year was the Seoul Games. Karlson's focus was Milan, where the world lightweight rowing championships would be held. No one seemed much interested in her chances there.

In her 2,000-meter race at the world championships in Milan in 1988, Karlson took the lead at the 1,000-meter mark and kept pulling away. With 500 meters to go, she started to think, *Oh my God, I'm winning the world championships.* This was her greatest moment in sports, her first gold medal in international competition, an achievement that had made all her work worthwhile. Heads did turn in Milan. But when Karlson got home, the best lightweight single sculler in the world attracted almost no attention at all. She found being the lightweight gold medalist in an Olympic year frustrating. When she lost her status as an unknown, she wanted everyone to be aware. But the American public was focused on the Olympic Games and had no idea of the lightweight world championships in rowing. Everyone who knew she rowed kept asking her about the Olympics. "It was tedious."

✦ ✦ ✦

Beneath their antagonism for each other and the difference in their personalities, Kris Karlson and Carey Beth (C.B.) Sands shared an amazing ability to focus on whatever goal they chose and an unshakeable belief in their own competence. Sands believed that most women considered luck the greatest factor in any success they had while men thought they had earned their good fortune. She was determined to think like a man. Sands rowed at Smith College and made her first national team in 1983. At five-seven and 125 pounds, she rowed in the lightweight category and, once she became a top-ranked sculler, stayed there. When she and Chris Ernst won the gold medal in the lightweight double at the world championships in 1986, Sands was not at all surprised. "I was surprised when I made the team in '83. After that, I had a certain belief in myself. The experiences I had had in rowing had always been successful. I had always believed it was there."

After winning the gold medal, Sands moved to Fountainebleu, outside Paris, to attend business school at the Institut European d'Administration des Affairs (INSEAD). Other students there laughed at her when she told them she planned to train two to four hours a day while she pursued her studies. The school itself is intensely competitive, with students pressed for any time outside their studies. She biked with the French biking team, trained with the local track and swim teams and entered her first half-marathon. She found the atmosphere perfect for an athlete and felt she was in better shape going into the 1987 world championships than she had been the year before.

Sands teamed up with Ernst again in 1987. She returned to the U.S. for six weeks so that they could train together. They were having some trouble in the boat; it didn't seem to move along the way it had the year before, and neither of them knew why. At the world championships, Sands and Ernst finished third.

The bronze medal finish in 1987 was hard on Sands. And her results in 1988 were devastating. With her new partner, Nina Streeter, Sands finished seventh in the lightweight double at the world championships. This was unacceptable. She knew she was capable of much better. She needed a different partner, one with as much talent and desire as she had. Ouside the boat, she and Nina Streeter had a great time together. But Streeter's behavior in the boat infuriated Sands. Streeter liked to think of herself as the underdog; Sands took her inspiration from knowing that she was good, possibly the best. Streeter liked to talk in the boat; Sands hated talking.

Sands knew she needed a partner who thought exactly the same way about rowing as she did. She wanted someone who was fast. She wanted someone who could train on her own and get up to speed in the double quickly. Sands had taken a marketing job with the French overseas department of Proctor and Gamble in Geneva, Switzerland. She routinely worked ten-hour days and spent a third of her time on the road, traveling to places like Martinique and Guadeloupe, with a transatlantic trip at least once a month. Other rowers doubted that she could train enough to be competitive herself, much less find someone willing to work around her schedule to train with her. But she was sure she could prove the doubters wrong.

Sands began to search for a suitable partner. She mulled over her choices as she got up early every morning to work out on the ergometer in her kitchen. When she could manage a workout on the water, as she was changing her clothes in the backseats of taxi cabs in order to arrive dressed and on time for her business appointments, she went over the roster of lightweight scullers. She listed all the possible candidates as she did everything she could to follow Korzeniowski's training schedule. If she was on the road and the workout that day called for rowing at a hundred percent for eight minutes, she would run as fast as she could for eight minutes. Some days she would jump rope for ninety minutes in her hotel room (she usually requested the ground floor). On weekends, she would go where the Swiss national team was training and row four times a day. With all the work she was doing, she wanted a partner she could depend on.

Finally, Sands realized she had only one choice. She could

not ignore the speed and self-confidence of one of her least favorite people on the U.S. rowing team. Sands would have to ask
Kris Karlson to row in the double with her.

"Why? What would possess me to do a fool thing like
that?" was Karlson's initial reaction to Sands's proposal, which
came in a letter from John Marden in the spring of 1989. "I
couldn't imagine putting the two of us in the same boat and us
getting along."

Marden thought that a Karlson/Sands double would benefit
both rowers. "I thought it would be good for Kris to row with
Carey Beth in the double. Kris has trouble at the catch and with
rhythm. She has no sense of flow in the boat. And she doesn't
know how to slow the slide and hold herself off her feet. She
zooms up the slide and slams into the water. Carey Beth had a
lot to learn about pure aggression, pulling those handles toward
you as hard and fast as you can."

Marden was coaching lightweight scullers for the Swiss national team. He had recently joined Sands in Switzerland after
having lived and coached in Florida during the year Sands was
in business school at INSEAD. He and Sands had both applied
to INSEAD, but Marden's application had been rejected. "We
had made a pact that we'd both go even if we both didn't get in.
But I just couldn't do it psychologically. I went to Florida to
coach. We saw each other every eleventh week or so."

Karlson's plans for 1989 were to race her single and to defend her world championship. She would be taking the summer
off before going into her last year of medical school. She had to
decide where to do her residency and in what kind of medicine.
It was to be a summer of consolidating her gains and figuring
out what goals were worth the next effort. Even if she wanted to
try rowing a double with C.B. Sands (which she did not), the
logistics would be formidable. She was in Connecticut. Sands
was in Geneva. Should Karlson travel to Geneva to train (which
she had no intention of doing), Sands's work schedule would
make practices in the double difficult. Marden, acting as the

go-between for Sands and Karlson, suggested that the two try rowing together in the heavyweight double trials, scheduled for June in Indianapolis, Indiana, just for fun. Karlson began to see a short-term goal developing: "to prove I could row a double."

Marden and Sands arrived in the U.S., picked Karlson up in Connecticut, strapped a borrowed double to the top of the car and drove to Indianapolis. Karlson had told Sands she would row with her at heavyweight doubles trials and, perhaps, at nationals, which were also in Indianapolis, right after the trials. That was all she promised. Sands encouraged her to take one step at a time but began to hold out the carrot of two gold medals at the world championships. Sands: "I had to get her trust. I told her that my goal for the summer was that she win two gold medals. That put everything in a new perspective for her."

Karlson and Sands practiced together five times before the trials. From the moment that they got into a boat and rowed together, Karlson's short-term goal began to stretch into the longer term. When they won the heavyweight doubles trials, Karlson forgot any reluctance she had about rowing with Sands at nationals. Karlson: "I couldn't believe how good that boat felt. It's not that often you row a boat together that well. I thought, 'I don't know if I can give this up.'"

Members of the U.S. rowing team do not normally row in more than one event at a international regattas. If someone rows in two events, she is taking a seat away from someone else on the team. Also, because racing places such demands on the athlete's system, recovering in time to repeat a peak performance in a regatta is difficult. Before nationals in Indianapolis, Karlson was unsure about whether she should push for permission to row in two events at the world championships. At nationals, she won her singles race by nine seconds; she and Sands won the doubles race by eight seconds. With such decisive margins, she felt she had the right to ask for an exception to the one-event-per-athlete rule. She was definitely the person to defend her title in the single. And why should a slower team represent the United States in the double?

Eventually, the executive and lightweight committees of the U.S. Rowing Association could not argue against speed. Karlson was allowed to compete in two events. Before that decision was definite, however, she and Sands had to complete the process of what they had begun calling "jumping through hoops." They had to win the lightweight doubles trials. Then Karlson had to win the lightweight singles trials. Karlson also wanted to go to a regatta in Lucerne to get an early season check on the international competition in the lightweight single.

Committed to rowing together, the two women parted after nationals, each with a checklist of objectives to accomplish in the three weeks before the lightweight double trials. Karlson went to Lucerne where she had a bad race, finishing second to a woman from Italy. She flew from Lucerne to Boston, where Sands picked her up at the airport and took her right to the boat. Trials for the double were four days later. They won by eight seconds. Sands said, "Check." One objective accomplished. Three weeks later, Karlson won the singles trials. Sands said, "Check." They got official word that Karlson could compete in two events at the world championships. Sands said, "Check."

The day after she won the singles trials, Karlson flew to Zurich and caught a train for St. Moritz, where she met up with Sands and Marden. Sands had taken a two-month leave from her job to train. The three of them would spend the next three weeks together, training in an altitude similar to that in Bled, Yugoslavia, site of the world championships. They all lived together in a small room that magnified the personality differences between Sands and Karlson. An incident that occurred on the second day of their stay in St. Moritz set the tone for the rest of the time there. Sands and Karlson had an argument over food. Sands, making a good salary at Proctor and Gamble, believed that the best arrangement for their temporary communal household was to share household expenses without strict accounting methods. Karlson, on the other hand, living on student loans, her parents' generosity and a small athlete's stipend, preferred knowing that she was getting exactly what she paid for. Sands: "Kris watches every penny. She doesn't trust the distributing gods to give her her fair share." On the second day in St. Moritz, in front of Marden, the two women started arguing over who had paid for what food. They were yelling. Sands ended the argument by saying, "All right. You buy your own food and cook it yourself and keep it in your own little corner." Then she walked out.

Sands and Karlson did not see one another again that day until their scheduled afternoon practice in the double. Marden was anxious about whether they would even get into the boat together. Both women showed up on time, put their boat into the water and climbed into it as if nothing had happened. Marden approached them and asked tentatively if everything was all right between them.

Sands said: "We're in the boat. Everything is fine."

Karlson said: "Yeah, I love C.B."

That incident cemented what each came to call their business relationship. Sands: "We were able to do everything in a business-like manner. It's hard for women to do that. We said that we wanted to win. We had trouble getting along outside the boat, but we didn't let that bother us in the boat." Karlson: "With C.B. in the boat, it was a professional relationship. We each knew what the other person wanted out of it. Nothing was worth arguing over in the boat unless it was something about rowing."

✦ ✦ ✦

Karlson loved training in St. Moritz. She did one workout in her single and one in the double with Sands every day. She could measure her progress in both boats and see that two gold medals from the 1989 world championships could, indeed, be hers.

Marden worked with both women, separately and together. He emphasized technique. Sands wanted Karlson to learn the visualization techniques that her former partner, Chris Ernst, had taught her. Sands described the way the visualizations with Ernst had worked: "When we rowed together, she was in the bow. At the end of a workout, she would visualize a race, would make up a story about what was happening. You take a race maybe seven minutes long, and as you paddle along for that time you imagine different scenarios and how you would handle them. You always win. The point of the whole process is to go through all the possible scenarios. Then talk about how you re-acted afterwards. It puts you in sync and makes you understand certain things about your partner. You find places where you can really lock into each other. As a result of all these visualiza-tions, we never said a word during the actual race. If you sat us down after the race and asked us what went on in our minds af-ter the first 250 meters, the second 250 meters, etc., I'd bet my year's salary that we'd be thinking the same thing."

In the Sands/Karlson double, Sands rowed in the bow and conducted their visualization sessions at the end of each work-out. On a typical day, as they were rowing along, she might say: "Okay, 750 to go. We're out in front and the New Zealand boat has just made a move on us. And that makes me really happy because we're going to make a move on them. They've gained a foot on us. And that makes me really happy because we're going to move three feet on them."

Through daily practice together and visualization exercises, Sands and Karlson learned to move as one unit in the boat and to respond to each other without words. They knew they were fast. The only thing that could undermine their performance in a race would be getting behind and forgetting how fast they were. They practiced handling situations in which they were not rowing well. According to Sands, "Our strategy then would be in the first 250 meters to take the stroke rate down maybe as low as twenty-eight for five strokes until we got it together, and then back up to thirty-six."

The more they practiced, the more Sands loved rowing with Karlson. They were both completely focused on doing everything necessary to make the boat go faster. Neither one of them liked to talk in the boat. They both refused to imagine that anyone in the world might beat them. Their race plan was simple: Get ahead and stay ahead.

✦ ✦ ✦

At the world championships in Bled, the lightweight singles race was one day and the lightweight doubles the next. In the six-boat singles final, Karlson was in lane four. The Italian woman who had beaten her at Lucerne was in lane one. For the first time in her racing career, Karlson was first off the starting line. "I was thinking about anticipating the 'p' in 'partez.' I jumped the start just enough but not enough to get caught. Before, I'd always waited for 'partez' to be through."

At the 500 meter mark, Karlson took a look around and saw that she was in the lead. She thought: *This is great. No one passes me in a race.* Typically, she was a middle-of-the-pack racer, going out at a moderate pace and then efficiently and relentlessly moving through the leading boats at the end of the race. She usually started high, rowing at forty strokes a minute for the first twenty strokes, then took ten strokes at thirty-six and rowed at a thirty-three in the middle of the course. When she realized she was in the lead at 500 meters, her thinking was: "I just wanted to keep widening the distance, to have enough margin at the last 500 to withstand their sprints."

Still in the lead with 500 meters to go, she looked around one last time and then bore down on the finish line. "I'm thinking: 'I have a doubles race tomorrow. Let's not do anything stupid. I'm just going to hang on.' I took the rate up, but it wasn't a burn-down-the-barn-doors sprint." She won the race by two seconds, successfully defending her world championship title. She was pleased but not ecstatic, the way she had been in 1988.

She was quoted in the press as saying: "It was so exciting when I won last year, but unfortunately I couldn't recapture that same feeling when I won this year because it was expected."

Marden thought that Karlson's nonchalant response to winning the singles race was a good sign; it indicated that she was focused on winning two gold medals and making history for the U.S. women's rowing program. He had thought all along that rowing in two events at the world championships would be the best thing for her. "The psychological difficulties of returning and defending a title are so strong that an athlete, no matter how talented, can be unnerved. Because Kris was doing double-eventing, it gave her something else to focus on, to distract her from the burden of being the defending single titleholder."

Sands was thrilled with Karlson's victory. It met another objective on her list. She congratulated Karlson and said, "Check." The next day, Sands and Karlson stayed away from each other until it was time to get into the boat to warm up and head toward the starting line. Karlson likes to be extremely calm and quiet before a race. Sands likes to listen to extremely loud music. Sands did have some concern over whether Karlson would be tired after her effort the day before. But she had known since nationals back in Indianapolis in June that she would rather row with a tired Kris Karlson than with anyone else. She told herself she would be alert to signs that her partner was tired and push her to get a bigger lead at the beginning of the race.

The race in the double turned out to be surprisingly similar to the race Karlson had rowed in the single the day before. Karlson and Sands had a good start and were ahead after the first 500 meters. Karlson: "I don't look around in the double as much as I do in the single because I know C.B. doesn't like it. But at 500 meters, I thought: 'Okay. Here I am again in the lead.'"

Sands thought her partner was tired, but she did not start to push her until 900 meters. "Then we made a pretty big move."

They had agreed before the race that either one of them could call for an increase in the stroke rate when she thought the time had come for the sprint to the finish. Karlson had decided during the race that she would wait for Sands to call the rate up. Karlson: "I could see all the other boats. I knew how badly she wanted that gold medal. When she called it up, I would do it."

The Karlson/Sands lightweight double finished three seconds ahead of the women from New Zealand, their closest competitors. Karlson and Sands had exchanged four words during the whole 2,000 meters. Sands had said "settle" twice at the beginning of the race. Karlson had said "settle" once. Then Sands had said "up."

Once they were across the finish line, struggling to breathe and letting the realization of their victory wash over them, Karlson shook the sweat out of her blond curls and screamed, "Check." Sands was startled and immediately looked around to see if they were about to hit another boat or run aground. Then she realized that she was not the only one with the mental checklist. Karlson had just ticked off the last item.

◆ ◆ ◆

In teaming up to row in the double at the world championships, Karlson and Sands managed to push beyond their mismatched personalities and their rivalry to a common ground where they needed to bring out the best in each other to excel. They think their accomplishment contains a lesson for all women.

Sands: "When choosing teams, men pick who they think will win; women pick their friends."

Karlson: "You can't always just row with your friends. People who row with their friends are not fast."

Sands: "People, especially women, would be amazed that I could row with Kris Karlson, someone I didn't even like. I work with a lot of people I don't like. What's important is that we have the same business goals."

Karlson: "We'll never be best friends. But our relationship is better now that we've rowed together."

Sands: "We're friends now, Kris Karlson and I. I think she has changed a lot."

✦ ✦ ✦

In 1989, Kris Karlson was named Female Athlete of the Year by the U.S. Rowing Association. She received the award early in December at the San Francisco Hilton at the rowing association's annual convention. The evening of the awards ceremony, while the hotel staff was arranging the tables in the dining room where the ceremony would be held, Karlson was in the next room, set up as an exhibition hall, doing her daily workout on an ergometer that she had asked an exhibitor's permission to use. Sticking with her training regimen no matter where she is or what else she has to do has gone beyond self-discipline for Karlson. It has become a necessity. Nothing else feels right if she is unable to get in her workout. "If I don't do this workout, somebody out there is doing this workout and they're going to be faster than me. To get this far, you have to be too boneheaded to stop."

After 1989, since she was unwilling to stop rowing, Karlson had to decide what challenges to take on next. She felt that she had accomplished all she could as a lightweight rower. Being virtually ignored for her accomplishments in 1988 because of the Olympics still rankled. Even more bothersome was the attitude of some in the rowing community about lightweight events. Because lightweight rowing is not an Olympic sport, the Eastern bloc countries did not put any training emphasis on it and often did not compete. Before the demise of the Eastern bloc, athletes from those countries were often considered the only real international competition. On top in the pecking order in the rowing world were heavyweight men who could hold their own against East German and Soviet rowers. Next came lightweight men, just because they are men. Then came heavyweight women who compete against East Germans and Soviets. Then lightweight women.

Karlson wanted to see if she could move up in the pecking order. She decided to row in 1990 as a heavyweight. That would be her short-term goal. As a more distant goal, she saw herself winning a medal at the 1992 Olympics.

✦ ✦ ✦

When she joined the ranks of the heavyweight women single scullers in 1990, Karlson became part of a group that specializes at winning silver medals at the Olympic Games. In two of the three Olympics in which U.S. women have competed in the single, they have finished second to Eastern bloc scullers.

Joan Lind of Long Beach, California, was the first U.S. silver medalist in the women's single at the 1976 Olympics in Montreal. Lind began sculling in 1970 and did not give up competition until after the 1984 Olympics. She was the model for an entire generation of single scullers. Lind was a product of the Long Beach Rowing Association, where Tom McKibbon, who had won the European championships (precursor to the world championships) in the double in 1969, was set on developing a group of beautiful and fast women scullers. McKibbon insisted on excellence. He sent his scullers out to run hills and put them on a weightlifting program. He worked them hard on the water. He also insisted that they adhere to an appearance standard that he found acceptable. He banned baggy shorts and gave the women Beach pink leotards with a little star on them. He was also fanatical about protecting the women from the grease stains that rowers get on the backs of their legs as they slide on their seats. McKibbon devised a way to shield the women from those stains.

His dress code may have been silly, but McKibbon's coaching inspired the women in Long Beach to excel. Lind: "Tom instilled in me the thought of seeing how good I could be. He gave me so much positive reinforcement and kept the sport so interesting. He gave me so many things to work on technically and physically. It was an adventure. A total mind, total body adventure. You can't buy that type of adventure."

Lind practiced in the single, as did the other Long Beach scullers. She was, however, terrified at the thought of racing that boat.

In her 1,000-meter final in the 1976 Olympics, Lind finished six-tenths of a second behind the East German sculler Christine Scheiblich. It was a dramatic race, with Lind starting off slowly and then rowing through everyone and nearly overtaking Scheiblich at the end.

The other U.S. Olympic silver medalist among women's single scullers was Anne Marden, who made her first national team in 1979. Marden, who is John Marden's older sister and who preceded C.B. Sands as a graduate of the business school at INSEAD, was working as an analyst for J.P. Morgan Investment Management, Inc., in London while she trained for the U.S. national team. Since her work required travel, she would borrow boats wherever she went, find coaches and negotiate inexpensive club memberships. When she was in London, she could step out the door of her cottage on the Thames and go for a row. Many nights in London she ran the ten miles home from her office and then took her boat out. She considered rowing a calming influence in her life. "Rowing has given me much more serenity than a lot of people have."

Marden's Olympic silver medal performance came in 1988 in Seoul. She had taken a two-month leave without pay from her work to train for the Games. She knew she would be going up against Eastern bloc athletes who had done fourteen water sessions and six land sessions a week and rowed seventeen miles a day, every day of the year, whose job it was to row and who had a strong support system of coaches and trainers. Marden, like other American rowers, had trained on her own all winter and spring and then had come together with the rest of the U.S. team for a crash program to prepare for competition. She had built her own support systems—one on the Thames in London, one on the Seine at Fountainebleu and one on the Merrimack near her parents' home in Concord, Massachusetts.

She left the team for awhile to train in the California Sierras on Donner Lake, to prepare for the altitude at Seoul. She was totally focused on her goal. The four-digit code for her bank machine card was the fastest time recorded in 1987 by the East German sculler. Every time she punched in that number, she was reminded of what she needed to do to win at Seoul.

In the final at the Seoul Olympics, Marden was in lane two. Jutta Behrendt from East Germany was in lane three. Magdalena Gueorguieva from Bulgaria was in lane one. After the first thirty strokes of the 2,000-meter race, Marden knew she was guaranteed the bronze medal, the one everyone had predicted she would win. She had accomplished the first part of her race plan, which was to go out hard and catch Marioara Popesou from Romania as soon as possible. By the 1,000-meter mark, Popesou was falling back. Behrendt and Gueorguieva were way out in front. "I knew very well that the media, my family and the rowing community were all expecting and praying for a bronze. I hated playing this 'as expected' game, but the East German and the Bulgarian were nowhere in sight, so anything better than a bronze seemed out of the question."

When she reached the beginning of the last 500 meters, she wondered if she should bother to sprint. She could win the bronze without sprinting. But she had told her coach she would sprint and had promised that she would never stop trying. With 200 meters to go, she heard shouts from the shore. "In lane three the Bulgarian was just ahead of me. She had been passed by the East German. This time I really did sit up and kick. My strokes were sloppy and I jabbed that water a few times, but I started to move past her."

Marden knew that she had finished second because Behrendt broke Gueorguieva at the end of the race. She was, nevertheless, pleased to stand on the awards platform and bow her head to accept the silver medal.

Anne Marden is one of the barriers Kris Karlson faces in her quest to make the 1992 Olympic team and win a medal. Nobody gives Karlson any odds of beating Marden in the single. Marden is shorter (five-seven) than Karlson (five-nine) but outweighs her by close to thirty pounds, all of it muscle.

For 1990, Karlson switched her weightlifting routine from endurance weights to heavy weights, aiming to add bulk and strength. She got up to 138 pounds. Her family still called her Bean. She had a rough summer of competition. Anne Marden beat her whenever they raced against each other. The European scullers also beat her. But Karlson was not discouraged. Rowing with C.B. Sands had taught her an invaluable lesson, namely, that much of the time to get what you want, you need other people. In 1990, Karlson was not only making the transition from lightweight to heavyweight; she was also becoming more of a team player.

At the beginning of the season, she approached another sculler, Alison Townley, about the possibility of their rowing a double together. Townley, who was the stroke of the 1988 Olympic eight, which turned in a dismal performance in Seoul, had been working on sculling for a year. She loved the purity of rowing in a single and the chance to fail or succeed by what she alone could do. But she also knew that Anne Marden was likely to be faster, at least in 1990. Townley is five-ten and weighs 160 pounds and has no physical reason not to be competitive with Marden or any other heavyweight sculler. Her lack of experience racing the single is what would slow her down. She and Karlson struck a bargain at the beginning of the season. They would both go for the heavyweight single world championship title, but if neither one of them won the chance to represent the U.S. in the single at the worlds, then they would team up to row the double.

Townley: "Kris was great. She was really honest. We're completely honest with each other. We're out to kill each other.

But if the best thing for medaling is to team up, then we'll do it. If I'm going to row in a small boat with someone, I want to be with someone crazier than me. Kris is crazier than me. The way she trains . . . so intensely."

The 1990 racing season worked itself out according to a scenario that Karlson, the realist, had visualized. Anne Marden rowed the single for the U.S. at the world championships. Karlson and Townley rowed the double. Marden placed third. Karlson and Townley won a silver medal. They were a surprisingly strong team, considering their lack of time together in the boat. The world championships were only their third race together, and they had yet to smooth out their teamwork.

For the 1991 world championships, once again Marden was the women's single sculler for the U.S. She placed fourth. Karlson and Townley rowed the double and had a disappointing regatta. They did not make the finals and placed eighth overall.

Karlson did not dwell on her disappointment over the world championships. She returned to Hartford, Connecticut, to continue her medical residency in family practice at St. Francis Hospital and to begin her long winter of training. Whenever she got the chance, Karlson climbed into her car, the square-backed Volkswagen with the sculling blades on the roof, and drove across Hartford to the Trinity College boathouse where she kept her single. She did the scheduled workouts on the cold, gray Connecticut River, in the shadow of oil tankers making deliveries all up and down the shore. If she was on call and unable to get to the water, she went up to the cardiac unit at St. Francis and worked out on the ergometer. She also trained on her ergometer at home, when she happened to be there with time to do a workout.

As she worked out and felt the pain, "the lactic acid pain, the burning pain that doesn't go away right away when you stop," she was happy. "When you stop, you're beyond tired; you're so tired that you feel good." She was doing something every day toward her goal of winning a medal at the 1992

Olympics. She was doing the best she could. Everything else was beyond her control, which made her work even harder at what she could control. Sometimes she thought of Anne Marden, halfway around the world and working just as hard. After all, Karlson and Marden were two of a kind—bright, ambitious, talented women who had found something they had a chance to be the best in the world at and were not about to let that chance pass them by. Even though her making the team in 1992 was not a sure bet, Karlson had to believe in her chances. She could, within the intensity of a workout, imagine a scene twenty years down the road. She is examining a patient, who notices the rowing pictures on her office wall and asks, "Were you ever in the Olympics?" Dr. Karlson smiles and says, "Yes."

Lou Daly, shown here in 1988 after winning a gold medal at the master's world championships in Strathclyde, Scotland, started rowing at the age of forty-seven. She races in both sweep and sculling events and has won numerous medals in each. Daly's approach to the sport rivals the intensity of an elite athlete twenty or thirty years younger.

Lou Daly

A<small>T HEC EDMUNDSON PAVILION</small> on the University of Washington campus in Seattle, a person must climb forty-eight steps to get from the arena floor to the top row of bleachers. Athletes often run these steps as part of their training. They go around the pavilion, running up the steep flights between all twenty-three bleacher sections. Lou Daly is among the athletes running the Hec Edmundson stairs. Three days a week she goes into the pavilion and runs stairs for thirty minutes. On a very good day, she zooms up fifty flights, more than twice around the arena. During an average workout, she conquers between thirty-five and forty-five flights. She goes as hard and as fast as she can for the full thirty minutes, no matter how wobbly her knees or how woozy her oxygen-starved brain.

On days when she is not running stairs, Daly lifts weights. One day's weight workout is for increasing the strength in her legs; another is for her arms. She sets goals and meets them, no matter what. One day she had a goal of doing forty cleans, a lift that involves squatting to pick up a weighted bar, pulling the bar up to the chin and then lowering it. Before she reached her goal of forty, she felt something go wrong in her back. She continued to squat, lift and lower until she had done her forty cleans. The next day her back was in complete spasm. She called in her medical team and told them to do whatever necessary to get her back in shape for a race coming up in ten days.

Daly runs stairs and lifts weights so that her body will respond the way she wants it to when she is rowing a boat. The
stairs and the weights are supplements to the three mornings a
week when she is on the water by six, sweep rowing, usually in
an eight. The stairs and the weights are supplements, too, to
her primary activity during the other four days of the week,
which is working out in a single. Daly is that rare rower who
does both sweep rowing and sculling competitively.

And something else is rare about Daly—she is in her fifties,
a woman with three grown children, training the way an athlete
in her twenties would. She pushes herself to excel at rowing for
all the same reasons any athlete strives to get stronger and faster: The effort gives her a sense of control and mastery that other
aspects of life do not offer. When she is racing in a boat, the
complexities of the world drop away. All that matters are the finesse of her stroke and the power she can put behind it. She
knows immediately how well she has performed, with both an
objective measurement—where she places in the field of racers
at the finish line—and a subjective evaluation of the feel of each
stroke. She feels the rush of adrenalin that is a thrill in itself,
but then she does something even more thrilling—bends that
energy to her will, using it to move the boat most efficiently.
Able to shut out distraction and doubt, she can open herself to
those incomparable moments when everything clicks, whether
she is sculling and her stroke is seamless, a graceful gesture that
sends the boat skimming through the water, or rowing in an
eight whose speed transcends the combined efforts of the rowers
and whose unity temporarily suspends individual personalities.

For these feelings, Daly is willing to push herself up fifty
flights of stairs in thirty minutes or lift weights beyond the
time when her back screams for her to stop. She is rare, but she
is not unique. Daly rows with and races against other women
her age who may not go to the training extremes she does but
who, nevertheless, know the same feelings that drive her to see
how good she can get. Hundreds of women in cities around the

country get up before five to stretch out and be on the water by dawn. In their boats, they forget everything else but whether their oars are properly squared as they catch the water. They welcome their coaches' constant corrections, piercing the early morning stillness and startling shorebirds. They race against their teammates for seats in the fastest boat, and they rely on those same teammates for support that embraces more than rowing. They go on road trips together to compete in regattas, some as far away as Europe. They have found a place of their own, where families, careers and politics do not intrude.

Some of these other rowers might protest that Lou Daly is a fanatic in her pursuit of rowing excellence, but their label for her may be only a shield against their own zeal. A coach of masters women says she has seen every woman in her group lose sight of all reality but rowing. "I've caught all of them going a little over the edge at one time or another. I've seen them let go of everything else and care ridiculous amounts about rowing."

✦ ✦ ✦

When Lou Daly discovered rowing, the rest of her life was disintegrating into chaos. She had functioned primarily as a wife and mother for twenty-five years, but those roles were changing. Her children were gone, either in college or on their own. And her husband had just entered an alcohol treatment program, under the pressure of an intervention that Daly led. A week after her husband went into treatment, Daly heard about an adult rowing program run by the Seattle Parks and Recreation Department on Green Lake, in the middle of the city. She signed up and within a week was rowing six days out of every seven. "I still remember sitting in the shell in my second class. I had this gut feeling. I thought, 'This is my sport. This is what I've been looking for.' It was like coming home."

By the time of this homecoming, which was January of 1985, Daly had tried just about every sport. Between the ages of thirteen and fifteen, while she was attending a finishing school in Switzerland, she had developed a passion for skiing. When she returned to the States, she was the only female on the ski patrol in the Cascade Mountains in Washington state. At the University of Washington in Seattle, where she majored in English, she had participated in synchronized swimming for four years. As she was growing up and into adulthood, she had fenced, ridden horses, played tennis, swum and sailed. (Her mother, Hortense B. Harley, raced sailboats in the 1920s, one of the first women in the Northwest to compete in that sport.)

Daly has a need to be physically active, and in January of 1985 that need was compounded by the stress in her uncertain life. Ballet had been her primary physical release for ten years. She had studied and worked hard at mastering the dance form. But once she got into a rowing shell, she realized how little she was getting back from the commitment she was giving ballet. "I was no good at ballet. I was just doing an exercise class. That's what it added up to. I didn't have the sylph-like figure that's required."

Daly's body was not the ideal long and muscular rower's physique either. She likes to describe herself as "five-six-and-a-half—close to five-seven in the morning and by evening closer to five-six." She weighs around 142 when she is in racing condition. Even though she isn't tall, she has long legs and arms, which she found more useful in rowing than in ballet. "I always used to say that you had to have the three Ts to succeed at something—technique, talent and tenacity. A couple of years ago, a friend of mine added two more—timing and a teacher. Of the five Ts, in ballet I had two. I had no technique and no talent. I was in the wrong place at the wrong time. I did have a good teacher and plenty of tenacity. But there comes a time when you realize that no matter how much you love something, if you're no good at it, you shouldn't continue."

Right away rowing felt like something she could be good at. She had balance and a sense of her body from ballet training. But mainly she had tenacity, which rowing rewards perhaps more than any other sport. Daly's daughter Laura, who was rowing for the Massachusetts Institute of Technology when her mother discovered the sport, says that natural athletic abilities are not the most important ingredients in making a good rower. "With rowing people can succeed because they've decided that's what they're going to do and proceeded to do it. With Mom, that's what happened."

Laura Daly watched from across the country with a mixture of amusement, admiration and relief as her mother became totally immersed in rowing. "I think focusing on rowing helped her a lot with what she was going through with my father. Rowing was something she knew was in her control. It also gave her a circle of friends. She would tell me, 'I have a whole bunch of women friends my age now who are going through the same things that I am.' And rowing was a real confidence booster for her. She knew that she was good at rowing because she had worked at it. She knew she had the talent to really focus in on something."

As Lou Daly's involvement in rowing deepened, Laura Daly's lessened. When she graduated from MIT with degrees in chemical engineering and biology in 1986, she had rowed there for four years and was ready to move on to other things. "I am very much of a generalist. Rowing is one of many things that I do. If you want to see a rowing fanatic, you talk to my mother."

✦ ✦ ✦

Lou Daly was two months shy of her forty-seventh birthday when she discovered rowing. She was past her athletic peak, but she had the kind of personality that instantly latches onto the sport. She was obsessive about detail and compulsive about learning everything she could. Lou Daly and rowing were a perfect fit. And being in Seattle put Daly in the perfect place to develop her new-found passion.

In 1985, Seattle was pioneering the development of rowing for masters women. Masters is a category identified by the U.S.

Rowing Association (USRA) to include anyone twenty-seven or older. The USRA found the need to create such a category in the late 1970s when the fitness movement discovered rowing as a benign form of total-body exercise for people of all ages. Those who had rowed in college forgot the agony of that experience and took up their oars again. People who had never rowed tried it and liked it. Soon, regattas were adding events for the older adults who wanted to race.

Among these older adults was a whole group of women that had been completely overlooked during the time that sport was opening up to women's participation. These were women born in the 1930s and 1940s. They came of age when woman's primary role in sport was cheerleader. They had gone to regattas and yelled for their boyfriends and husbands to do well. Then they had gone to regattas and cheered for their sons. Increasingly, they saw their daughters out on the water and pulled for them as they raced for the finish line. These women were the support system for all the other people who rowed. They drove young rowers to practice. They organized regattas and made sure that everything ran smoothly. They handed out ribbons and medals. And one day, they decided that if rowing was so much fun, they ought to be able to do it, too.

The first group of masters women in Seattle was formed in 1982 when Lou Bradley and Sally Laura extracted a promise from University of Washington crew coach Dick Erickson that he would teach them how to row. The two women were on the organizing committee for a huge Seattle regatta when they persuaded Erickson to set a date for their first lesson. Bradley and Laura took twenty-two other women with them to the University of Washington crew house on that date. Erickson was not there; he had forgotten. Bradley and Laura called his office and got him to the boathouse. Erickson did not know what to make of this group of women. As soon as he arrived, he began thinking how ridiculous some of them looked. Lou Bradley, for instance, was wearing her sailing clothes and a life jacket. He figured he would send them out in the rain for an hour and a half and never see them again. Two days later, they were back with two more women.

While Erickson worked with this group, which eventually became the Conibear Rowing Club (named after the University of Washington crew house on Lake Washington), another group was forming at another spot on the lake. Martha Beattie, who had rowed at Dartmouth and was coaching girls crew at Lakeside School, a private prep school on the north end of Lake Washington, held a family rowing weekend to raise money for the crew program. She offered anyone willing to make a donation the chance to row in an eight. Beattie: "I thought some of the moms would like to get in a boat and see how it feels." Two of the moms, Penny Lewis and Gretchen Hull, thought it felt so good that they wanted more. They asked Beattie to teach them and some of their friends how to row. In the fall of 1984, Martha's Moms started with twelve women whose average age was forty-eight. Their logo was an apple pie with oars crossed in front of it.

Beattie, who was used to working with teen-aged athletes, found coaching this group of women a delight. "In some ways it was easier to teach them. They were so anxious to learn and so self-deprecating. Younger kids are so full of confidence that they can do anything that sometimes they don't listen well. These women learned quickly. I didn't treat them any different-ly from the way I treated kids going to the world champion-ships. I would really lay into them at practice. The ones that I was hardest on would come off the water and thank me after practice. They would say, 'I appreciate the attention so much. I'll work to get better.' Most of them had never had a coach be-fore of any kind."

Hull was fifty-two when she started rowing under Beattie's guidance. She had watched her husband and two of her three sons row. (One of her sons was on the 1980 Olympic team.) As she picked up on the technique and began to see the whole group improve, she discovered a feeling of pure pleasure that she had not gotten out of the Junior League or hospital volunteering. "From my early thirties, I was spending time doing things I thought I ought to do but that I didn't really enjoy doing. I loved how rowing made me feel. It's like nothing I'd ever experienced before as far as pulling together. It works when you work together. You belong to a group and support one another. You have a physical outlet. I was getting the things that I didn't get enough of when I was a young woman."

Hull was not alone in her feelings about the sport, and Martha Beattie suddenly had a group of serious older athletes who wanted to row on a regular basis. They requested and got a land training program that would bolster their performance on the water. Beattie encouraged them to run or ride bikes and to cross-country ski in the winter. She cautioned some of them against lifting weights because of the danger of injury, but otherwise she was not worried about the impact of rowing on their bodies. It is a non-contact sport. "It's a very gentle sport. You can do it until you're eighty." When people talk about how demanding rowing is, they're talking about what the sport asks of an athlete's aerobic capacity.

Beattie was eager for her group to race. As a rower who had been good enough to go to selection camp for the Olympic team in 1976, she knew the draw of competition. She wanted Martha's Moms to have the satisfaction of testing themselves in a race. "You're out there slaving away for hours and hours practicing and doing all that land training. You want that reward of staying with someone in a race. You want the adrenalin flow, the nerves before the race, the elation after the race." As a coach, she also wanted the chance to see how her team was doing compared with other groups of women.

Martha's Moms had only a few months' rowing experience when they entered their first regatta at Green Lake. Theirs was one of four boats in the masters women's eights category. Beattie, who was pregnant, was the coxswain. "I was not what you'd call a light coxswain." Before the race she warned them not to look around at their competition as they rowed. "Every time you look out of the boat, the chance of catching a crab is 100 percent greater," she said. She remembers how "tunneled in" all the women were as they participated in their first race.

Gretchen Hull was in that eight. "That first race we were just scared to death. It was cold and rainy, terrible water. We made a pact that we were going to finish the race and not make Martha embarrassed."

Nobody remembers where Martha's Moms finished in that race. Hull knows only that they finished. "And we were okay. It just whetted our appetites. We thought, 'That wasn't so bad. We can do better than that.'"

Martha's Moms was the group that Lou Daly chose to row with after her introduction to the sport through the Seattle Parks program. On the first morning that she showed up for practice with the Moms, in the spring of 1985, she saw a banner on the Lakeside boathouse, "It's a boy," announcing the birth of Beattie's first child, Sam.

Daly was hooked on the sport by the time she sought out the Moms. She was looking for people who were just as passionate about rowing as she was. If she did not find exactly the same level of intensity, she found a group that allowed and supported her passion. Beattie noticed Daly's talent right away. "She had a smoothness and a natural ability from the beginning." Beattie also noticed her intensity. "She was always coming up to me with all these questions. And I remember at the end of that first season, she said to me, 'I just want you to know that this is VERY important to me.'"

Some of the Moms teased Daly about being "on the upper end of fanaticism" when she joined the group. She was not sure at first how to take this teasing. So determined was she to excel at the sport that she could not tolerate anyone else's letting up for a minute. "Nothing is more frustrating than to be out in the boat totally focused and to hear from back near the bow somewhere: 'Don't you think we should send so and so a birthday card.'"

Within a few practice sessions, she was stroking the eight and snapping at the other crew members when the boat was lurching or not setting up just right. She also had a bad habit of telling the coxswain what to do. "If I could feel the power drop, I would tell her. My theory was: 'If I don't tell the cox, who will?' Then I got totally bawled out by the coach who told me I had to give the cox the space to find out what she was capable of."

Daly quickly realized that she needed the cooperation of everyone in the boat and that she would have to make room for attitudes that differed from her own if she wanted to do her best in rowing. While, on the one hand, the sport was giving her a shot at mastery and control, on the other hand, it was demanding that she learn to rely on other people. Opening up to the various dispositions in a diverse group of women was a new experience for her, as was trusting anyone. "I was a snob. I had led an isolated life." She had also endured a lonely, troubled childhood. Her mother, who married four times, had a drinking problem. When she herself married, she moved from one dysfunctional home into another. She focused on being a good executive wife (her husband ran her family's enterprise, one of the largest cemetery businesses in the country) and a good mother (her three children were born within thirty months of each other). She returned to school to get a master's degree in architecture, spending six years juggling her family's needs with her own.

"The codependent thinks, 'if only I try harder, things will get better.'" With her kids gone, her husband in treatment and her future uncertain, Daly was beginning to question the way she had been thinking. She seized upon rowing to teach her the lessons she needed to learn to move into a new phase in her life. And the sport seemed to cooperate by giving her the right teachers at the right time.

In 1985, the year that Daly started rowing, one of her daughter's teammates at MIT moved to Seattle to live with the Dalys and to train for the national team. Daly immediately identified with what Liz Bradley, her young houseguest, was doing. "Liz was an inspiration. She showed me how to follow a passion. She was following a passion and dedicating her life to it. I saw through her it was possible to set goals for yourself and achieve them. Growing up in a dysfunctional home, you don't learn how to do that; you don't set goals because nothing is stable."

With her own passion affirmed by Bradley's, Daly pushed harder during practice sessions with the Moms and during her own workouts on land. The Moms had decided to compete in the national masters championship regatta, which was being held in Seattle in 1985. Daly was stroking the eight and trying to understand everything there was to know about sweep rowing and stroking.

A good stroke, according to Daly, "has to row with great consistency. She has to have a metronome in her head so that she knows exactly when she's rowing at thirty-eight strokes a minute. She has to understand ratio—the relationship between the drive and the recovery. A lot of people don't understand what ratio is, and you get this godawful lurching in the boat. The stroke also has to be somebody people have confidence in. The trick is not to run the boat like a cruise director but to set an example. A lot of it has to do with attitude. Attitude is very contagious."

As Daly was trying to absorb all she could about rowing and stroking a boat, she felt the Moms fall into place behind her. She discovered that once the boat was set for the championship regatta, all the women in it were totally committed to working as hard as they could to be ready for the race. There was no idle chatter in the boat during practice. All the rowers were focused on refining their technique and making the boat move as effectively and as fast as possible. In the stroke seat, Daly could feel

the commitment in the boat. She began to trust the other rowers and to see that when she corrected someone else, she was
only expressing "the rower's eternal thought, the ultimate
conceit—if everybody else in the boat would just get her act together, we'd do great." She began to lighten up and even enjoy
being teased for her extreme level of dedication. No one in her
family had teased in a good-natured way. Once she figured out
that the Moms admired her and counted on her the way they admired and counted on everyone else in the group, she liked their
teasing.

At nationals in 1985, Martha's Moms finished third. "We
got a bronze medal," Daly says. "We were thrilled. We
wouldn't come back down to earth for six days."

Watching the women in her group respond to racing confirmed Beattie in her decision to gear their program toward regattas. "Racing is something very new to a lot of people in my
group. They're of an age where they just sort of missed out on
the whole women's sports movement. Racing gives them this
self-image of a truly competitive athlete. It's very gratifying.
They're not pretty little girls playing half-court basketball in
the 1950s. They're athletes."

Knowing the intense work that preparing for a season of
racing requires, Beattie insisted that her rowers take time away
from the sport. She wanted them to have enough balance in
their lives to keep them from burning out on rowing. Her
schedule called for a three-month break in the winter and a
month off in the spring. Daly, who was just beginning to learn
about the sport, could not see any need for a break. In fact, she
thought a break would be counterproductive; she might forget
everything she had learned about technique. When the rest of
the Moms stopped sweep rowing, Daly decided she would learn
how to scull.

✦ ✦ ✦

If Lou Daly had found the perfect fit between personality and
sport when she found rowing, she found the perfect fit between

personality and coach when she found Frank Cunningham, who uses words like obsessive and compulsive when he talks about the rower's personality. Cunningham characterizes himself as obsessive and compulsive. "I'm certainly obsessive about rowing. It was the one sport that I could do."

Cunningham rowed at Harvard in the 1940s. (His 1947 Harvard varsity crew is in the rowing hall of fame.) When he moved to Seattle in 1948, he helped set up a rowing program for boys at Green Lake and settled into a life-long coaching career, constantly thinking about the rowing stroke and how to perfect it and about the sport itself and the way it should be pursued. Rowing is his passion, and he considers forty years in the sport a minimum apprenticeship. He speaks about the sport almost as if it is a religion and definitely as if it is an art form. He can hear a variety of music in a rowing shell. "You are aware of the different song the boat sings. You use the blades to tune the boat."

Cunningham had taught Laura Daly at Lakeside and, therefore, had what he calls a "rather formal and limited acquaintance" with Lou Daly. Their relationship changed the moment she showed up at Lake Washington Rowing Club for sculling lessons. She had endless questions about the sport, and he had endless answers.

Daly loved the logical style in which Cunningham taught. She loved hearing about the mechanics and the physics of the rowing stroke. Cunningham's method of teaching capitalized on women's strengths rather than men's. In fact, Cunningham had nothing but unkind remarks to make about the way most men row: "When you see a man rowing, you don't want to use him as a model. You want to realize he's doing the best he can. He's very stiff. It's just pathetic. Partly it's his hip girth and the habit of sitting down all the time instead of hunkering, squatting, bending. You sit in a chair a lot and you'll never have any flexibility. Women going through an ordinary day, especially if they're dealing with children, develop a lot of flexibility. And they retain most of the flexibility they have in their hips. By the time I get through teaching a man, he's rowing like a woman."

One of the first things Daly learned from Cunningham was that she was using her back wrong. This was aggravating an old injury—she had ruptured a disk shoveling mud. Cunningham showed her how to row without straining her back. "She was trying to shove the boat ahead with a hooped back. I suggested that she bend from the hips and learn how to brace her back so she didn't put a strain on the muscles that are prone to go into spasm."

Cunningham, since he was a masters rower himself and fifteen years older than Daly, knew what an older body could be expected to do and knew, too, that flawless technique could make up for shortcomings in strength and athleticism. Daly loved the minutiae of technical instruction. She loved the subtleties and nuances that Cunningham insisted she learn. He had her rowing in a single, learning to balance the boat, seeing how changes in technique affected how well she performed, how fast she moved the boat, how soon she tired. She was fascinated: "The precision of the sport had great appeal for me. Sculling is very technically oriented. I love it, being a detail-oriented person."

Besides appealing to the more exacting part of her personality, single sculling helped Daly develop confidence in her ability to do things on her own. While she was learning in sweep rowing with Martha's Moms to work as part of a team and to trust other people, in sculling she was learning to rely on herself. "Scullers," according to Daly, "are far different. They have different personalities than sweep rowers. Scullers tend to be loners. They're independent and capable of solving all the problems associated with rowing." If they are going to race, single scullers have to do everything themselves—get their boats to the regatta, rig the boats, attend the coxswains' meeting, get the boats into the water, plan the strategy, motivate themselves, get the boats out of the water afterward. They usually have to find their own coaches. The payoff of rowing in a single is, as Daly sees it, the knowledge that you alone are responsible for making the boat go fast, if it is going fast. "In a sweep boat, if you're going fast, you wonder what part you're playing in that speed."

Not long after she started learning how to scull, Daly wanted to race in a single. As Beattie had encouraged her and the Moms to enter regattas to reward themselves for their long hours of practice, Cunningham encouraged Daly to test her speed against others. Cunningham: "If you get into a boat that's designed to go fast and you're taken with the idea of getting speed out of the boat, you naturally want to get up alongside somebody and see what you can do against them. Racing will drive you to new levels of speed."

Although it had not occurred to him that older women would want to race boats when he started the boys' crew program at Green Lake, Cunningham was delighted by what he saw among women who came later to the sport. "Their enjoyment is absolutely pure. They strike me as being at the stage I was when I was sixteen, presented with the option of athletics for the first time. You can see it in their eyes—they're just dancing. They get into a competitive situation and feel the adrenalin rush, and it's more exciting than anything they've ever felt before."

In 1987, Daly entered her first national singles competition, after having competed in a single only twice. The masters national regatta was at Lake Placid, New York. Her daughter drove from Boston to cheer for her. Daly was so far ahead of her closest competitor that she did not have to sprint to the finish. "After the 500-meter mark, I just concentrated on doing the prettiest rowing that I could. Afterwards, an old friend of the family, who lived in Lake Placid and used to coach rowing, called my mother and said, 'That's the prettiest rowing I've seen in years.'" The 1987 masters nationals was definitely Daly's regatta, for not only did she win the singles title, but she also stroked two Martha's Moms sweep boats—an eight and a four—

that won gold medals in their categories.

A couple of months after her triumphs at Lake Placid, Daly separated from her husband and moved into a houseboat on Lake Union in Seattle. For her fiftieth birthday, on March 16, 1988, she gave herself a new Pocock wooden racing single. She could launch the single from the deck of her new home, which was, not incidentally, located right next door to Rowing Northwest, a center for recreational scullers. When she first moved in, she had to fight the temptation to run outside every time someone rowed by and yell, "No, no. You're doing that all wrong. That's not the way you do it." Then she would remember that these were recreational rowers, and she would flop down onto the white sofa in her sunken living room and concentrate instead on her view of the Cascade Mountains across the water.

✦ ✦ ✦

"People will tell you I'm an addict," Lou Daly says, without denying the accusation. Her commitment to rowing, after more than six years in the sport, is no less intense than the six-day-a-week involvement she craved when she discovered the sport and could not get enough of it. "In crew, you keep hitting these levels. Then you discover a higher one. In training, people are taken beyond the capacity they think they have. I like that. There's not a fixed limit. It's all in your head."

Rowing is Daly's single most important activity. It is more of a vocation than her work, which is architecture. She plans her architecture projects around her training and regatta travel schedule. "I couldn't be a full-time architect and still do the things in rowing that I want to do. With all that's involved, rowing is exhausting."

Besides her training, which can take up to four hours a day during racing season, Daly has to be constantly on the alert for "the optimal fuel." She experiments with her diet and pays close attention to what her body tells her about its nutritional needs. "If my body says broccoli, I go out and buy broccoli." She avoids fat, and eats fresh vegetables and fruits, plus bread, potatoes, pasta, fish, chicken and turkey. She seasons with pepper and lemon juice instead of salt. When she is training, she usually eats four to five small meals a day. "And I always eat something before I go out to practice. It's usually a banana in my car on the way." Daly believes that what she eats and drinks makes a difference in the way she performs on race day. The last week before a race she cuts out all dairy products, which she believes build phlegm in the lungs and add to the buildup of lactic acid in the muscles. She also stops drinking carbonated beverages the last week before a race. She stays away from caffeine generally and drinks gallons of water. When she is training hard, she uses a nutritional supplement to replace the salts and potassium her body is losing. If she is participating in more than one race in a day, she eats Power Bars, dense, Seattle-made concoctions that promise increased energy and are popular with cyclists and marathon runners.

Daly's preoccupation with shaping her body into a precision rowing machine includes sessions with a Rolfer and extra time for warm-up stretches before a workout and cool-down stretches afterward. She is careful of her back. "Pain is a hard teacher. When there's something that you love that you can't do because you've injured yourself, you learn to take care of yourself."

With all the time she devotes to rowing, including naps because of the demands of training, she still manages to keep a number of architectural projects going for the satisfaction of that work and the income it brings. She passed the written portions of her state boards in architecture early in the eighties, and in 1988 she passed her oral exams and finally became a registered architect. She works on small projects, adding decks and hot tubs, redoing interiors, remodeling a home after a fire. She enjoys design and holds two patents—one on a form for people to use in genealogical research and the other ("You'll laugh at this," she predicts) on a hanging unit for mausoleum vases.

One of the aspects of rowing that holds Daly's interest is the elusive nature of technical mastery of the sport. Her sculling coach Frank Cunningham has seen her row perfectly for short stretches. "Then you turn your back, and she's got a little wrinkle in there." Daly is a harsher critic of her efforts than anyone else. One of her problems, she says, is that she is too slow getting out of the bow, which means that she doesn't bring her hands around quickly enough at the finish of her stroke. Instead, she holds her layback too long and pushes down on the bow of the boat, slowing it. As she works on bringing her hands around more quickly, she is alert to problems elsewhere in her stroke. She knows there will always be something to work on, and that prospect cheers her.

Thinking constantly about the flaws in her stroke is another one of Daly's rowing problems. "My coaches are always telling me, 'Lou, you think too much.' You have to train your body to feel it, not to think it." Cunningham, in particular, has urged her to stop intellectualizing. "She needs to just get out there and go into a zen state of mind. She tries too hard to achieve the ideal. Or she may be trying to please the teacher. We've suggested that she come down with three or four martinis under her belt, anything to stun the intellect or back it off a bit. What we're trying to do is show people how to move the way animals move. They don't have any intellect. They are spontaneous. You've got to achieve that animal grace. You've got to turn yourself into an animal when you're out there in the boat."

Daly agrees with Cunningham's analysis but has trouble with the zen of rowing. "The cerebral sort that I am, it's hard to let go," she says.

In 1988, Daly went to the masters world championships in Scotland and rowed her single well enough to win a gold medal, making her the best woman single sculler in her age group in the world. (She also won golds in the four and the eight that she rowed in at worlds that year.) Once she had reached that pinnacle, she had to set other goals for herself. She began to race her single in the open category, rather than masters. This meant competing against younger athletes. In open competition, she usually finishes about the middle of the pack. She thinks she can improve by learning more about strategy.

Racing in a single is a far greater challenge to her than racing as part of a crew. "In the past I've finished an eights race and tasted the blood in my lungs. Sure, it's exhausting for maybe twenty or thirty minutes or an hour afterwards. You come across the line totally exhausted, but you recover quickly. In a single, the mental exhaustion combined with the physical, may wipe you out for a day or two. Part of that is your total responsibility for everything. And it's a different strain on your body. In a single you can't let up for a second, or the boat dies." The hardest part of a singles race for her is between the 300- and the 500-meter mark. "I start to think about all the things I didn't do. I didn't lift enough weights. I didn't do enough stairs. And if I'm in an open race, up against twenty-year-olds, I think, 'Why am I doing this? I hate it.' Then I begin to think about all the different things the coaches have told me. Getting from 300 to 500 is hell, especially if you're not in the lead." By 500 meters, she figures she's halfway home and can probably make the finish line. By 750, she has only thirty to forty strokes left and can certainly do those. "Then I tell myself to sprint. I wonder if I can. I don't think I can. Well, I'll try."

In the single, Daly has learned just how far she can get by relying on herself. But it is the community of sweep rowers that has given her the greatest return on her investment. She likes to speak in almost mystical terms about the feeling of union in a boat. "It's a psychic feeling. You adjust to each other without ever talking about it. It's almost eerie." When rowers are totally in sync, something that she calls cavitation occurs. "When the boat cavitates, it is moving so efficiently through the water that a fine layer of air bubbles is created between the hull of the boat and the water, and the boat moves faster with less energy. You can feel it. It's like sitting in champagne. Once you've felt it, there's no mistaking it. You keep trying for it again and again."

She has experienced this feeling three times in races. The first was in 1987 at the masters national championships in Lake Placid in a Martha's Moms four. "We had a very good start. We knew it was incredible by 300 meters. We had the lead by 500. I still remember Poo's (Penrose, the coxswain) voice. When she gets excited, her voice goes way up and she says something like, 'This is what we came for.' We knew we had the lead. We knew we were gaining with every stroke. It was total elation. Everybody knew that we had done what we came to do. There was no way anybody could beat us. You could tell without looking around that everybody was rowing with this grin on their faces. There's a certain energy that radiates throughout the entire boat."

The second cavitational experience that she remembers occurred in 1988 at Seattle's Opening Day Regatta, a popular event with several hundred thousand spectators. Daly was stroking a Martha's Moms eight. "We went out and started our warm-up. The boat cavitated. We knew the boat was setting up beautifully. People were totally concentrated in the boat. We had a marvelous race. We knew we were rowing to our max. It doesn't matter how exhausted you are. There's a hidden source of energy you can always tap. It's just an incredible experience. We went precisely at the stroke rate the coach had called. We started at thirty-eight, settled at thirty and finished at thirty-six. It was like someone had slipped us a drug or something, some go juice. It was like the culmination of something you work hard for, having shared training and having built relationships and friendships, having built a team of people you know you can rely on. And they know they can rely on you."

In 1989, the Moms rowed in the Head of the Charles in Boston, the largest single-day regatta in the world. As many as half a million people line the banks of the Charles River to watch the best crews from all over the world race for three miles. The Moms had a four in the race, and Daly was stroking. The Moms had arrived in Boston a couple of days before the regatta so they could practice. For some reason, they were having problems rowing together and couldn't figure out what was wrong. They were all experienced rowers who had firsthand knowledge of what an exceptional row was. Maybe the weather was getting to them. Strong winds came up from different directions each day. They were on an unfamiliar course, in wretched conditions. On race day, they rowed out to warm up, feeling uncertain about how they would perform. As they were taking their first warm-up strokes, the weather finally broke. The skies cleared, and the wind died. The Moms crossed the starting line flying. "We started rowing and built up to full power. We all felt it: it was just magic. Every single stroke in that three miles was perfect; well, maybe I can think of two strokes of mine that I could have done better. It was like we were in a time capsule apart from everyone else. Such intense concentration. You know you're doing the very best you were trained to do." The Charles River winds underneath five bridges during the course of the race. On each bridge the Moms' fans were shouting down, "Go Moms." "It was absolutely intoxicating, a straight adrenalin high. It's another world within a world. You know that you're invincible."

Coupled with these transcendental experiences are the "giggly fun times" of road trips with a group of women who are temporarily free of all responsibilities but getting themselves to the regatta and rowing. Daly has traveled with the Moms to regional regattas all over the Pacific Northwest and to national and international regattas in Boston, San Diego, Oakland, Lake Placid, Miami and Strathclyde, Scotland. And back home in Seattle, she has found among the Moms friendships and a community of women that sustains her. "I know I have a support group there who will understand, but not in an invasive way. It's an incredible group of women."

The Moms welcome new rowers into their program every

year, and the group, which was diverse from the beginning, has grown even more so. Cosette Harms, who joined in 1988 when she was forty-five, says the Moms range from "people who sell their couch to pay for their trip to a regatta to people who come from generations of incredible wealth. Rowing may be the only thing these women have in common." Harms had watched the Moms practicing and wanted to join for several years but waited until her two sons were old enough to get themselves off to school. She remembers driving by the lake one rainy morning and seeing "a group of crazy ladies, sopping wet." It was the Moms, coming in from practice. They were getting their boats out of the water. The women lifted an eight up over their heads and, as they turned it over, water poured out all over them. They were laughing. "Those have got to be soul sisters for me," Harms thought. "I love that kind of thing because it's so bizarre and so funny. If they're out there doing that, I'm missing out."

She joined for the exercise and found the camaraderie that she had imagined would be there. She races, but sometimes, particularly at the start, she wonders why. "I don't like tasting blood afterwards and coughing and having to breathe so hard and feeling so sweaty and totally destroyed. What I like about racing is that it's over with quick. But I do admit it's a thrill to be ahead in a race. You get this tremendous urge to make it four, five, six seats ahead."

Racing is something that none of the Moms is forced to do, but that all of them, so far, have chosen to do. The rewards of racing seem to be available to all ages of women. "It sure beats watching the grandkids," one of Martha's Moms shouted to a men's college crew after her boat had held off their boat during the Head of the Lake Regatta in Seattle. "Oh, to be fifty again," said a Mom in her sixties after her first regatta. The Moms are oriented toward racing, with most of the coaching attention going to those who are getting ready for a regatta. Martha Beattie, the head coach, originally pushed the Moms to race with the idea that they should have the same kind of rewards she had experienced from racing in college. As her life changed and she stayed with the group, her ideas about why racing is important changed. "I know now as the mother of three young kids that you don't get a lot of very objective strokes for what you are accomplishing in the house and with your children. A gold medal in a race is so tangible you can hardly stand it."

Lou Daly knows about the tangible rewards of competition. She also acknowledges the intangibles, like the support she has gotten from the Moms for her own efforts in rowing and for the changes she has been making in her life. Since she first joined the Moms, she has mellowed and is not so quick to snap when a boat she is in lurches from side to side. "Commitment and the desire to improve are much more important than the level of rowing people are at." She knows that rowing has gotten her through some stressful, tough times. In the beginning, she used the sport as a physical release for emotional energy and as a diversion from her problems. By the time her marriage of thirty years ended officially in a divorce in 1990, she had learned to accept emotional support from the women with whom she rowed. In fact, she had learned a whole new way of relating to women her age. Before she got into rowing, she related to other women as what she calls "an extension of the family unit," as a wife or as a mother. Once she began to row and began to receive individual attention and encouragement for what she could do, she started to relate differently. "There's something very special about the people in crew. When we're together, the outside world drops away."

✦ ✦ ✦

Rowing's main lesson for Lou Daly—that she can trust herself and other people—was not an easy one for a woman who had spent her entire life protecting herself from the unreliability of those she loved. It was not an easy lesson for a woman given to concentrating on detail and believing that if she worked hard enough, all the details she had within her grasp would add up to something worth giving a life to. Gradually, though, within the nurturing community that Martha's Moms provided, Lou Daly learned that other people can be relied on and can share a commitment that enlarges everyone involved. She also learned—but this was the hardest part—that other people actually wanted her to do the best that she could. She allowed a young woman her daughter's age to drive that lesson home to her.

Cecily Coughlan started coaching Martha's Moms in the fall of 1986, the year she graduated from Brown University. She had rowed at Brown and had competed against the MIT crews for which Laura Daly rowed. Coughlan moved to Seattle to study sculling with Frank Cunningham. Almost from the first day she arrived in the city, she was also working with the Moms, serving as an enthusiastic assistant to coach Martha Beattie. "I wanted to give back to that generation that opened up the doors for me." Coughlan found that in giving to the generation that was her mother's age, she was also getting a great deal in return. For one thing, she was learning how to coach. "The Moms essentially were my training ground. They were very gentle and good at giving me feedback. There was a lot of humor at the boathouse." Lou Daly, in particular, was helping her find the words to express herself as coach. "Lou demands an eloquence from anyone who is coaching her. She demands an answer."

When Coughlan first came to the Moms, she was quiet and slightly in awe of the women she was coaching. Daly, in her single-minded quest for the perfect rowing stroke, was one of the more overwhelming Moms. "There's this drama in her life, this power. She is very passionate about life. Anything she does, she does a hundred percent."

The eagerness of all the Moms to learn how to row better and the commitment they brought to the sport encouraged Coughlan to develop a variety of ways to express the concepts that she wanted to get across. Some responded well to imagery;

others needed more sophisticated analyses. Coughlan adapted her coaching to the individual needs of the Moms. By early 1989, after two seasons with the Moms, including travel with them to regattas where they were extremely successful, Coughlan was becoming more confident and assertive. When Lou Daly asked her for special coaching for a very important race, Coughlan was flattered and not a little apprehensive about the prospect. Daly wanted to break ten minutes in a 2,500-meter ergometer race, something no woman in her age category had ever done.

A rowing ergometer is a machine that allows people to simulate the rowing motion and measure how much power their muscles are supplying. It is a simple machine that looks like a round-headed dachshund straining at its leash. The rower sits on a seat that slides, puts her feet in footstretchers and pulls with both hands on a handle that is attached to a cord attached to a flywheel. A digital readout on the ergometer translates the speed and heft of each pull into a stroke rate and distance traveled.

Because rowers do not lose their compulsion to race during winters when the weather prohibits their being on the water, they invented ergometer competitions, the best-known of which is the CRASH-B Sprints, held every February in Boston. CRASH-B stands for Charles River All-Star Has-Beens and was organized by former Olympians and national team rowers. Lou Daly wanted to break the ten-minute barrier at the CRASH-Bs, where rowers from all over the world travel to compete. Sometimes as many as sixty people are pulling on ergometers at the same time. Officials set each ergometer at 2,500 meters, and competitors pull away until the readout is zero. The ergometer readout also shows split times for each 500 meters.

Daly had been inspired to train for the CRASH-Bs by her chiropractor, Dan Nelson. He had her warming up on an ergometer before she lifted weights as part of a rehabilitation program for her back. He would watch as she strained at the machine and ask if she thought she could go any faster. She would say, "Of course I can." After seeing how she bumped up her speed through several of these exchanges, Nelson dared her to try for the CRASH-Bs. Daly couldn't resist the challenge.

In order to be in the CRASH-Bs, Daly first had to qualify in regional competition. Seattle's event, called Ergomania, is held in early February, and Daly asked Coughlan to coach her during the event. What she wanted, basically, was someone to stand behind her and say encouraging words as she struggled to pull the readout down to zero in less than ten minutes. She already had her plan, which was to go out hard, settle, then finish hard, just as she would in an on-the-water race. Coughlan, however, was working on other ideas. She had experimented on the ergometer with another athlete, and she realized that the machine defeats people about the sixth or seventh minute into a 2,500-meter piece. "You've got so much energy at the beginning that you're afraid if you don't use it, you won't have it at the end. So you go out faster than you should. By the sixth or seventh minute, your brain isn't getting enough oxygen and the doubts start creeping in. That's where most people have trouble."

About two hours before the regional competition, Coughlan told Daly what she thought her strategy should be. She suggested that she take the first three 500-meter splits at a steady two minutes each, then pick up the pace in the fourth 500 and sprint home in the fifth. Coughlan did not spend a great deal of time trying to persuade Daly of the correctness of the strategy. "Just do it, Lou," she told her before the race.

The plan went against all of Daly's training and practicing. It went against all of her instincts. Nevertheless, Daly followed Coughlan's strategy. She held her rate steady at two minutes per 500 meters through the first 1,500 meters. She kept looking at a monitor, which showed how the other seven competitors were doing, and seeing that she was nowhere near the lead. "In the fourth 500 meters, I started driving it down. Everybody else was dying. I drove everybody else right off their sprockets.

What a great feeling." She finished in 9:53.3, which broke the previous record for her age group by a minute and ten seconds. When she went to Boston for the CRASH-Bs, she followed the same strategy and duplicated her time.

Coughlan: "I was asking quite a lot of her to hold back. I'm grateful that she had the courage to do that. To have someone with that much life experience put her fate in my hands was a confidence booster for me."

Daly: "She's the coach. I trusted her."

✦ ✦ ✦

Lou Daly has a case full of medals and ribbons that she has won at various regattas. It is made of cedar ("white cedar, the same wood my shell is made of") and lined with blue velvet. Her ex-husband built it for her. "It's the nicest work he ever did." The handles on the front are slender oars. It folds out into three panels. On one side are all her small ribbons, stacked on top of each other. On the other side are bigger ribbons. In the center are her many medals.

Daly knows that all these medals and ribbons go only part of the way toward explaining her passion for rowing. She fell in love with the sport because it was there when she needed it, and it was complex enough to engage many different aspects of her personality. There are times when she regrets not having had the chance to see how her twenty-year-old body might have responded to the challenges of rowing. But even coming as late as she did to the sport, she has gained a sense of mastery from it, as well as a sense of self-acceptance.

As Cecily Coughlan says, "I think that in some ways rowing started and accompanied a process of self-exploration for Lou. I've seen her move towards a form of grace with herself, a peace with herself." Rowing offers anyone willing to open herself to it the chance to explore values like community, self-sufficiency, commitment and trust. Lou Daly found all those things in great measure in rowing. And she found more. Rowing for Lou Daly is an art, the highest form of self-expression. It is a place where she can define herself in terms that she carries with her to everything else she does. Sometimes the lines between rowing and the rest of life are blurred, and Lou Daly finds herself wondering: "Does life imitate rowing? Or does rowing imitate life?"

PADDLING

So much is possible with a small boat and a lightweight paddle. A woman can go to the Olympics via this craft, or she can explore the world.

If she wants to go to the Olympics, competitive kayaking offers different events for different temperaments. For the athlete who likes to focus on an all-out sprint, tracing one butterfly shape with her two-bladed paddle over and over again as fast as she can, putting as much push into that motion as her bursting lungs and burning muscles will bear, there is flatwater kayaking, 500 meters to the finish. Flatwater kayaking is for the woman who loves straight-ahead, uncomplicated speed and head-to-head competition with equally talented and dedicated athletes. Marcia Jones, Francine Fox and Gloriane Perrier were the first American women to translate their love for flat-out flatwater kayaking to Olympic medals. That was in 1964. Nearly thirty years later, Traci Phillips pushes to shave hundredths of seconds off her time and to live up to the Jones-Fox-Perrier legacy.

For the woman who likes her speed with an edge of danger and a syncopated rhythm, there is white water slalom kayaking, a race through a series of gates—the fastest run wins. In white water slalom, the athlete tries to find the most fluid line in a tumble of foam, strives to place her paddle where her eye directs, rides a sweep of water one moment and battles against the current the next. The white water slalom paddler is all balance and control in the midst of chaos. She is also the most self-contained and patient of athletes, sometimes having to wait twenty years between the offering of Olympic events in her sport. Cathy Hearn is the quintessential white water slalom paddler, having made her sport into a way of being in the world.

If a woman wants to explore, a canoe or kayak can take her into exotic lands and the uncharted territory of her heart. Valerie Fons paddled from the top to the bottom of the earth and found that when her usual sources of comfort were gone, she had the mettle and the ingenuity to create inspiration from the material at hand—women's voices in a Caribbean church choir, the soft fur of a puppy, gifts that strangers placed under the Christmas tree on her canoe. In thirty-three months of paddling oceans and rivers away from everything she knew, she discovered the song that she wanted to sing for the rest of her life. It was a song about fear as the doorway to dreams and about ways of gathering the courage to move through that door.

In two months of travel by canoe through the last great wilderness on the North American continent, down one of the wildest rivers in the world to the Arctic Ocean, seven women learned that life stripped of the trappings of civilization is startling in its intensity. These women went to the Back River to push their physical, emotional and spiritual limits. The river carried them further than they imagined possible.

Marcia Jones paddled to a bronze medal finish at the 1964 Tokyo Olympics in the women's flatwater single kayaking event. She was the first American woman to win a medal in the sport. After she retired from competition, she coached a new generation of paddlers and produced six Olympians.

After practicing daily side by side in singles on the Potomac River, Gloriane Perrier (left) and Francine Fox went to the 1964 Tokyo Olympics and won a silver medal in the double. Perrier, who was thirty-five when she won the silver, retired from competition in 1967 and coached her own group of Olympian flatwater paddlers. Fox, who was fifteen at the Tokyo Olympics, continued her racing career in a single. She was Marcia Jones's primary competition until they both retired in 1974.

Marcia Jones, Francine Fox and Gloriane Perrier

~

IN THE SUMMER OF 1960, a nineteen-year-old swimmer, who was not quite fast enough to make the U.S. Olympic team, went to Rome to watch the athletes who had qualified for the most celebrated amateur athletic event in the world. She was there at her mother's insistence. Given her choice, she would have been back home at swimming practice. She *was* going to be an Olympic athlete one day. She had started dreaming of that day when she was ten years old.

Her mother knew about her dream and had done all that was within her considerable means to help her and her older sister, who also had Olympic aspirations, develop their athletic abilities. A break from training to watch the Rome Olympics, her mother thought, might be just what the two young women needed to return to their quest newly inspired.

One day, the three of them took the train from Rome out into the countryside. They arrived at a lake that was in the crater of a volcano. They walked through orange trees, looking for the best spot from which to view an event that was new to all of them. The event was canoeing. The mother was determined to expose her daughters to as many Olympic possibilities as she could find. Right away, the nineteen-year-old was intrigued by the physiques of the paddlers she saw. They had powerful upper bodies, like swimmers'. She liked the graceful rhythm of the paddlers as they took their warm-up strokes after putting their slender boats into the water.

Women paddlers had two events that day—the single kayak (K1W) and the double (K2W), each a 500-meter race. Women's kayaking events had been added to the Olympic Games in 1948, twelve years after flatwater canoe and kayak races for men became a permanent part of the Olympics. American women did not participate in the first three Olympiads for which they were eligible. In 1952, a young woman, Ruth De-Forest, had qualified to go. But the American Canoe Association, which governed Olympic participation in the sport in the U.S., decided that she could not make the trip to Helsinki without a chaperone, which it did not want to send. So a male kayaker was added to the team instead. In 1956, the American Canoe Association once again refused to spend the money to send women, even though several had qualified in national trials. Finally, in 1960, three women went to the Rome Olympics as the U.S. representatives in flatwater canoeing (a term that covers both canoe and kayak races). These women were selected from a small group of serious competitors, maybe fifty altogether. Most women had never heard of the sport, which was essentially a 500-meter sprint in a narrow, enclosed boat shaped like the needle of a compass.

The woman paddling the single that day for the U.S. in Rome was Gloriane Perrier, thirty-one years old and facing the first international competition of her career. Her boat looked different from the rest of the boats going to the starting line for a qualifying heat. It was a wider model that the Europeans recognized as a cruising kayak, one meant for leisurely, steady paddles. Gloriane's primary mission at the Rome Olympics was to get down the course without tipping. She had a powerful upper body, the equal of any European or Soviet paddler's. But she lacked balance. She felt top-heavy in narrow boats. Her cruising kayak put her at a disadvantage for speed, but it would save her from having to swim to the finish line.

The gun went off, and Gloriane began plowing her double-bladed paddle through the water. There was a wind, which churned the water and worked to her advantage for a few seconds since she was the only competitor in a stable boat. The rest of the paddlers, however, quickly found their rhythm and balance in their sleek pointy mahogany kayaks. They streaked past the American. The best paddler from the U.S. did not make the finals.

By the end of that heat, the nineteen-year-old swimmer in the audience had become very much interested in kayaking—and not just from a spectator's point of view. She had heard the murmurs from other spectators when they spotted the American's unorthodox boat. At first, she was embarrassed for her country. Then she began to feel that she could save America further embarrassment. She was young and strong. She had been training for nearly ten years as a serious athlete. She had the right physique. Surely, she could turn in a better performance than the one she had just seen. How hard could it be to keep one of those slender kayaks upright?

In the years to come, Gloriane Perrier would develop a sincere dislike for the story of how young Marcia Jones discovered the sport of kayaking at the 1960 Rome Olympics. But Gloriane would not let that story discourage the affection or decrease the respect she came to feel for Marcia. The two women would become great friends and together would inspire and teach a new generation of American women paddlers. They would team up with a third paddler, one who was not at the Rome Olympics, to become world-class competitors in the sport of flatwater kayaking. Perrier, Jones and Francine Fox would astonish the paddling world in 1964 at the Tokyo Olympics. They would do what no other American women had done before or have done since—they would win medals in kayaking against the best paddlers in the world. And that would be only the beginning of their contributions to the sport and to other women who wanted to be competitive paddlers.

✦ ✦ ✦

Marcia Jones was born in Oklahoma in 1941. Her mother's family had been part of the Oklahoma land rush and had claimed some oil-producing acreage. According to Marcia, her mother was "very independent and stubborn" and had an office downtown. She did not call herself a feminist, but she may have been one. Her name was Mary Francis, and she kept it at that when she married Ingram Jones.

Mary Francis had a law degree from the University of Michigan and a pilot's license. From her office in Oklahoma City, she managed the family's real estate holdings. Ingram Jones was an electrical engineer who worked in Venezuela. In the summers, Mary Francis would take her two daughters, Sperry, older by twenty-two months, and Marcia, to visit their father.

In Venezuela the summer that Marcia was ten, she and Sperry took swimming lessons. Their coach told their mother that they showed promise in the sport. Back home at the end of the summer, Mary Francis started the Oklahoma City Swim Club, now called the Kerr-McGee Swim Club. The two Jones girls began to think of themselves as athletes. They trained every day and competed in races. Marcia was good at freestyle and breast stroke; Sperry specialized in back stroke and butterfly. By the time she was thirteen, Marcia was good enough to beat Venezuela's national swimming champion. She had several scrapbooks stuffed with press clippings about her idols, the top swimmers of the time. She wanted to be just like them and to fulfill her athletic potential in the Olympic Games.

Mary Francis did everything she could to support her daughters' desire to excel as swimmers. She was pleased that they had found a healthy, constructive way to spend their time. She took them to all the races that they wanted to enter, and she got involved in the organizations that supported amateur swimming in the U.S. Marcia thought she was the ideal parent, not pushy but willing to supply anything her daughters said they needed.

Matt Mann, the swim coach who had been at the University

of Michigan when Mary Francis was in law school there, was at the University of Oklahoma when her daughters were becoming serious about the sport. Mary Francis called him and said she had two daughters who wanted to make the Olympic team. He told her to send Sperry and Marcia to Camp Ak-O-Mak, a swim camp that he and his daughter ran in northern Ontario. The camp motto was: "We do not sew beads on belts."

At this very serious swim camp, Marcia and Sperry Jones were among the first girls to do the hard workouts that the boys did. They raced against the boys, too. After a few years, there were enough serious swimmers in the girls' camp to give the Jones sisters tough competition. In fact, the competition got a little too tough. Marcia and Sperry were not the fastest girls.

By 1960, even though she was not saying so out loud, Marcia was discouraged about her chances of going to the Olympics as a swimmer. She was ready to find another sport to which she could devote all her determination and intensity. When she discovered kayaking at the Rome Olympics, she found the ideal sport. She had natural balance and rhythm, and she was one of the few women in the country at the time willing to devote a substantial portion of her time and resources to training.

As soon as Mary Francis and Marcia and Sperry Jones returned to the States after the Rome Olympics, Mary Francis was on the phone to Ray Dodge, who lived in Niles, Michigan, and imported kayaks from Denmark. She ordered boats for her daughters, and she bought them a lakefront lot for a training site. She took them to Niles, which is in the southwest corner of the state, to meet Dodge and to see about kayaking instruction. "My daughters would like to learn how to kayak because they want to go to the Olympics," Mary Francis told Ray Dodge. He put the two young women and two experienced paddlers into a four-person kayak and sent the group out across a lake. Marcia thought her lungs would burst as she struggled to keep up with the veteran paddlers. But there was no way that she was going to ask them to slow down or to stop for a minute. She knew her sister would not ask for special treatment either. They both survived that first test in a kayak and were eager for more.

Marcia put her new racing kayak into the Huron River in Ann Arbor, Michigan, for her first solo paddle. No one was around to watch. She rolled the boat. She swam back to the dock, righted the boat and climbed in again. She moved slowly, pushing the needle-like kayak along the dock to the end. Then she raised her double-bladed paddle, held her breath and dipped her left arm to take a stroke. She rolled right into the water again. This went on for a week. Marcia despaired of ever getting 500 yards from the dock without tipping. No matter how slowly or carefully she moved, she fell out of the boat every time. At the end of the week, she took the boat to a pond where the water was even rougher than in the river. The wake from motorboats tossed her kayak. And she continued to fall out of the boat. She counted the number of spills that day—twenty-five. She felt more like a swimmer than a kayaker. But she persisted. After her twenty-fifth swim, she righted the boat, got back in and paddled. She kept paddling. She paddled until her arms were tired. After that day in the pond, she rarely fell out of a kayak.

Marcia was a natural at kayaking. She had good upper body strength, and she fell into the rhythm of the two-fisted stroke right away. Her first instructor was Don Dodge, Ray's son and a national champion. He worked with Marcia on her stroke during the summer of 1961 and helped her get ready for her first competition—nationals, in Washington, D.C. She had been paddling for only six weeks or so when she won the junior division. (The category "junior" was not based on age, but rather on skill level. A paddler had to win the juniors before being allowed to compete in the senior division.) Marcia raced in the senior division, too, at the 1961 nationals and placed third. Gloriane Perrier was first in her wide-bottomed boat. She noticed Marcia: "Her style was—I don't want to say perfect, but it was close. Every motion was accurate. Her reach was good. And her mental attitude was right—she was unrelenting."

Several months after nationals, Marcia Jones lost her instructor, Don Dodge. Don was a student at the Eastman School of Music in Rochester, New York, and when he went back to school in the fall of 1961, he attended a class picnic on Lake Ontario. He decided that he'd like to paddle across the lake. The wind came up, and he never returned.

After Don Dodge died, Marcia continued her training efforts, applying the principles she had learned in swimming to increase her strength, endurance and cardiovascular capacities. After so many years of being in training, she had a physical need to work out and felt guilty if she didn't. She and and her sister Sperry paddled together when they were both enrolled at the University of Michigan. They liked to do locomotive drills, where they would take twenty hard strokes and rest for twenty, then thirty furious strokes and thirty easy and so on, all the way up to one hundred. They pushed each other to their limits because they were both intensely competitive, particularly against each other. Sperry thought that, being older, she should be able to beat Marcia. And she could, over long distances. But in sprints, Sperry always finished second to her little sister.

In 1962, Marcia went to nationals again. This time a thirteen-year-old named Francine Fox beat her for the women's single kayak (K1W) title. Marcia was shocked: "She was a big strong girl. She worked hard. She was right there on my left-hand side, and I couldn't pass her." That 1962 race was the last K1W national title race that Marcia Jones lost for the next eleven years. Losing to a teenager who had even less experience than she shook Marcia into focusing on kayaking more than ever. She transferred from the University of Michigan to Michigan State, to which Ray Dodge had donated a fleet of kayaks in his son's memory. This took some of the pressure off of her scholastic competition with Sperry, who was definitely the better student.

Her first year at Michigan State, she met Bill Smoke, a rower who wanted to go to the Olympics more than anything. He

had rowed in lightweight boats (where the average weight per
rower is 155 pounds or less) for the Detroit Boat Club, but because the Olympic Games do not have events for lightweights,
he was casting about for another sport. He had heard about Ray
Dodge and, with some of his Detroit Boat Club lightweight
teammates, traveled to Niles to see about instruction in kayaking. Dodge suggested that the boys go to Michigan State in
East Lansing and look up Marcia Jones. She could teach them
how to paddle, he said.

Bill Smoke was instantly impressed with Marcia Jones's
strength and technique. "She knows how to move a boat. She
has that fluid style that makes a boat go. You've got to have
strength and balance and the determination to put it all together. You're pulling with one hand, pushing with the other and
balancing with your legs." He rigged up a pulley system that
would allow them to train indoors in a thirty-yard pool in the
winter. They would do ten-second sprints on a paddling board,
using paddles with holes in them to reduce resistance, then pull
themselves back to the start. Marcia and Bill both wanted more
than anything else to make an Olympic team, and they were
prepared to work hard toward that end.

In 1963, Marcia started lifting weights, two hours a day,
three days a week. She worked with a weight training coach at
Michigan State. She liked feeling her body get stronger. "It's a
neat accomplishment. I like bodies that can do something, that
are capable and strong." She also moved to Philadelphia for the
summer to train on the Schuylkill River, storing her kayak at
the Vesper Boat Club. Her mother knew Jack Kelly, Vesper's
most famous rower, who invited the Jones sisters to train alongside his athletes. Being in Philadelphia made travel to regattas
easier, since all the major ones were on the East Coast. When
she won the national K1W title in 1963, the determined Marcia Jones was happy to have achieved the vital first step toward
her ultimate goal of getting to the Olympics.

By 1964, Marcia Jones was unbeatable in the women's single in the U.S. At the Olympic trials, she won her spot on the team easily. The veteran Gloriane Perrier and her young partner Francine Fox qualified to represent the U.S. in the double. Sperry Jones finished fourth in the trials and had to make another Olympic trip as a spectator, sitting with her mother.

◆ ◆ ◆

As a young woman, Gloriane Perrier had never thought about being in the Olympics. She loved sports, and she loved winning. But she had only a vague idea of the Olympics. She thought the Games were limited to running and swimming events. She knew that softball, her favorite sport, was not included. Growing up in Maine, Gloriane tried every kind of athletic endeavor, including ice hockey, and had excelled at them all. When she left Maine in 1950 at age twenty-one and moved to Washington, D.C., to work as a secretary for the Army Signal Corps in the Pentagon, she began playing softball in several high-powered women's leagues. She had thought about going into accounting, but the fiscal year started in July, right in the middle of softball season. Gloriane, who could catch a ball deep in center field and throw a strike to the plate, did not intend to let anything like a job interfere with her softball. By remaining a secretary, she could get time off to travel to tournaments and play on different teams. She played every position except catcher. Batters dreaded seeing her on the pitcher's mound. She could fling the ball at great velocity toward the plate, but she did not have the best control. She was most effective in the outfield, where her powerful right arm intimidated base runners.

Gloriane had a strong upper body. She was tall—five-ten-and-a-half—and weighed around 155 pounds. She had broad shoulders and narrow hips. One day she watched a track team practice at a field in her neighborhood. Several young women were working on their javelin throws. When the coach saw Gloriane, he asked if she had ever thrown a javelin. She said,

"No." He invited her to try. She hoisted the javelin and let it fly. Her one fling easily outdistanced any that the track team members had managed.

Gloriane played basketball during the winter to stay in shape for softball. On the basketball court, she was just as exuberant as she was on the softball field. She would come off the court, breathless and sweating, and her coach would say, "Oh, Glo, that was a wonderful game of football you just played."

Gloriane Perrier began to learn more about the Olympic Games when she decided to try bowling. She signed up for a league organized through the Pentagon. A man named Frank Havens, who had won the silver medal in the 10,000-meter men's single canoe race in the 1948 Olympics and the gold medal in the same event in the 1952 Games, bowled for the same league. He was impressed with the way Gloriane threw her bowling ball. Often, it hit the pins on the fly. Occasionally, she would hurl it so that it bounced right in front of the pins and scattered them. The pin setters would scatter also when they saw Gloriane taking aim. According to Frank, "Gloriane threw with such great gusto that they had problems getting guys who would set the pins for her. A lot of times she would loft the ball. Every time she threw it, she really let it go. She was an overachiever."

Frank Havens belonged to the Washington Canoe Club, which had a boathouse on the Potomac River right under the Key Bridge in the Georgetown section of the city. He was always looking for people who might make good paddlers, especially people who would train with the zeal that he did. Gloriane Perrier seemed perfect for the sport. She had the right build and the right amount of enthusiasm. The owner of the bowling alley said to Frank, "Why don't you see if you can't get this Perrier woman interested in something besides bowling. She is ruining my alley." Frank immediately suggested to Gloriane that she might like to try kayaking. She had never heard the word kayaking before. She asked what it meant.

"Canoeing," Frank said.

She replied, "Oh, God, that's sissy."

Frank defended his sport and again invited her to try it. So, on a Sunday afternoon, in the spring of 1959, Gloriane Perrier went to the Washington Canoe Club and tried paddling a double kayak with Frank Havens. He could feel right away how strong she was. He sensed, though, that she might have problems with balance. Havens suggested that she try a single. She instantly tipped. This made her mad and intent on trying again. Frank helped her get the water out of her kayak. She got back in and tipped in again. She couldn't leave the float, even though she tried again and again, about twenty-one times in all. She was sure that people walking by thought she was taking swimming lessons.

Her own lack of skill at keeping a kayak upright annoyed her, but the sight of others, obviously younger and weaker than she, paddling kayaks without any apparent problems infuriated Gloriane and made her determined to conquer the sport. She began to go to the Washington Canoe Club every day to work out in a training single, which offered more stability than a racing kayak. Frank Havens was delighted: "I was looking for all the competition I could get. Glo was always there."

Training with Frank was fun for Gloriane. They paddled for an hour or an hour and fifteen minutes, once a day, as hard as they could. They would return to the float exhausted, hardly able to get out of their boats. Gloriane loved the feeling of complete relaxation that exhaustion brought. She would laugh at the end of her workouts.

A couple of months after she started paddling with Frank, Gloriane Perrier was in her first race. She hadn't intended to race, but Frank had tricked her into it. He got her to the regatta in Philadelphia by telling her she would just be watching. Then, because the Washington Canoe Club needed points and the women's single kayak race had only two paddlers in it, he persuaded her to be the third paddler. She would automatically get a medal, and the club would get a point if she could just cross the finish line. He said, "Oh, Glo, do me a favor. All you have to do is stay up, and we will get one point." As she paddled to the starting line, with her two competitors waiting and watching, she flipped. The two paddled over and helped her get back in, encouraging her to stay in the race. "All you have to do is stay up, and you'll get a medal," they said. She got to the starting line. When the referee said, "Are you ready?" she felt like saying, "No way." But the gun went off, and she automatically started paddling. She concentrated on keeping her body still and straight and digging her paddle smoothly into the water. And she crossed the finish line in third place. As she paddled toward the reviewing stand to receive her bronze medal, she flipped again.

By the next year, Gloriane Perrier was less wobbly. She would never have good balance in a kayak, but she compensated by paddling a cruising boat and being so much stronger than any other woman paddler in the U.S. At the Olympic trials in 1960, she won the K1W and the honor of representing the U.S. in that event in Rome. Two women from Ohio—Mary Ann DuChai and Diane Jerome—would paddle the double.

As Gloriane trained on the Potomac River in 1960, word began to get out about how fast she was. She was routinely doing 500 meters in 2:07 and sometimes, 2:05. In her heavy, steady boat, she was going faster than the best time recorded by the Soviet woman who was the current world champion with a time of 2:07. Soviet women had won every K1W Olympic event since 1948. The women on the 1960 Soviet team heard about the times this strong new American woman was posting on the Potomac and were eager to learn more about her. When the U.S. team arrived in Rome for the Olympics, the Soviet champion and her teammates asked to see "Miss Gloriane." Miss Gloriane appeared, and the Soviet champion and her teammates were impressed by her physique. Gloriane's arms were bigger than the champion's, or any of her teammates' for that matter, and she casually flexed her muscles a few times as she was being inspected. She was extremely anxious about being at her first international competition, but she was not about to let her competition know that. Then the Soviet champion and her teammates asked to see Miss Gloriane's kayak. The group walked over to the place where the boats were being uncrated. Gloriane pointed to her kayak. The Soviet champion and her teammates looked perplexed. They consulted among themselves and then asked, through an interpreter, "Where is your other boat?" She replied that she had no other boat. The Soviet champion and her teammates smiled nervously at each other and left. For the next three days, they made sure that they were on the water when Gloriane did her workouts in her lumbering craft. They followed her as she paddled. The Soviet champion soon realized that Gloriane would be no competition, and the results of the heats confirmed that realization. Gloriane's times on the Potomac were faster than in the Olympics because of a push from the river's current. When she lost in the heats, Gloriane was actually relieved. She had been slow, and she had been an object of curiosity because of her recreational boat. But at least she had not humiliated herself or her country. She had gotten through the biggest competition of her life without falling in the water. Finishing last was an accomplishment for Gloriane, whose main worry was finishing at all.

Gloriane had a wonderful time at the 1960 Olympics in Rome. She learned that she was a member of an international community, one that ignored the "iron curtain" that was then separating one group of countries from another. She made friends and received encouragement and support from all sorts of people. Her problems with balance were obvious, as was her tremendous power. One of her K1W competitors, Ingrid Hartman from West Germany, advised her to give up the single and paddle in a double so that she would not have to sacrifice so much of her power to her struggle for balance. Ingrid even offered to help her choose a partner. She told Gloriane that she would visit her in Washington, train with her and tell her who among American women paddlers would make a good partner.

◆ ◆ ◆

In the summer of 1962, when Ingrid Hartman was Gloriane Perrier's houseguest in Washington, D.C., Francine Fox had been paddling at the Washington Canoe Club for less than six months. She was thirteen years old, a precocious kid who was a grade ahead of her age group. A junior high classmate of hers had persuaded her to try kayaking after noticing how well she moved in their gymnastics class. Francine was big for her age—five-eight and 160 pounds.

Frank Havens was happy to have Francine at the club because she was a natural at paddling. "The kid had super moves. Everything looked the way it was supposed to. She had great balance and good style."

Francine paddled for a couple of months in a double with Debbie Smith, the classmate who had invited her to the club. Then she moved into a single. Her first time in a tippy racing single, she paddled right away from the dock with barely a wobble. Soon, Francine was training with a group of former Olympians, including Frank Havens, Gloriane Perrier and Charles Lundmark. Lundmark noticed Francine's dedication and hard work. She seemed to thrive on the physical demands of the sport. Lundmark knew that every success she had in a kayak was encouraging her to train harder. She was built for kayaking, and she picked up all the techniques quickly, with little effort.

All Francine knew was how much she loved kayaking. She enjoyed being physical and exerting herself and being sore and going back for more. Her parents were divorced, and she lived with her mother, who "barely eked out a living." Nevertheless, when Francine wanted a paddle, her mother found the means to buy her one. And eventually she helped her daughter buy a kayak.

In July of 1962, six months after she first picked up a paddle, Francine Fox won the senior women's single kayaking championship. She beat Marcia Jones for the first and what turned out to be the only time at nationals. That performance definitely influenced Gloriane Perrier, who had been watching Francine's development as a paddler and had been trying to make a decision about finding a paddling partner. Gloriane was amazed at the youngster's balance. Gloriane's friend and adviser Ingrid Hartman thought that Francine was too young to be a good partner. "Get yourself a twenty-one-year-old," she advised. Gloriane told her that no twenty-one-year-olds with great paddling potential had appeared. In that case, Hartman shrugged, go with Francine. "She is the one because she is not afraid of anything," Hartman commented.

Francine, who was looking for potential partners herself, was not aware that Gloriane was considering asking her to paddle a double. She had discovered that she liked team boats better than singles and that she needed a partner to push her. In a double, she tried to out-pull the woman with whom she was paddling. In a single, she didn't work so hard.

The more Francine considered the other women paddlers at the Washington Canoe Club, the more convinced she was that Gloriane was the partner for her. Gloriane was stronger than anyone else there, had more experience and definitely was determined to get faster and improve upon her performance at the 1960 Olympics. The fact that Gloriane was twenty years older did not seem important to Francine.

In 1963, the precocious teen and the wobbly Olympian teamed up—each one thinking the partnership was her idea—and promised each other they would be competing together in the Tokyo Olympics in 1964.

✦ ✦ ✦

Gloriane Perrier, Francine Fox and Marcia Jones went to Tokyo a month before the Games so that they could get acclimated and focus solely on their paddling. Before leaving the U.S., they had trained across the country from each other—Gloriane and Francine in Washington, D.C., and Marcia in Newport Beach, California. Marcia's mother had found a German coach in Newport Beach and sent both her daughters to train with him for two months. Marcia and Sperry were the only two women in the training camp. Bill Smoke was there, along with a group of men who hoped to make the Olympic team. They paddled twelve to fifteen miles a day and had eleven workouts a week, with Saturday afternoon and Sunday off. Marcia was content: "All we did was eat, sleep and kayak."

Marcia and Sperry raced against men in single canoes (C1— wider and heavier than a single kayak and propelled by a single-bladed paddle), who are about the same speed as women in single kayaks. Bill Smoke marveled at how hard the Jones sisters trained. He thought the Europeans, who considered American women too soft for a sport like kayaking, would be surprised. The biggest danger with Marcia and Sperry Jones, in Smoke's opinion, was overtraining. They tended to burn themselves out in their workouts because they did not know how to give anything less than everything, and they did not know about pacing their training to allow their bodies to peak on the day of the big competitive event. Throughout her career, Marcia would turn in her best times in her workouts.

At the Washington Canoe Club, Gloriane Perrier and Francine Fox were paddling hard every day for an hour or so, getting help from other paddlers at the club and trying to push their double faster down the Potomac. Gloriane was paddling in the bow of the boat where her job was to steer with the foot rudder and to set the stroke rate. Gloriane believed in working hard on the water, but she could not spend her whole day training. She had a job. By 1964, she was thirty-five and beginning her fifteenth year as a secretary, working in the Pentagon. Francine had school to attend until summer vacation. She was fifteen and would enter her senior year in the fall.

The U.S. Olympic paddling team in 1964 was made up of

three women and eight men. Even though women had been competing alongside men at the national championship level for more than ten years, the U.S. governing body for the sport had apparently taken no notice that women had different require- ments in the way the uniforms were cut. The uniform commit- tee issued men's shorts and a man's tank top for everyone on the team, giving the women a small, a medium and a large from which to choose. The large was the only one that came close to fitting any of them. Francine got it. Since Marcia was the small- est at five-six and 130 pounds, she wore the small. She was up- set at the way it fit and at the committee's insensitivity to the women on the team. It seemed to her that the comittee paid more attention to the way the women would look off the race course than the way they would look performing the task for which they were going to Tokyo. The girdles and gloves that the committee issued for the three women were evidence of this attitude. Marcia packed her girdle and her gloves reluctantly since she did not intend to wear them much. The one Olympic- issue item that she liked was the belt buckle with the Olympic rings on it. She decided to wear that whenever she could and to focus on it. She was determined to make the most of the Olym- pic experience that had been her dream for so long.

On the day that she marched into the stadium for opening ceremonies with the rest of the athletes, Marcia Jones cried, first with excitement and then with some regret because the rest of the American contingent seemed so casual about the event that meant so much to her. She had wanted to march in step, the way athletes from other countries do. But the American ath- letes surrounding her sauntered. She held her head up and walked along in the middle of the pack, not the best place, she learned, for seeing and being seen—the right hand side of the parade was a better vantage point for the marching athlete. When the white doves were set free to flutter up and out of the stadium, she noticed that the veteran Olympians pulled out newspapers and covered their heads. She would know to carry a newspaper with her next time. Marcia was extending her dream as she was living it; she knew that one Olympics would not be enough.

Even though she had participated in the spectacle of the Olympics once before, Gloriane Perrier was no less moved by her second appearance at the Games. She loved all the fanfare: "Oh god, it's gorgeous. All the athletes. You know that you're among the best."

Francine Fox was in awe of all the other athletes at the Tokyo Olympics, but she tried to concentrate on her own workouts during the month that she, Marcia and Gloriane spent training together. Her only previous international competition had been in Canada, where she hadn't seen the Soviets, the Hungarians, the Romanians, the Czechs or the Germans, the traditional paddling powerhouses. She was slightly intimidated by their reputations and their toughness. But she concentrated on her own training. She wanted to do her best. The fact that expectations for the American women were not high took some of the pressure off her.

During their month of training together in Tokyo, all three of the American women noticed that the other teams seemed to do more than just paddle for their workouts. The Americans would be lying in their beds in the morning and hear all the other teams out running in the streets. Marcia wondered whether she should be doing something different to get ready for the most important races of her career. The coach of the U.S. team was not much help. He spent very little time with the women on the team and seemed indifferent to their desire to perform well. Marcia accused him of not being willing to spend eight dollars an hour to rent a launch and go out on the water with the women.

The American women did everything they knew to do. They were basically self-taught anyway and didn't expect coaching. Sometimes when coaching was offered, they refused to listen, thinking that they knew better. After all, they had gotten to the Olympics following their own advice. One day, the women received an offer of help from the coach of the Italian team, Kahlman Blaho. He said that he had been watching their workouts and thought they had a good chance of performing well in the upcoming races. He also told them that he wanted to move to the United States. He had fled Hungary for Italy during the revolt of 1956, and he was ready to move across the Atlantic.

After the women accepted his offer of help, the first thing he did was suggest that they pair up in different combinations to see which pair made the double go fastest. When he timed each of the three combinations, he discovered that Marcia and Gloriane were the fastest. Marcia, however, did not want to be in a team boat. And Gloriane was loyal to Francine. "I told her when she was twelve, for godsake, that we would paddle in the Olympics together," Gloriane said.

If Gloriane and Francine were to paddle together in the double, Kahlman said, Francine should move into the bow to relieve Gloriane of any responsibility but supplying raw power. The two paddlers complied with his recommendation and switched places. The three paddlers uncharacteristically did exactly what Kahlman suggested in the workout plans that he organized for them. Much of his coaching concentrated on their attitudes. He encouraged them and kept them focused. He knew how to pace their workouts so that they would peak on the day of the finals.

Because all the paddlers, with the exception of the Soviet team, did their workouts on the same body of water at the same time, they had a good idea before the competition ever began of who was going to get medals. The Romanian coach would stand with his stopwatch pointed at the Bulgarian paddler doing 500 meter sprints. The Czech coach would time the German team. The Soviet women were the favorites, but no one knew for sure how fast they were. Marcia was scheduled to race against the Soviet Ludmilla Khvedosiuk in her heat. She knew that she was competitive with the other women in the field. If in the heat she could stay ahead of them and close to Khvedosiuk, she might have a chance at a medal in the finals. She wanted a medal. "I had made the team. Now that was no longer good enough." When she finished second to Khvedosiuk in her heat, she knew a medal was possible. "I thought I had a chance. I was hoping I wouldn't mess up."

In the final, Marcia was in the second lane. There were nine boats in the race. In Tokyo, race officials laid on platforms and held each kayak to make sure that the boats were lined up evenly for the start. Marcia was not used to being held at the starting line. She thought the official was going to tip her boat. She demanded that he let go. There was a false start, and all the paddlers returned to the line. She was more nervous than she had ever been before a race.

The gun went off again, and this time all the boats pulled cleanly away from the line. Marcia quickly moved into fourth place. Her strokes were fast and powerful, steady and even. A paddler from Sweden was right behind her. Marcia could hear every breath the Swedish woman took. With one hundred meters to go, Marcia looked around. The Russian woman was way ahead. The Romanian was half a boat length ahead. The German was right beside her.

Somehow, Marcia found the extra strength to kick up her sprint at the end. Never before had she been able to give more in the last hundred meters of a race. But this was her chance at an Olympic medal. It might be her only chance. She paddled as hard and fast as she possibly could. When she crossed the finish line, gasping and completely drained, she did not know whether she had overtaken the German. She looked up at the dock. Gloriane was standing there, jumping up and down and screaming, "You got it. You got third."

Marcia's bronze medal finish inspired Francine and Gloriane and gave them confidence. The night before the race, Gloriane had gotten a tip from a West German paddler who was her friend. The West German coach was the starter, so the tip went, and was going to be a stickler about following the starting rule in the upcoming final. The rule is that the paddlers go on the gun. The reality is that they start pulling away on the "Are" of "Are you ready?" Gloriane told Francine that they would wait until the gun went off to start. This way, she figured, everyone but their boat and the German boat would get a penalty for a false start. The other major strategy that the American double planned to employ in the race was to start steady and finish hard. This was their new-found coach's strategy, as opposed to Gloriane's, whose usual race plan was to get ahead and stay ahead. Gloriane liked to show her tremendous strength in the first half and just hang on for the second half of a race. She didn't like to come from behind.

The Germans were in lane nine, and the Americans in lane three. The starting judge began, "Are you ready?" Seven boats were off before the gun. Only lanes three and nine held. The seven quick starters were penalized for a false start. Gloriane smiled. On the second start, the judge began, "Are you ready?" The Germans were out of there, and Gloriane was furious that she and all the other paddlers had waited for the gun. There was no false start called. Her friend had tricked her.

The Americans had a strong start, if a couple of beats later than the Germans. They looked good through the first 200 meters. The fifteen-year-old paddling in the bow was setting a pace that would conserve her thirty-five-year-old partner's incredible power. She was also keeping the boat stable. As they paddled through the inevitable pain of the next 200 meters, the two Americans knew they were moving well and passing boats. It was a rainy, foggy day and Gloriane could barely see Francine in front of her as they churned down the course. Gloriane was not sure how many boats were in front of them. Francine knew she was doing her best and having the race of her life—that was all that mattered. For the last hundred meters, she picked up the pace and unleashed Gloriane's power. The Americans saw the Romanian double on their left. They dug in harder and passed that boat. As they crossed the finish line, they looked around and didn't see anyone else in front of them—until the Germans came paddling back to congratulate them on their silver medal.

The three American women won their medals on a day when other American athletes were doing little of note at the Tokyo Olympics. Consequently, the three got a great deal more press than they were used to or than they might otherwise have received. Marcia, being closer to the ideal of feminine beauty than her two teammates, was the darling of the press. Stories gushed about "pretty Marcia Jones" and her medal-winning performance. They marveled that, despite her delicate appearance, she actually was strong enough to paddle past hefty European athletes. The stories downplayed, if they mentioned at all, the hours she had put in lifting weights and the incredible strength she had in her upper body. She was invited to appear on the game show, *To Tell the Truth*, where she tried to keep her identity from the four panelists. She fooled only one of them, however, because the two decoys appearing with her knew nothing about sports.

Winning that silver medal was Gloriane's proudest moment. She had business cards printed identifying her as an Olympic silver medalist. When she returned to the Washington Canoe Club, people wanted her to teach them how to paddle and wanted to know her training secrets. "How much jogging do you do?" they asked. "I don't jog," she replied. "How much weight do you lift?" "I never lift weights." Her training secret was to paddle hard on every stroke in every practice and to believe that she could be among the fastest paddlers in the world.

✦ ✦ ✦

By winning medals in kayaking in the Olympics, Francine Fox, Gloriane Perrier and Marcia Jones attracted attention to the sport and drew other women into it. All three continued to compete after 1964—with Marcia compiling her impressive string of national championships unbroken until 1974—but their greatest contribution to the sport was their encouragement of a new generation of women paddlers.

Marcia Jones and Bill Smoke married in 1965 and devoted the next five years to promoting the sport through which they had met and which had fulfilled their dreams of being Olympic athletes. He became chairman of the national flatwater committee, and she was treasurer. They started a newsletter for competitive paddlers in the U.S.; Sperry Jones was the editor.

Marcia and Bill bought a piece of land with trees and pasture that rolled down to the St. Joseph's River in Buchanan, Michigan, a small town just up the river from South Bend, Indiana. They built a spacious wooden house on the river bank, and Marcia could paddle in her backyard. Bill turned a couple of horses' watering troughs into paddling tanks, and he and Marcia hauled them to shopping malls so that people could try the sport. They both touted the sport at countless Kiwanis and Lions Club meetings, and the area around Buchanan gradually became a center for kayaking.

As she spread the word about her sport, Marcia continued to train. She wanted to go to the Olympics in Mexico City in 1968. Sperry, who came closest to beating her sister in 1965 when she tied with Marcia in the national championship race, also wanted to go. Their mother once again facilitated their pursuit of the Olympic dream. Mary Francis had begun looking for a place where they could train at an altitude similar to Mexico City's almost as soon as the '64 Olympics was over. When they both made the Olympic team in '68, they went to the Colorado site their mother had secured for them. Mary Francis did not live long enough to sit among the spectators and watch both her daughters compete in the Olympics. She died early in 1968 in a house fire.

Marcia would make one more Olympic team (1972) before

ending her competitive career, but she would not match or better her 1964 Tokyo performance. Even while she was competing, more and more of her energies were going into coaching. In 1969, Ray Dodge's youngest daughter wanted to learn how to paddle. Marcia agreed to coach her, and invited some other youngsters to be part of a small kayak club that she started at her house. The kids would arrive every day at four, and Marcia would send them to the garage to paddle in the twelve-foot-long watering troughs modified into paddling tanks. When they gained enough proficiency, she put them on the river, which is a muddy, slow-moving stream most of the year. She ran this club for ten years and produced six Olympians: Greg Barton, Bruce Barton, Pete Deyo, Julie Leach, Ann Turner and Candi Clark. Greg Barton, who won two gold medals at the Seoul Olympics in 1988, started paddling with Marcia when he was ten. He and his brother would travel to Buchanan from their home in Homer, Michigan, one hundred miles north. They would pitch a tent on the Smoke land and spend the summer working on their conditioning and technique. Greg Barton gives Marcia, his first instructor, much of the credit for his success as a paddler. She spotted him at a marathon canoe race, in which his parents were participating, and invited him and his brother to her place to learn Olympic paddling.

While Marcia Jones Smoke was developing Olympians in Buchanan, Gloriane Perrier was doing the same in the Washington, D.C., area. She began coaching soon after she returned from Tokyo in 1964. Her presence at the Washington Canoe Club attracted young paddlers who wanted to go to the Olympics. If those paddlers could survive her workouts, they had a good shot at the Games.

Gloriane believed in punishingly hard workouts. A typical session would be ten 500-meter sprints with only a few seconds in between each one. She would not permit any laggards on the course. "When you can do a two-minute race, don't give me a 2:02. Give me a 1:59," she screamed. She wore ten stopwatches around her neck and seemed to be aware of everything that was going on with every paddler. Frank Havens thought she was the best coach in the country.

Gloriane retired from competition in 1967 because she stopped winning. "If I'm not coming in first, I don't want to race." She pushed the kids she coached to do better than she had. She wanted perfection—and she wanted her version of it. There was no other way to paddle but Gloriane's. Quite a few kids could not finish her workouts. She was not asking them to do more than she had done, but she had been a phenomenal athlete, with uncommon strength and will. The kids would stop paddling and start crying and then drop out of the junior program.

Theresa Haught was twelve when she signed up for coaching from Gloriane. She cried during workouts, but her tears welled up from anger, not surrender. She would whisper through her clenched teeth, "I'm going to show Glo that I can do it." Even if she was doing one of Gloriane's favorite workouts—ninety times ten seconds at high intensity alternating with ten seconds of rest—on a frigid day on the Potomac, when her hands were frozen to the paddle, Theresa persevered. If she complained, Gloriane talked about her own paddling and how hard she had worked. Theresa would cry, but she was always back the next day. Soon, she began winning races and eventually made two Olympic teams.

Nancy Purvis and Linda Murray were two other Olympians whom Gloriane coached. She saw herself and Francine Fox in the two young women who wanted to paddle a double in the Olympics. Gloriane, who did all her coaching without pay, bought a boat for Nancy and Linda to race. She told them there was nothing they could not do. In fact, she assured them that they could do better than she and Francine had done; they could win the gold medal that she and Francine had missed. She insisted that they aim for a world record. Every Thursday night, she would cook dinner for them at her apartment and give them strawberry shortcake for dessert.

When Nancy and Linda made the team that would go to the 1972 Olympics in Munich, Gloriane hoped to be named coach of the women's Olympic team. After all, she had gotten half of the four-woman team ready to qualify for the Olympics. The U.S. Olympic committee for canoeing and kayaking, however, had another idea and selected a swimming coach, who had no kayaking background, to travel to Munich with the women athletes and coach them there. Although Gloriane herself does not say that being overlooked as the Olympic team coach that year caused her to get out of the sport, those close to her don't hesitate to comment that she got a raw political deal. Gloriane paid her own way to the Olympics to cheer for her double. She gave her training schedule—including the instruction to feed the athletes strawberry shortcake every Thursday night—to the swimming coach. Nancy and Linda did not win the gold medal that Gloriane and Francine had missed. In 1972, their boat did not make the finals.

◆ ◆ ◆

After the 1964 Olympics, Francine Fox finished her senior year of high school and started paddling at the Potomac Boat Club instead of its next-door neighbor, the Washington Canoe Club, ending her partnership with Gloriane. She had turned sixteen and wanted to pursue interests outside kayaking. She continued to race, primarily in a single, until 1974, even though she did not win. She loved everything about paddling—the feeling of the rhythmic exertion, the hard work, being out on the water. She pushed Marcia Jones Smoke, who benefitted from that pressure: "Francine was always there. I could never let up because I didn't want her to beat me."

Francine couldn't train as hard as Marcia because she couldn't afford it. Sports were a luxury for her, something she could do once she was sure the bills were going to be paid. She went to college in the Washington area and got a masters de-

gree in German language and literature. She married John Van
Dyke, who paddled at the Potomac Boat Club and was on the
1972 Olympic team, which Francine had failed to make.

The Van Dykes now live in Carlsbad, California, and have
two teenaged children, Johnny and Angela. The whole family is
active in sports, but the two Olympian paddlers are not pushing
their children to concentrate on any one activity. Francine believes in letting her children find their own strengths as athletes, just as she was allowed to. She and her husband paddle for
recreation and race in triathlons. They have horses, and one of
their favorite events is the annual Ride and Tie, in which two
people alternate between running and riding one horse thirty-
two miles over a mountain trail.

Francine teaches algebra and geometry in high school and
also has one period of physical education, a conditioning class.
She says that after pushing hard all of her life, she discovered
another way of existing in August of 1990. She was forty-one,
and her friends sent her to a Colorado mountaintop for a week-
long seminar that teaches taking one day at a time and savoring
each moment. The seminar made a big impression on her and
allowed her to be easier on herself. She has no regrets, however,
about the way she pushed her young self to learn to paddle and
to get to the Olympic Games. "I wouldn't trade a day or a
stroke for anything else. I'm eternally grateful that life gave me
that opportunity. I loved what I was doing and the people I was
with at the time."

Marcia Jones Smoke retired from competition the same year
that Francine Fox Van Dyke did. Her daughter Jenny was born
in 1974, and her son Jeff, three years later. She gave up coaching when she had two small children to tend. Soon, she was doing for her children what her mother did for her, giving them
all the encouragement and resources they needed to excel at
whatever sport they chose. She and Bill Smoke divorced in
1990, but she and the kids still live in the house on the St. Joe
River. There they have a covered twenty-five-yard pool in

which to practice their swimming and a field and goal in which to practice their soccer, as well as several horses, which Jenny shows and jumps, four dogs, two cats, four chickens and, occasionally, pigs for 4-H projects.

While Marcia says she has not pushed her kids to compete, she has helped to make sports the focus of their lives. "Sports are something really tangible. They have given me a purpose, something I can pass on to the kids." Both Jeff and Jenny are excellent athletes, preferring the triathlon to other events. Jeff has already won the Iron Kid junior championship, and Jenny says she would like to go to the Olympics when the triathlon becomes an Olympic event. Neither of Marcia's children likes to kayak. "It's boring," Jenny says.

Marcia attends every event in which her children participate. She loves to watch them. "I get a big thrill out of watching my children compete. It's a different type of thrill from when you're competing yourself. I did what I wanted to do in kayaking. I was satisfied. Then the kids came along, and now I can do things with them. I like to watch people in athletics. I like to watch people excel."

Marcia still likes to kayak, though she does not just get in the boat and paddle around. "I'm not the kind that can sit in a kayak and go along the coast line for two weeks at a time. Once you're an athlete, it's hard to go out and cruise up and down the river and go slow. I have to have a workout. I'll do 5,000 meters to see how my time compares with that of long ago." She paddles three times a week, runs three times a week and also plays tennis. And in an Olympic year, she goes to the Games as a spectator.

Gloriane Perrier stopped coaching in 1973. Her father died that year, and when she went home to Maine for the funeral, she discovered that her frugal parents had more than half a million dollars in a bank, collecting five-and-a-quarter percent interest. "I was amazed that my parents, whom I always thought were poor, had that much money," she says. "Of course, being from

Maine, they're very secretive!" She persuaded her mother to let her invest the money in something more lucrative, and thus belatedly began the career in finance that she had sacrificed for softball and then kayaking many years before. She became an expert in treasury notes ("I would get a gold medal for investing in treasury notes if it was an Olympic event") and, buoyed by her success with her parents' money, she began investing for her kayaking pals. She has invested more than five million dollars for other people, never charging anyone for her services. "I do it for nothing, because I don't want to work for you. I want to work for myself."

"She likes to play with that computer and make money," Frank Havens says. He has profited from her investment advice. "She makes money for everyone she knows."

Gloriane retired from her secretarial job in 1983, after thirty-three years. She no longer paddles because of problems with her back, but she does jog and walk. She corresponds with European friends that she made in international competition and divides her time between her home in Leavenworth, Kansas, the house she grew up in in Maine (her mother died in 1989, and her sister still lives there) and her brother's home in Florida. She has a friend, a major in the Army, for whom Gloriane invested in treasury notes, enabling her to retire before the age of forty. The two of them plan to visit all the places where Gloriane raced. "I've been to all these countries and never seen anything," Gloriane says. "All that was on my mind was to win the race."

❖ ❖ ❖

At the 1984 Olympic Games in Los Angeles, Marcia Jones Smoke and Francine Fox Van Dyke met at at the paddling venue. The two women hadn't seen each other for more than ten years and had a lot of reminiscing to do as they walked together along Lake Casitas, ducking under the boats that various paddlers were carrying to and from the water. They talked about their time in Tokyo as Olympians together. They talked about Gloriane, with whom Marcia had stayed in touch. As they strolled, they began to pay attention to the announcer on the public address system. He was reading off the names of all the U.S. Olympic medalists in paddling. He talked about Ernie Riedel in 1936; Frank Havens, Steve Lysak and Steve Mack-nowski in 1948; and Frank Havens again in 1952. Marcia and Francine smiled at each other in anticipation of hearing their names next. They knew that their year, 1964, was coming up. They stopped walking and waited for the announcer to broadcast the fact of their accomplishment in Tokyo. "We thought it would be kind of neat to hear our names," Marcia says. What they heard, however, did not please them. The announcer dismissed their Olympic year by saying merely that three women had won medals in 1964. He did not mention those women by name. He did not mention the bronze medal for the single and the silver medal for the double. He did not mention that the three women were the only U.S. medalists in paddling that Olympic year.

Marcia was stunned at the omission. Francine was immediately angry. As soon as Marcia got over her shock, the two of them began to look for people who could do something about the insult. They did not blame the announcer; he was just a hired voice. They blamed the people in charge of the event, people whom they knew. Marcia knew the omission of their names wasn't malicious but was an oversight typical of the way the competitive paddling community regarded women. The disregard of women had been evident in 1952 and 1956 when women qualified for the Olympics but the American Canoe Association refused to spend the money to send them to the Games. It was obvious in 1964 when the three women who made the Olympic team were issued men's uniforms and ignored by the U.S. coach. Apparently, the attitude was still in play in 1984 when a script handed to an announcer contained the names of male medalists in the sport but not the names of the female medalists. "It was like women didn't count," Marcia says.

Francine and Marcia were not about to tolerate such an attitude. They went straight to the people who controlled what was said over the public address system at Lake Casitas and told them how they felt. And the next day, the announcer made sure that he named Marcia Jones, Francine Fox and Gloriane Perrier as the three medalists in kayaking for the United States in 1964. Those three had surprised the world one day in 1964, and they had started something for American women. Their names were important reminders that women could excel when they chose to do so. Perhaps some young woman among the spectators would, upon hearing those names, get an idea about being an Olympian herself.

Traci Phillips is an outstanding athlete who discovered the Olympic sport of flatwater kayaking when she was twenty-one. After six months of training in her new sport, she made the U.S. national team in 1986. She has been the top U.S. women's single flatwater kayaker since 1987.

Traci Phillips

~

TRACI PHILLIPS is heir to the tradition of excellence that Marcia Jones, Gloriane Perrier and Francine Fox established for American women in flatwater paddling. But this thoroughly modern athlete, the best hope among United States women for a flatwater medal in the 1992 Barcelona Olympics, has more support and encouragement for her single-minded pursuit of faster racing times than her three predecessors ever would have dreamed. Phillips, who does not come from a wealthy family, is nevertheless able to spend all of her time training and living as an athlete. Grants from the U.S. Olympic Committee and from private sponsors pay her way.

This support is not without its drawbacks for Phillips, who has discovered that having all the time in the world to train can be hazardous to her athletic endowment. Her major hurdle in reaching her potential is burnout—she tends to overtrain. Because her number-one goal is to win a medal in flatwater kayaking at the Barcelona Olympics, Phillips has had to find a way to stay in shape without burning out in her chosen sport. Her solution is unique. In the fall, when the kayak racing season is over, she puts her boat in storage and turns her athletic focus to the luge, a sport that requires her to ride a sled as fast as she can down 750 meters of icy curves.

Phillips, a small, determined-looking young woman with straight blonde hair that hangs to her waist, spends her winters in Lake Placid, New York, practicing with the U.S. luge team. When she shows up at the luge run, she wraps her hair around her head and clamps a helmet over it. Then she places her sled, which is little more than two runners and a hammock, at the start and sits on it, bending her upper body forward as far as it will go. She grabs the stationary handles on either side of the luge track's starting line and begins to rock her sled back and forth, sliding it forward as she leans back and backward as she bends forward. She is working up momentum for the fling that will send her and her tiny sled flying down the track.

The explosiveness that she needs to have a good start in the luge is similar to the burst of unleashed power that she aims for at the start of a 500-meter flatwater kayak race. Both sports demand tremendous upper body strength, coordination and speed at the start. In kayak racing, Phillips sits in the cockpit of a slender, temperamental, seventeen-foot, twenty-seven-pound boat. The second she hears the starting gun, she begins paddling at about 130 strokes a minute. She wields the double-bladed kayaking paddle with all the precision of a mowing machine; the kayak, which tips easily, does not wobble even slightly under her control. Phillips digs her blade into the water at each stroke, extending and rotating her upper body for maximum power as she hauls the kayak past the planted paddle. She pulls the blade out of the water with a clean, sure motion, quickly recovers her balance and sets up for the next stroke on the other side of the boat.

Both the luge and kayaking require a crucial transition after the start. In the luge, the athlete must move from a forward-leaning, seated position to lying flat on her back for the ride down the track. To see the blur of white through which she is hurtling, she lifts her head enough to look out over her toes. She must make this transition from sitting forward to lying back without slowing the sled or losing control of its course. Once she is in position for the rest of the run, she steers by shifting her body weight on the sled, by pulling on handles and by using the pressure from her legs against the runners to point the sled down the proper line. There is one line on the track that is the fastest way to the bottom of the run, and that's what she is straining with all her wit and might to find. She wants to find that line and allow the sled to gain momentum the way a rolling snowball gathers mass.

In kayaking, the transition is more subtle. Phillips must drop her rate to a more sustainable 116 strokes per minute for the body of the race. She must hit it just right, reducing the rate without losing power. The transition is quick—the time between the last stroke at 130 and the next at 116. It requires a highly developed sense of timing and an internal metronome. As she drops the stroke rate, Phillips keeps her pace consistent and her body steady, eliminating extraneous movements and leans, using her legs to twist her torso into position and her arms as the conduit for the thrust that only the larger muscles of her upper body can supply. She hears the steady splash of the blade into the water; each entry sounds like a small explosion. Boom. Boom. Boom. Boom.

After the start and the transition in both the luge and flatwater kayaking comes the hard part, the part in which the athlete must relax and get on top of the adrenalin rush that can otherwise overwhelm her. When Phillips talks about relaxing in either sport, she is not describing what most people would consider mellowing out. Relaxing on a luge run means shutting out everything but the feel of the perfect line down the run. It means shutting out how fragile her body feels stretched against a tiny sled that is traveling at seventy miles per hour through hairpin curves and S curves, swinging left and right and back again. It means shutting out everything but where the pressure is on each curve, where the push is so that the sled bursts out of the curve hell-bent for whatever twists come next. The way to learn to relax on a luge run is to crash, according to Phillips. "Once you crash a few times, you're really not afraid. It looks worse than it is." Crash and learn—that's her philosophy for mastering the luge. Once the fear of crashing is gone, the athlete can stop steeling her body against the terrible pull of gravity. She can stay loose and loopy, like the line she seeks. She can relax and rely on her reflexes to react in time to the next curve on the course.

In kayaking, Phillips has to relax on each stroke. Her tendency is to grip the paddle so hard with her right hand that the power coming from her body and through her arm runs up against a knot that impedes its flow. She has to tell herself to let the color back into her knuckles and give her strength room to run. She begins reminding herself to relax at about ten strokes into the race. At the 300-meter mark she intensifies those reminders. This is the place in the race where the pain of the effort asserts itself. The muscles in Phillips's body begin screaming for her to stop. First her forearms start to burn. Then her shoulders. Then her lower back, stomach and abdominal muscles. Quickly, the conflagration spreads to consume her entire body. She tells herself that she must relax, shut out the pain and force her body to increase the exertion against which it is howling. She concentrates on welcoming the pain as a sign that she is working as hard as she should be. Then she tries to replace it with the feeling of speed. For the finish, she needs to be able to pick up the stroke rate to about 120 and put incredible strength into each of those rapid thrusts of the blade.

Mental strength in both the luge and in flatwater kayak racing is the factor that makes one international competitor faster than another. At the elite level, the athletes are usually physically equal, having trained the same muscles for the same purposes. The athlete who can best relax and focus on either the fastest line down the luge run or the power in each stroke in a kayak race will be the winner. Phillips, who has been among the top U.S. women flatwater paddlers since 1987 and who finished sixth in the single in the 1988 Olympics, is focusing on her mental preparation as she trains for the 1992 Olympics. The kayak in which she practices and races wears a big green and yellow neon sticker reading "Mind Right." The sticker is right in front of the cockpit where Phillips can see it on each stroke. The quote is from the movie *Cool Hand Luke*. In the movie, Luke is put to work digging a ditch and filling it back in after a failed attempt to escape from prison. The guard supervising this Sisyphian chore repeatedly asks him, "Got your mind right yet, Luke?"

Training in the luge has helped Phillips get her mind right for paddling. She learned how to relax because the luge demands a certain letting go. She learned how to focus because the luge demands close attention to nuances. She learned her lessons in the luge so well that what was originally an off-season diversion to keep her sharp for kayaking has become a passion in itself. Because of her formidable athletic talent and her relentless competitive spirit, Phillips has won a place on the development team that supplies the athletes for the U.S. Luge Team. After the '92 Barcelona Olympics, where she will try to become the first American woman since Marcia Jones, Gloriane Perrier and Francine Fox in 1964 to win an Olympic medal in flatwater kayaking, she will be aiming for the 1994 winter Olympic trials in the luge. Her goal is to be among the top ten women lugers in the U.S. in 1994. And that probably won't be the end of her pursuit of the elusive perfect line on the luge run.

✦ ✦ ✦

Traci Phillips has always excelled at every sport she tries. Her mother, Marjorie Howe, says that her physical gifts were evident almost from the time she was born on August 1, 1964, in Honolulu, Hawaii. She was an active baby who loved to play. "She was sitting up at four months. She was a lot of fun and very aggressive. I'd give her something to do, and she'd just love it. She was walking at nine months. When she was ten months old, I took her with me to the swimming lessons I used to teach. She would walk right over to the pool and fall into the water. She was never afraid of the water."

When Traci was two, she learned how to swim. Her mother was teaching a class in which Traci desperately wanted to take part, but Howe refused to let her into the class because she was too young. Little Traci would stand outside the pool fence and watch as her mother taught the big kids how to swim. Then when the lessons were over and the students were splashing around in the pool, Traci would dash in and insist that her mother watch her repeat everything the big kids had just learned. "Mommy, watch me," she would say. She wanted to prove she could do everything Howe's students did so she could be in the class. Her mother relented and let her join. "I told her she couldn't be disruptive. She turned out to be my best student."

Marjorie Howe, who had grown up in Woodland, California, a town of 6,000, was delighted to have a daughter so eager to learn about sports. Howe had not participated in any organized athletics until she went to college. "Where I grew up, you played with your dolls and that was it." In college, she learned how to ski. Eventually, she became a ski instructor at Squaw Valley and took Traci to the slopes with her. Traci was skiing down the big hill at Squaw Valley by the time she was four.

Traci's determination to stick with something until she succeeded amazed her mother. At five, Traci got her first bicycle and wanted ride it right away without training wheels. "She thought training wheels were the worst thing that could happen to a bicycle," Howe says. While Howe watched from the kitchen, Traci taught herself how to ride. "She didn't want anybody to help her. I didn't dare go out there. By the end of the day, she had a few scratches on her, but she could ride that bicycle. She was very happy."

Marjorie Howe moved back with her daughter to Honolulu when Traci was eight. Howe immediately joined the Outrigger Canoe Club, which offered a variety of sports for children. Traci first tried volleyball on the club's so-called baby court. Little kids stayed there all day and threw themselves after the volleyball as it landed in the sand. Traci spent nearly every afternoon on the baby volleyball court. Traci also learned how to surf at the Outrigger Canoe Club. She met a man in his sixties who was willing to teach her, and soon every day after elementary school she and her pal Bill would be out in the surf. She then took up canoeing as soon as she could find somebody to teach her how to steer. Between the ages of ten and eighteen, Traci did as much outrigger canoeing, surfing and playing sand volleyball as she could: In a typical weekend, Traci would participate in a surfing contest, a canoe regatta and a volleyball tournament. She excelled at all three sports, winning state championships in each of them. She also took up racquetball and was a three-time Hawaiian champion in that sport.

Although athletics was definitely Traci's main interest when she was growing up, she also managed to get good grades until her senior year in high school when she gave up everything else to concentrate on whether the surf was up and what tournaments or races she could enter. She tried college—enrolling at the University of Hawaii as a drama major—but she lasted only a year. She didn't like sitting in a classroom or taking tests.

Marjorie Howe wanted Traci to be around sports and to be active, but she was unprepared for her daughter's intense competitive spirit and her perfectionism: "She wanted to win all the time. She had to win."

Traci did not discover the Olympic sport of flatwater kayaking until she was twenty-one. She was surf-skiing on the Ala Wai Canal in Honolulu when an old friend asked if she would like to try paddling the racing kayak he had just brought over from California. "Sure," she said, eager as always to try a new sport. As soon as she got into that kayak, she felt an immediate connection, a sense of excitement that all the other sports at which she excelled had not given her. She knew very little about how to paddle a racing kayak, and she was having trouble keeping the tippy boat upright. But even as she took her first few wobbly strokes, she had the feeling that she had found a sport that would allow the fullest expression of her athletic potential. All the time she was growing up, Traci had been certain that one day she would participate in the Olympics. The sports she had competed in, however, were not Olympic events. The one thing she knew about the kayak she was trying to paddle was that it was the type of boat raced in the Olympics. If she could master this slender craft, it just might take her to the Olympics.

In January of 1986, a month after her introduction in Hawaii to the racing kayak, Traci moved to Newport Beach, California, to train with Billy Whitford, the coach for several women paddlers who had gone on to make the Olympic team. She told Whitford that her goal was to make the 1988 Olympic team and that she was prepared to do anything to work toward that objective. Her mother had agreed to help her financially during her first year of all-out training.

Whitford wondered whether Phillips would have the patience to learn a difficult new sport at her age: "You've got to be willing to walk before you run again when you're learning a new sport. With kids, it's easy to start something new. When you're older, it's harder. You get into a boat and you flip, flip, flip. Finally, you get over flipping but you're not as fast as the others. She wanted to get in and just run, run, run. But you can't just get into these boats and rely on your natural talent. It takes an extreme amount of patience and dedication."

Phillips let her frustration show during those first months of learning how to paddle. Sheila Conover, who had been on the 1984 Olympic team and who was a hopeful for 1988, found Phillips very difficult to train with and noted her "big attitude problem with bad days." Conover also became Phillips's best friend almost immediately. She liked the way Phillips would go off on conversational tangents unrelated to paddling—like talking about how she thought she must have been a USO entertainer in a previous life or how her greatest ambition was to tap dance to all of Benny Goodman's records. "Traci is one of the silliest people I know," Conover says. Conover also admired Phillips's determination to learn how to paddle. She welcomed the idea of competition from Phillips because it would push *her* to get faster. She excused Phillips's outbursts in practice because she believed that to be good an athlete has to be self-absorbed and unwilling to accept anything but perfection.

Conover had made a relatively rapid rise to the top among U.S. women paddlers, and she knew that Phillips had the talent to do the same. Like Phillips, she had paddled outrigger canoes before trying kayaks. She was eighteen when she took up the sport in 1981. "I wasn't very good at first. I did a lot of swimming and thought [kayaking] was a crazy sport." She sought Billy Whitford's coaching, and, within six months of learning how to paddle, won the junior nationals and finished ninth at the junior world championships. Three years later she was on the Olympic team, representing the U.S. in the single (K1W) and in the four (K4W), which was a new Olympic event for women in 1984. She finished sixth in the KW1 and fourth in the K4W (with Leslie Klein, Ann Turner and Shirley Dery).

At five-nine and 150 pounds, Conover was larger than the five-four, 122-pound Phillips. She was only a year older but had five more years of paddling experience. She helped Phillips figure out some of the tricky technical aspects of the sport. Phillips looked at Conover and at other women who had been the best U.S. paddlers and who would be trying for the 1988 Olympics and thought that she was just as good an athlete. She knew that her size would not necessarily be a drawback. "Good kayakers come in all sizes. That's why I like kayaking." She figured she had more determination than anyone else who was trying to make the team.

To be internationally competitive in flatwater kayaking usually takes years of intense conditioning and technique work. Phillips, with her background in other sports, had a good conditioning base on which to build. Her cardiovascular system, her muscular endurance and her flexibility—the three most important physiological factors in the sport—were in excellent shape. When she began learning how to race in a kayak, she was a mature athlete both physically and mentally. Her task was to work on paddling technique and on balance.

"Kayaking is not traditionally a strong sport in America the way it is in Europe," says Billy Whitford. "It's not a scholastic or collegiate or professional sport. Consequently, we don't have a great deal of depth among our elite paddlers. Traci, with that competitive drive of hers, realized that physically she had what it took to make a name for herself quickly in paddling."

As Phillips began working on technique, she wanted to understand everything right away. Besides getting help from Whitford and Conover, she kept after her new boyfriend, Greg Barton, to give her advice. Barton had been paddling racing kayaks since he was a kid in Michigan. He had traveled from his home in Homer to take lessons with Marcia Jones Smoke in Niles. He was also an engineer who enjoyed talking about the biomechanics of the stroke and who worked on paddle designs. "I hounded him all the time," Phillips says. "I was always asking questions."

Kayaking technique allows room for individual style, but certain basics must underlie that style. The paddler sits in the kayak's cockpit with her body leaning slightly forward and her knees slightly bent. She must coordinate the movement of her arms and body and aim for a stroke that is symmetrical on both the right and left sides. The blades should trace an outline that resembles a butterfly's wings. The stroke has four different parts: set-up, catch, power and recovery. The recovery occurs when the paddler is switching from one side of the stroke to the other. In the recovery position, the paddle shaft is horizontal at the paddler's shoulder level. The stroke starts when the paddler pushes her off-side (away from the stroke) knee down to force her hip to begin rotating toward the side of the boat where the blade is going to enter the water. She leans farther forward with her upper body, rotating so that her on-side (the side of the stroke) shoulder is extended. The more rotation she gets from her body, the more power she will put into the blade. The recovery position is extremely unstable because the paddle is out of the water. If the paddler moves her body even slightly to either side of the kayak, the boat will tip. In the set-up phase, the paddler drops her on-side arm, fully extended, towards the water. All the motion for the set-up comes from her on-side shoulder rotation. At the catch, the paddle hits the water at about a forty-five-degree angle and moves quickly to ninety degrees. The paddler pushes her on-side leg down on the footrest to get more power from the stroke and shifts her entire center of gravity to the stroke side. She pushes with her off-side hand and pulls with her on-side hand. Keeping her pulling arm straight, she must remember to use her body first in the stroke. In the power phase of the stroke, she pulls the paddle straight back, keeping her hand level with the water, then pumps with her on-side knee and begins rotating her body toward the other side of the kayak. She brings the paddle out of the water cleanly and decisively, twisting the blade slightly.

When she started working with Whitford, Phillips spent hours in her boat working on technique. She observed that some of the fastest paddlers had less than perfect technique but tremendous power at the catch. She concentrated on getting more and more distance from each stroke that she took. Six months after she began paddling, she went to trials for the team that would represent the U.S. in international competition in 1986. Her performance earned her a place on that team. She had been lifting weights and running, but more significantly she was in her kayak as much as possible, taking stroke after stroke, until she got the technique down and then could put power behind it. That first year, her times for 500-meter races were around 2:20. Sheila Conover had finished in sixth place in the 1984 Olympics with a time of 2:02.38. The winner of that Olympic race, a Swedish paddler, posted a time of 1:58.72. Phillips realized when she traveled with the team to Europe in the summer of 1986 how much faster she would have to get if she hoped to be competitive with the best women paddlers in the world. She was determined to spend the off-season getting faster.

Because she wanted to train full-time for the 1987 racing season, Phillips had to find a way to support herself. Her mother suggested that she look for sponsors. One of her sisters-in-law, who worked in advertising, helped her put together a letter about her determination to make the 1988 Olympic team and a resume. Phillips sent this package to all the organizations and wealthy individuals she could think of who might be willing to assist in financing her Olympic effort. Her first sponsor was the Outrigger Canoe Club of Honolulu, which had been so influential in getting her involved in athletics in the first place. She also made contact with a philanthropist whom she now calls her "secret sponsor." She was one of the few athletes who had approached him about money for training; he responded almost immediately and has been giving her financial support ever since.

Phillips had an outstanding racing season in 1987. She won three gold medals at nationals and was suddenly the top woman single kayak paddler in the U.S. She did well in international competition that year, winning two gold medals at the Pan American Games and finishing seventh in the K1W at the pre-Olympic regatta in Seoul. She was named the Canoe/Kayak Female Athlete of the Year and was the winner of a Women's Sports Foundation's Up and Coming Award in the speed and power category.

All these achievements came at great expense. Phillips was stressed and sick by the end of the year. She had trained extremely hard and had worried endlessly about whether she would be faster than her competition. When she went home to Honolulu for Christmas, her mother was frightened by how tired she seemed. "When I saw her, she had no energy whatsoever. She was depressed. She didn't know what was wrong with her."

Phillips began a battery of medical tests to try to determine why she felt so bad. Her iron level was low, so doctors initially diagnosed anemia. Other doctors told her she had the Epstein-Barr Syndrome; then they said she probably had mononucleosis. She never did get a conclusive diagnosis. On her own, she began reevaluating her training and taking vitamins. "I think basically it was a stress thing," her mother says. "She pushed herself too hard. She overtrained. She knew that she had to have experience in the boat. The girls in Europe have been training for ten to fifteen years. Traci had one year in the boat when she became number one in the U.S."

Even though she felt as if she couldn't spend another minute in her kayak, Phillips did not want to abandon her goal of paddling the K1W in the 1988 Olympics. She doggedly stuck to her training schedule. Several generous grants allowed her to train full-time once again. The Outrigger Duke Kahanamoku Foundation gave Phillips $400 a month for eight months, and her secret sponsor gave her $10,000. She also received a $2,500 Olympic training grant from the U.S. Canoe and Kayak Team. Without money worries, she still managed to fret. She knew that a paddler named Cathy Marino, who had been given a chance to win a medal in the 1984 Olympics before she hurt her shoulder, had recovered from that injury and was training hard to make the 1988 team. Marino, a five-seven, 153-pound paddler who worked as a firefighter for the City of Long Beach, had a reputation for being the gutsiest competitor among the U.S. women. Seven years older than Phillips, Marino had decided that 1988 would be her year. She started training seriously in November of 1987, telling everyone she had never trained harder.

Phillips, who was training with the male paddlers on the team, worried constantly over how fast Cathy Marino was. She also worried about Sheila Conover and Shirley Dery-Batlik. She tried to focus on her own training and to forget about the other women, but she couldn't. Greg Barton suggested that she go train with her competition to find out exactly how fast everyone else was. She didn't like that idea and continued to fret.

At the Olympic trials in 1988, she lost the singles race by three-hundredths of a second to Cathy Marino. She knew that her attitude was the culprit. "I was not confident going into those trials. I knew that Cathy would be faster than before." Phillips's performance at the trials was good enough to win her a place on the Olympic team, which meant that she had fulfilled a childhood dream. But she felt no elation and no sense of accomplishment. She was tired and disappointed in her performance.

When the team got to Seoul, Korea, Phillips was wondering whether her effort to be in the Olympics had been worth the pain. She was struggling with this question even as she walked with the team into the stadium tunnel that led to the opening ceremonies. As she neared the portal to the stadium, she felt her doubts drift away like one of the thousands of balloons released to celebrate this gathering of the world's greatest athletes. In an article that she wrote for the Outrigger Canoe Club's newsletter, she admitted to being hit by a wave of emotion when she and the American team burst out of the tunnel to the thunderous cheers of the crowd. Reflecting on all the times she had watched the Olympics on television, she wrote: "Now, I was the watched, I was among the men and women whose names and faces would hold the imaginations and dreams of people all over the world."

Phillips had a second restorative moment at the 1988 Olympics. Paul Podgorski, who was coach for the entire U.S. Canoe and Kayak Team, decided that Phillips should represent the U.S. in the women's single kayaking event, even though Cathy Marino had beaten her in the trials. He wanted Marino to race in the double and the four. Marino protested his decision but did not prevail in a hearing before a U.S. Olympic Committee panel.

Of the twenty competitors in the women's single kayaking

field (K1W) in Seoul, nine would make the finals. Not many people expected the inexperienced Traci Phillips to be among the final nine. Phillips, however, was beginning to think differently. Now that she was the K1W racer for the U.S. team, she was determined to make the finals. Doing her warm-up routine before getting into her boat for the heat, she looked like a fighter going into the ring, jumping up and down and jabbing at the air. She raced well enough in the heats to make the semifinal. When she crossed the finish line in the top three in her semi-final, she shot her fist skyward, exalting in her accomplishment. In two-and-a-half years, she had gone from beginner to Olympic finalist in flatwater kayak racing.

How Phillips performed in the final was almost beside the point to her. She knew that she didn't have a chance to win, as her times were still not close to the fastest European paddlers. In the final, as she sat in her kayak at the starting line, she looked around at the other paddlers and felt an impulse to giggle. She was completely relaxed; they looked as if they were lined up for the biggest test of their athletic careers. For Phillips, the biggest test of this Olympics was already behind her. She went out hard at the starting gun and stayed relaxed through the race, finishing sixth. Along the way, she was even calm enough to admire the paddling style of the winner, a woman from East Germany: "She was so long and so graceful. Every stroke was the same as the one before. If you've seen shots of a gazelle running in slow motion, that's what each stroke of hers was like. Each stroke was like the leap of a gazelle."

✦ ✦ ✦

Lake Placid is the ideal place for an athlete as single-minded as Traci Phillips. The village was the site of the winter Olympics in both 1932 and 1980, and this heritage is the part of Lake Placid's history that its current boosters choose to emphasize. "Sports capital of the world," visitors' brochures boast. Posters of the U.S. hockey team's dramatic and surprising 1980 win over the Soviets are on display in many of the shops along Main Street. The Hotel Marcy, a six-story structure also on Main Street, has given the walls of its stairwells over to fitness exhortations. Any guest choosing to climb the stairs to her room can read as she goes: "Stress can block calcium." "Alcohol can raise fat level." "Drink 8-10 glasses of water a day." "Dehydration causes pain, confusion and depression." "Deficiency of potassium could cause muscle cramps and weakness." "Drink to win: water the ideal replacement fluid."

Health and recreation were the major preoccupations of Lake Placid and the surrounding area before Olympic fever hit. In 1884, the first American cure cottage for tuberculosis opened in neighboring Saranac Lake. People with tuberculosis sought the clear cool Adirondack mountain air for relief of their symptoms. The first tuberculosis hospital in the country was built in Saranac Lake. Along with the cure cottages, the other distinctive architectural feature of the region around the turn of the century were the so-called camps, elaborate compounds maintained by the wealthy as summer homes. Occupants of these camps devoted themselves to the sporting life.

The cure cottages are gone, and the camps share the countryside with condos, but the Olympic spirit is as willing as ever in Lake Placid. Although the Olympic village that housed the athletes in 1980 is now a minimum security prison, other accommodations for athletes have been constructed. The U.S. Olympic Committee designated Lake Placid an official Olympic Training Center in 1982. The first phase of a thirteen-million-dollar, thirty-four-acre sports complex, which includes housing for more than 200 athletes, plus a dining room and support building, was completed in 1990. Phase two includes a multi-sport field house with sports medicine facilities and groomed outdoor fields. The center is the primary training site for winter Olympic sports—skiing and ski jumping, bobsled, luge, speed skating, hockey and biathalon.

Traci Phillips has everything she needs in Lake Placid—a

place to paddle, trails to run, a weight room in which to work out and reminders everywhere that being an Olympic athlete is one of the noblest goals a person can pursue. She lives in an apartment three floors above a Main Street storefront in Lake Placid. From the rear balcony, Phillips can look down on Mirror Lake where she practices her paddling in the spring, once the ice melts. She keeps her kayak on an outfitting company's rack right below the apartment. On a typical day early in the season, she tries to get at least one training session in her kayak. She rises at 6:30 a.m. and looks out to check the condition of the lake. Unless the water is being whipped to a froth by the wind, she will go out for a paddle after breakfast. She eats at the Olympic Training Center, which serves athletes three hot meals a day. Each dish offered in the cafeteria comes with information about its contents: calories, fat, carbohydrates, protein and sodium. If Phillips cannot paddle because of the weather, she goes to a fitness club several blocks down Main Street where she warms up thoroughly before beginning her routine. "When you get up in the morning, your muscles are like honey that has crystallized," she says. "Warming up is like putting that honey in warm water. I make sure that I warm up for twenty minutes and warm down for fifteen." At the fitness club, she lifts weights and spends time on the rowing ergometer. After lunch at the Olympic Training Center, she goes for a paddle in the afternoon. She will paddle even in a hail storm, as long as the water is calm enough not to swamp her boat. After dinner, she is in bed by 9:30.

For a time after the 1988 Olympics, Phillips was dating Steve Maher, a competitive luger who lives in Lake Placid. Maher, who was on the 1988 Olympic luge team, wanted Phillips to see what his sport was all about, so in the fall of 1988 he invited her to join the team in practicing starts. Phillips was intrigued to notice that because of the strength she had developed in kayaking, she had one of the fastest starts of any woman practicing with the team. That first winter she had time for only about a dozen days of riding down the luge run, but she decided that she would like to learn more about the sport, which seemed fun and quite different from kayaking. In the winter of 1989/90, after racing her kayak all summer, she returned to Lake Placid to line up for her turn down the luge run.

Luge has been characterized as riding down a mountain on a bar of soap. The course at Lake Placid, with its rough, bumpy surface, battered Phillips's body, giving her constant whiplash. "It's a weird sport, really stupid," Phillips says, but her tone indicates that she is completely captivated by it. She quickly learned that the perfect line down the course is an ideal that no one, no matter how accomplished, ever achieves. The challenge of getting as close to that ideal as possible was one that Phillips found irresistible.

She told her paddling coach, Paul Podgorski, that she was doing the luge as a training alternative to keep from being burned out in kayaking. Podgorski, who tried the luge when he was a youth in his native Poland and had broken his leg on one ill-timed run, shrugged and cautioned her to be careful. During that winter of 1989/90 in Lake Placid, Phillips made 150 luge runs. She competed in the national championships, where she finished twelfth. But she recorded her first run at under forty seconds. In the luge, a run under forty seconds is a fast run, a very competitive run. Phillips was thrilled to post her best time yet—39.88 seconds—at her first national competition.

When she returned to kayaking in the spring of 1990, Phillips felt rested. The diversion of the luge had helped her mental attitude, and she was excited about being back in her boat. She also felt physically fitter than ever, having lost some body fat during her winter riding the luge.

Perhaps most importantly, she had learned some useful techniques from luge competition about how to relax in her kayak. "You've got to relax your mind and body but still be explosive." When she relaxed on the luge, she could focus. She was going to try to achieve the same kind of relaxed focus in paddling during the 1990 season. She would explode off the starting line, make the transition to a quick steady pace that would keep her in contention during the body of the race, concentrate on her rhythm, on rotating her body and extending it, on transferring the power from the big muscles of her body through her arms to the blade. Boom. Boom. Boom. Boom. She would stay quick, steady and strong when the pain hit. She would tell herself that the pain was her main competitor and that overcoming it was the key to a strong finish. She would concentrate on feeling her power through the pain as she picked up the stroke rate at the end of the race.

Phillips was able to use the luge to learn about relaxing because she was new to the sport and had no expectations about how she should do. Her spectacular rise to the top among U.S. women paddlers had put tremendous pressure on her. After the 1988 Olympics, most of her serious U.S. competition retired, and she became the person to beat. She disliked being the fox instead of the hound, as she put it. When she is out in front of the pack, she says, she starts thinking too much: about the mechanics of the stroke, about the way pain can sabotage a paddler, about the times she failed to relax her right hand enough to let her power flow through it. But in the luge, where she was the hound and not expected to excel, she could let go and have fun. She discovered the gift of relaxing and realized she could take that gift with her when she switched in the spring to kayaking.

Taking this same mental approach in kayaking paid off for Phillips the first season after she used luge for her winter training. At the 1990 world kayaking championships, she finished only two-and-a-half seconds behind the Italian woman who won. That was the closest Phillips had ever been to the winner of a big international race. Even so, she placed eighth in the race. The international racing scene is intensely competitive. Mere hundredths of a second often separate the finishers. Phillips knew that she had to train even harder and get mentally tougher if she wanted to close the two-and-a-half-second gap.

In the winter of 1990/91 when she resumed her luge training, her intent was still to use the luge as a break from paddling. Meanwhile, Phillips had been named to the senior development team, which consists of lugers who are considered
potential national team members. Being on the senior development team meant that Phillips would receive coaching and
more time on the practice track. Even as she worked on her improving her luge times, she was mindful of her primary athletic
goal—getting faster in flatwater kayaking, which she considers
"the most beautiful and demanding of all sports."

No matter what she is doing, Phillips is generally thinking
about what types of training will help her make up the couple of
seconds that separate her from the world champion flatwater
kayak racer. She is at the point in her paddling career where
gains in speed are coming in smaller increments. "The closer
you get to the fast times, the harder your gains are," she says.
She wants to know everything she can about the way her body
works so that she can get the most out of it.

One of the main sources of Phillips's information about her
athlete's physiology has been Jay T. Kearney, director of sport
testing for the U.S. Olympic Committee. A former competitive
canoeist with a degree in sports physiology, Kearney pays special attention to the kinds of physiological traits paddlers need.
He tests Phillips at least twice a year and sometimes three times
to measure her progress in two key areas—maximum oxygen
uptake and ability to produce lactic acid. Flatwater kayak racers, according to Kearney, need physiological characteristics
similar to 800-meter runners: power and sustained muscular endurance. The better their maximum oxygen uptake, which is
their ability to use oxygen, to send it via heart and lungs to
muscle tissue during physical exercise, the better their performance . There is also a positive correlation between their ability
to produce lactic acid and their performance.

To test for oxygen uptake, or VO_2 max, Kearney outfits

Phillips with a mask equipped with a breathing apparatus attached to a bag. She goes as hard as she can for four minutes. During the fifth minute, she breathes into the bag. Kearney analyzes that air. To measure lactic acid, which is the waste product that builds up as the athlete depletes the energy stored in her muscles, Kearney has Phillips paddle 500 meters five times, the first at sixty percent, then seventy percent, then eighty, ninety and the last piece at a hundred percent. He pricks her finger after each piece to gather a blood sample.

Phillips keeps every statistic that Kearney has ever compiled on her. She has a scrapbook filled with his graphs and charts. They are both the evidence of her hard work and the measurements with which she plots her goals for the next training season. She wants to make the line on her VO_2 max graph soar to sixty by 1992, a lofty goal, according to Kearney. The normal (non-athlete) college-age American woman has a VO_2 max between thirty-five and forty; the world champion male flatwater kayaker has a VO_2 max of seventy-two.

Besides trying to improve her aerobic capacity, as measured by VO_2 max, Phillips also strives to increase her ability to function anaerobically, or without oxygen. Lactic acid accumulates in muscles when the athlete is working beyond her aerobic capacity. The presence of lactic acid causes the burning sensation that Phillips begins to feel about 300 meters into a race.

Phillips has two goals for her lactic acid production: one is to begin producing it only at the highest level of paddling intensity so that she is sure her aerobic capacity is at its maximum development. She has graphs from Kearney that indicate she is where she wants to be as far as this goal is concerned. These graphs show minimal rises in the amount of lactate as she increases her paddling intensity from sixty to seventy to eighty and even to ninety percent. Only when she is paddling as hard as she can does the amount of lactate in her body shoot up.

Her other goal is to produce and to be able to tolerate higher levels of lactic acid, which will add to the energy available to her during a race. Lactic acid is measured in millimoles. A normal person with no athletic background produces between seven and ten millimoles of lactate after running all out. The highest levels among kayakers, produced by men at the top of the sport, are between sixteen and eighteen. Women tend to produce less lactate. At the start of her 1990 season, Phillips's blood contained twelve millimoles of lactic acid after she had paddled at a hundred percent. She was not particularly pleased with that figure, but she was confident that she could increase it. "I can tolerate more pain." Eventually, lactate will cause the muscles to shut down; but the burning sensation sets in long before that happens. Phillips has to train herself to outpaddle the pain.

To increase her lactate tolerance, she does workouts that consist of ten seventy-second-long pieces at a hundred percent, with a twenty-second rest in between each one. "If you do it right, toward the end of these you're just burning. You can barely hang on to your paddle. The point is to be able to go harder longer before that pain sets in. To get your lactate high, you must be capable of pushing your body to that point of exhaustion."

Phillips trains with the men's paddling team instead of with the women's team because she wants training partners who are faster than she is and who will push her to go harder. Among women paddlers in the U.S., she has no one to chase. Phillips does all the workouts that the men do, which means that she is practicing for 1,000-meter events, the distance that men race, as opposed to the women's 500-meter events. "If I do the 1,000 meters when I train," she says, "then when I do 500s the next day they seem short."

When she is working out in her kayak, Phillips gives one hundred percent on each stroke. The intensity she puts into her training has won admiration from her coaches and her competition. "Traci works harder than anyone I know," says Cathy Marino, who is challenging Phillips again for the K1W spot on the 1992 Olympic team.

Phillips has seen her hard work pay off since she began training in her kayak in 1986. Every year her body can tolerate more work. And every year she can post faster times for the 500-meter kayak race. She has cut twenty-five seconds off her time since she started racing. By the end of the 1991 racing season, she had cut six seconds off her 1988 Olympics time. "That's a big difference," she says.

In 1991, at the world championships in Paris, she placed seventh, less than two seconds behind the winner from Germany. "I finished a lot closer than I did the year before, so I've improved," she says. She looks at the times of the paddlers who finished right in front of her and is both encouraged and frustrated by how close they were. She was three-hundreds of a second from sixth place and four-tenths of a second from fifth.

Phillips thinks of these European paddlers as she trains for the 1992 Olympic season. Where she was once in awe of them, now she sees them as vulnerable if she can only figure out what they're doing to be slightly faster than she is. She also thinks that an Olympic medal—the first one to be won by an American woman kayaker in twenty-eight years—is within her reach. "I'm more motivated," she says. "I'm excited because I'm so close."

Before she can go for that medal, however, she knows that she has to sprint past her American competition at the Olympic trials in the U.S. Getting up in the morning and looking down from her rear balcony onto Mirror Lake to check the paddling conditions, Phillips thinks about Cathy Marino or the other American women who would like to take her seat in the Olympic K1W. She knows that they will be doing their prescribed workouts and getting faster. On the mornings when she is not intrinsically inspired to train, the knowledge of her competition pushes her. If she gets up before dawn and starts to stretch out and begins to wonder, "Why am I doing this sport?" she immediately answers, "There are probably some girls training on the West Coast today."

So even when the spring temperature in Lake Placid is in

the low thirties and a light hail is falling, Traci Phillips finishes stretching, puts on all the waterproof clothes that she owns and goes down to the boat rack to get her kayak. She pulls the spray skirt up around her waist and then climbs into the boat. She puts her hands into the waterproof mittens attached to her paddle and pushes away from the dock. Right away, she is moving swiftly and smoothly. The big green and yellow neon sticker right under her nose cautions her to get her mind right. She is paddling as hard as she can, and her catches are coming as fast as the hail that falls all around her into the water.

Cathy Hearn won three gold medals in whitewater slalom kayaking at the world championships in 1979. She is one of two women in the world to accomplish such a feat. Hearn decided in 1972 that she wanted to be an Olympic whitewater paddler, but she had to wait twenty years for the chance, since whitewater paddling is an infrequent Olympic event.

Cathy Hearn

~

FOURTEEN-YEAR-OLD Cathy Hearn was riding down a dusty Montana road with her family during the summer of 1972 when an electrifying piece of news came over the car radio. Jamie McEwan, a kid she knew of from back home in the Washington, D.C., area, had just won a bronze medal in whitewater slalom canoeing at the Munich Olympics. As the car bumped along and the Hearn family absorbed the news in uncharacteristic silence, Cathy felt the course of her life take shape. She would do what Jamie McEwan had just done: She would win an Olympic medal in whitewater slalom paddling. Her decision in that moment was not the fleeting passion of an average teenager. It was an idea that took hold of her life and had an effect on everyone else in that car. It determined what her two younger brothers—Davey, ten-and-a-half months younger, and Billy, eight years younger—would do with their lives. It gave her father, Carter Hearn, a more willing paddling partner for the next few years. And it eventually inspired her mother, Mary Alice Hearn, to believe for herself what she had been instilling in her children: *You can do anything that you want to do.*

The sudden illumination of her future that Cathy Hearn received on that day in Montana was short on details, the most significant one being that whitewater slalom paddling was not a reliable Olympic event. For the chance to win an Olympic medal, as Jamie McEwan had done, Cathy would have to wait twenty years. Not until 1992 in Barcelona would slalom paddling be included in any subsequent Olympiad. The goal of winning an Olympic medal, however, began to recede in importance as Cathy Hearn discovered whitewater racing as a way of life, a chance to pursue the "rebel excellence" that her family encouraged and a way to relate to nature and to people all over the world. Because she pursued a vision of her future, presented with startling clarity during a single moment on a country road, Cathy Hearn has become one of those rare people whose life is of a single piece, who does not keep the place for her passion fenced off from the rest of her existence. Her passion is for making a small flat-bottomed kayak run fast and clean through a series of gates that hang over a tumble of water. Her life is devoted to the perfection of one of these two- to three-minute runs.

✦ ✦ ✦

Cathy Hearn was born on June 1, 1958, in Washington, D.C. When she was ten weeks old, her parents took her camping in Glacier Park. That was the beginning of her exposure to living simply in the outdoors. According to her mother, all the Hearn children "learned very early how to rough it and to make the best of the situation they were in and to persevere." Cathy's father was a geologist with the U.S. Geological Survey and took the family west for field work every summer. He was also a paddler, having taken up canoeing in high school. For recreation in the summers, the family went on paddling and camping trips. All of the Hearn children were told that as soon as they learned how to swim, they could paddle. While Carter went one direction to do his field work each day, Mary Alice took Cathy and Davey another direction to a small town in Montana for swimming lessons. Mary Alice paddled, too, but not with the fervor that her husband did. When the kids got older and started going to races with their dad, she handled the logistics. "Someone had to manage the whole thing," she says.

When Cathy was five, Carter took a canoeing class from the Canoe Cruisers Association (CCA) in Washington, D.C., the most active paddling club in the U.S. Shortly thereafter, he began racing on whitewater. Mary Alice took Cathy and Davey to races on the Potomac and the Youghiogheny to watch their father compete. Cathy got her first boat when she was nine, and she paddled with a group of CCA children. Her mother made sure that there was no pressure on her to paddle and that she was having fun on the water. Mary Alice had watched other kids whose parents pushed them to race. One little boy in particular had made an impression on her. "I remember that kid totally encased in a wetsuit, totally programmed to be a racer. There was so much invested in it by his parents. He'd get all ready to race, and then he'd puke."

When Cathy was ten, she accompanied her father nearly every other weekend to a swimming pool during the winter to practice paddling and rolling her kayak. She was interested in the sport, but it was only one of several pursuits that engaged her. She was also taking violin lessons and learning gymnastics. Her favorite events in gymnastics were the vault and the beam, two of the most difficult events but appealing to Cathy because the lines of kids at those pieces of equipment were shorter and she didn't have to wait to practice.

Cathy entered her first river race when she was twelve. She and her father paddled in a parent/child event on the north fork of the Potomac River near Petersburg, West Virginia. Carter reassured her that if she got tired during the race, she could stop paddling. She didn't stop, and they won the race, beating a father/son team.

Cathy Hearn knew, from an early age, that she wanted to be good at something. When at age fourteen she heard the news about Jamie McEwan's medal, she felt she had been pointed toward *the* activity worthy of her whole-hearted pursuit. "I knew I would grow too big to be in gymnastics, and the violin required too much time indoors." Paddling seemed to meet all her requirements in an enterprise that would hold her interest and give her a chance to excel.

Jamie McEwan was nineteen when he won the bronze medal in whitewater slalom at the Olympics in 1972. This was the first time a U.S. whitewater paddler had won any kind of medal in international competition. The sport had been dominated by Europeans since the first world championships in Switzerland in 1949. American paddlers did not compete internationally until 1957 and did not break into the top ten until ten years later, when Barbara Wright finished ninth in the K1W (women's single kayak) slalom. McEwan's medal created widespread interest in the sport, particularly in the Washington, D.C., area where he lived and where his mother, May, began coaching aspiring paddlers.

It was May McEwan who had given Jamie his start in paddling. She had taken up the sport when she was in her late forties and had become a masters national champion. She eventually raced in Europe. When Jamie returned home from the 1972 Olympics, his mother held a meeting for any kid who might be interested in training seriously for whitewater paddling. She showed them Jamie's medal and said, "See, this is what you can do."

Cathy Hearn was at that meeting and was even more inspired than she had been upon hearing the news of the medal. She began getting up at 4:30 a.m. once a week to go to a pool where May McEwan set up gates so that the kids could practice. Cathy remembers being influenced by May McEwan's gutsiness and her "go-for-it" attitude. "She had a tremendous influence on me. She was one of the first women I'd known who was really into athletics and who concentrated and was excellent and had fun doing it." Cathy had also heard of Barbara Wright and her accomplishments in paddling. She liked the fact that both May McEwan and Barbara Wright were "female and intellectual and doing something totally jungle" like running whitewater.

Cathy worked with May McEwan for a couple of years, going when she could to her afternoon sessions on the Potomac and to weekend sessions in a pool. She spent the summer of 1974 working at Valley Mill Day Camp, which the McEwan family ran. After her summer at the camp, where she ran rivers with Jamie McEwan and Angus Morrison, who had also been on the 1972 Olympic team, Cathy told her parents that she wanted to cut back on the number of hours she spent in school so that she could have more time to train. She arranged, through the girls' gym department at Walter Johnson High School in Montgomery County, Maryland, to do independent study instead of meeting standard gym requirements. "The main thing was to get out of gym because gym is so totally bogus. They used those belts to woggle off your fat. I said, 'Forget that. I'm out of here.'" To fulfill her independent study requirements, she kept a training log, a habit that would endure throughout her racing career. She was not sure how to train for competitive paddling because so little information was available. She read swimming magazines and applied what they said about intervals and pyramids to her sport. She also read about the way runners train, figuring that a two- to three-minute slalom race would be similar to a running race of that duration. She found other women paddlers in the D.C. area, like Carrie Ashton and Louise Holcombe from the 1972 Olympic team, who answered her questions and helped her progress as a paddler.

Carrie Ashton suggested that Cathy lift weights to develop the tremendous upper body strength that a whitewater paddler needs to maneuver on the river. For a time, Cathy joined Carrie and two other paddlers, Miki Piras and Mary Ann Walkup, in their weight-lifting sessions. The three more experienced paddlers taught her how to lift safely and explained the physiological principles involved in that kind of training. Because their gym was an hour's drive away, Cathy began looking for a place to lift weights closer to home. She asked to use the boys' weight room at her high school, but was denied permission. Then she discovered a junior high that would allow her to use its universal gym equipment. Her brother Davey, seeing how serious she was getting about training, went with her to the gym and to her afternoon paddling sessions either on the Potomac River or in the David Taylor Model Basin, a three-quarter-mile-long indoor pool that the Navy allows paddlers to use when it is not testing submarine models.

When Cathy first started lifting weights in the fall of 1974, she was the only girl in the gym. The rest of the lifters were high school boys, some of them paddlers and some football players. She was working almost exclusively on her upper body and getting results. The guys noticed the results and could not keep from making derisive comments. They began to call her "Muscles" and tease her. They shouted to each other that they would never go out with a "Dub," which is what they called female kayak racers (from the racing designation "K1W"). Cathy knew that the strength she was gaining was improving her paddling, but she found the boys' heckling almost unbearable. Years later she was able to look back on those early days in the gym and say, "Adolescent guys are insecure about their own masculinity. They want all women to look like *Sports Illustrated* swimsuit models." But at the time, she was not immune to the insecurities of adolescence herself. She lifted weights through the spring of 1975, but then she stopped completely for several years.

In the spring of 1975, when she was still lifting weights, Cathy was also riding her bicycle the ten miles to and from school every day and spending two to two-and-a-half hours a day doing gate work on the Potomac River, using the gates that Jon and Ron Lugbill had set up on the river. The Lugbills were young slalom canoe (C1) paddlers trying to make the U.S. team that would compete at the world championships. Jon Lugbill, who today is the top C1 paddler in the world, with Davey Hearn his closest competitor, turned fourteen in the spring of 1975. He had been racing for two years and had made the U.S. team at age thirteen. He was fearless, sometimes recklessly so, always taking the fastest, most aggressive line through the water and always trying the most difficult moves. He pushed anyone who paddled with him to behave in the same way, but Cathy Hearn did not have to be pushed. She loved playing in the fast-moving Potomac. She was right there with the Lugbills as they paddled gates five days a week and then played on the river the other two. Their river play included surfing, in which they cut back and forth on the crest of a wave, and doing enders (a maneuver in which the paddler buries the bow of the boat in the oncoming current and does a somersault). Cathy became one of the leaders of this group of young paddlers (which also included Stephen and Michael Garvis) who would eventually make the U.S. a presence in the whitewater world. She was one of the older paddlers in the group, and she had a car, which made everyone's getting to the river easier. But most of all, she had an attitude that being on the river, where she could learn how to read the best line through the water and try the difficult moves that would yield the fastest times, was the finest place in the world to be.

After spring training with the Lugbills in 1975, Cathy went to her first team trials, held on the nearby Youghiogheny River. At the end of the first day of racing, she was in sixth place. May McEwan told her that she had a good chance of making the national team if she kept up that kind of performance. The possibility alarmed Cathy. She performed poorly on her second day of racing and finished eleventh overall. "This woke me up to the idea that maybe what I was lacking was the mental stuff. I needed to believe a lot more [in myself] and be prepared for any eventuality."

That summer she and her brother Davey both went to Madawaska Canoe Camp in Canada for three weeks of instruction with European paddlers. Gisela Grothaus, who had won an Olympic silver medal in slalom and was a wildwater world champion, paid particular attention to Cathy, working with her on how to adapt what she saw the men doing on gates to her own body weight and style and showing her how to train. From Grothaus, she learned that concentration was the key to a good slalom run. She learned, too, that the vaunted European paddlers were not superhuman. Cathy appreciated Gisela Grothaus's zeal for the sport, but she also saw that the woman knew how to have fun, both on and off the water. Cathy realized that she did not have to sacrifice her sense of play to be one of the best in the world at her chosen sport.

In the summer of 1976, when Cathy had just graduated from high school, the group of kids from the Potomac went to California for nationals and, as Cathy says, "completely cleaned up." She won the women's canoe slalom (C1W) and finished third in the women's kayak slalom (K1W). Davey Hearn won the men's canoe slalom (C1) championship. Their success in California convinced the Potomac pack that their method of play/training and the paddling techniques they were developing were right. They had not had regular coaching and tended not to listen to people who offered advice. "We were mostly rebellious teenagers," Cathy says. "We didn't consider ourselves real athletes. We were in it for fun and because we liked to race—me and my brother and the Lugbills and the Garvises. And we'd had enough success to think our own training methods worked, which was to spend most of our time on whitewater."

The winter after their success at nationals in California, a man named Bill Endicott went to the model basin where Cathy and the boys were practicing their gate work and began to talk with them about the sport. He had been a national champion in C2 and a member of the U.S. whitewater team but had dropped out of competitive paddling in 1973 because he felt he lacked the "something special" to be a world-class athlete. He had written a history of whitewater paddling and managed the team one year. Then his father died, leaving him enough money to do whatever he wanted with his time. He decided to devote himself to the hotshot kids running Potomac whitewater.

Because Endicott agreed with the way they were already

training and because he asked questions and listened to their answers respectfully, Cathy and the boys accepted him as their coach. Endicott concentrated at first on the canoeists, since he had been a canoeist himself and the majority of the Potomac group were canoeists. Cathy, in fact, was the only serious kayaker. (In international events, women do not paddle canoes, which are harder to maneuver than kayaks. The canoe racer kneels in the covered cockpit of his craft and makes his way down the river using a one-bladed paddle. The kayaker sits and uses a two-bladed paddle.) Cathy listened intently to everything Endicott told the C1 paddlers and was grateful that he did not try to separate her from the rest of the group. Endicott was impressed with Cathy's strength and her dedication. "She was one of the leaders of that group, one of the best of the lot."

Endicott worked to get the paddlers ready for the world championships in Spittal, Austria, in the summer of 1977. Cathy took a year off between high school and college to work and train full-time. She went to several camps at the Nantahala Outdoor Center in the mountains of North Carolina, and she began lifting weights again. Endicott worked with her and the C1s on what he considered the three crucial skills in slalom paddling: eye/paddle coordination, which is the ability to recognize water formations and to put the paddle in exactly the right spot; good shoulder and torso strength and good hip flexors for ducking and dodging gates; and the right mental attitude, one that adjusts to quickly changing conditions and does not panic.

"You have to be able to stand on the shore and look at the water and figure out the way it's going to throw the boat. You need to be able to predict accurately what the water is going to do to you. Cathy has that in spades. She has an excellent understanding of the water and the position of the boat. The harder the whitewater, the better she does. She also has extraordinary upper body strength." What she lacked, when Endicott arrived, was the athletic mentality that would make her successful in races. He worked with her and all the paddlers on self-image training, helping them discover who they really were and then bringing their aspirations into line with that realistic self-image. "The nervous system acts as a computer automatically setting out to accomplish whatever goal you program into it. If you program it with a negative image, it will produce negative results. If you program it with a successful image, it will produce successful results," he told them.

His paddlers had some success at the world championships in 1977. The canoeists placed fourth in C1 and C2. Cathy finished tenth in K1W and won a bronze medal in the team slalom event. Her first medal was special to her, but she realized that if she wanted to win any more medals she would have to work on being consistent and being mentally prepared.

In the fall of 1977, Cathy went to Hampshire College in Amherst, Massachusetts, a small college where students design their own learning programs and receive written evaluations of their progress instead of grades. She decided to study the physiology and psychology of human performance and to concentrate on her paddling. She met three women in the New England area who were the kind of paddlers she wanted to be: Leslie Klein, Carol Fisher and Ann Turner.

Ann Turner had been on the Olympic flatwater paddling team in 1976. Cathy had heard about how strong she was and how fine a paddler. She had hoped to meet her but she had not expected such a warm reception. "Ann was an Olympic athlete who took me under her wing. She was really nice to me. She wanted to train with me." Ann Turner's encouragement of Cathy Hearn was not unique among paddlers and is a tradition that continues today. In the 1970s, the sport was not organized or wealthy enough to provide much direction to its best athletes. Consequently, U.S. paddlers worked with each other to improve so that they could challenge the Europeans. The U.S. national flatwater team did not have a full-time coach until 1982, and it was 1989 before the whitewater paddlers on the national team had a full-time coach. Women paddlers in the

1970s also crossed over from one type of paddling to another and, in some cases, competed in the same season in more than one type of event. Leslie Klein in 1977 was on both the flatwater and the whitewater teams. Many women who had started out in whitewater but were interested in being on the Olympic team switched to flatwater because the 500-meter flatwater sprint was the only Olympic event for women. Some, like Carol Fisher who wanted to compete only in downriver events, worked out with flatwater paddlers to get into racing shape. (Downriver is one category of whitewater racing; slalom is the other. In downriver, the course is at least eight miles long and predominantly whitewater. If the rapids are Class III, the downriver race qualifies as wildwater. The paddler is racing against the clock, fighting to keep the boat on the fastest line down the river.)

Carol Fisher, Leslie Klein and Ann Turner were the people Cathy Hearn needed to meet in 1977 when she was away from her pals on the Potomac for the first time. The three women were all older than Cathy and were experienced competitors. They made paddling their priority, training hard and lifting weights. At the time, Cathy was still having questions about her body image. She knew that she wanted to be a great paddler and that to do that she had to be strong, yet she was getting all kinds of signals from society that a strong body was not feminine. Cathy knew that she did not want to paint her fingernails, agonize over makeup or dress in clothing that limited how freely she could move. But she wondered how she could be a woman and still love to strap on a helmet and life jacket, step into a boat that she wore like a part of her body and shoot down a river, shouting for the thrill of it. Fisher, Turner and Klein showed her. They were all comfortable with their muscular bodies. They were all guts-out racers. And they managed to relate to men as more than buddies, a role Cathy feared would be hers eternally if she kept on developing as an athlete.

When Cathy went to nationals in 1978, she won a bronze

medal in K1W. She was disappointed in her performance, though, and felt that she had choked. The North America Cup (which consists of three races and is held during even-numbered years) was being held that year. Cathy decided that she would enter all the cup races and use them to concentrate on the mental part of her training. She set a goal for herself of being unbeatable. And she was, winning all three races. Those three victories marked the turning point in her career. She realized she could set a goal for herself and, by visualizing that goal often enough, she could reach it.

The next year, 1979, was a world championship year. World championships in whitewater racing are held during odd-numbered years. In 1979, the championships were to be held in Jonquière, Quebec. For the first time, Americans were expected to do well in international whitewater competition. Endicott's group on the Potomac had matured and gotten faster. And Linda Harrison, a paddler from Newark, Delaware, who had been third at the 1977 world championships in Spittal, was given a good shot at the gold medal at Jonquière. Even though Cathy had beaten her in all three races of the North America Cup in 1978, Linda had prevailed that year at nationals, where the pressure is often greater. She was known for her ability to do well under pressure, whereas Cathy did not have that reputation. Cathy, however, was encouraged by the results of her mental focus during the North America Cup, and she was determined to show the paddling world that she was capable of performing in a big race without choking. No whitewater race was bigger than the world championships.

✦ ✦ ✦

Cathy Hearn was twenty-one years old when she went to Jonquière to compete in the whitewater world championships in 1979. She had taken spring semester off from college to train. At Jonquière, there were four events in which she could possibly compete: individual slalom, team slalom (if she finished among the top three American women in individual slalom), individual wildwater and team wildwater (again, if she finished among the top three Americans in the individual competition).

She had decided to compete in wildwater as a diversion from her slalom racing. The most important race to her was the individual slalom, but she didn't want to dwell on that event for fear that her anxiety level would overcome the confidence she was trying to build. "I'd seen too many people put all their eggs in the one basket of winning the slalom and then be terribly disappointed when they didn't win. I felt that thinking about winning would put too much pressure on me."

In the spring, she trained in Washington, D.C., working with her old friends on the Potomac and with Bill Endicott. She coached gymnastics that spring, too, and did gymnastic workouts. Her training log for the year, which Endicott reprinted in his book on training and technique, *The Ultimate Run*, shows that she spent thirty-eight percent of her training time in the boat. When she was not paddling, she was skating, running, cross-country skiing, swimming, stretching or doing ballet or gymnastics. Endicott was impressed with the amount of training she was doing and with her general physical abilities. He had questions, though, about whether she was mentally prepared for Jonquière. "If you're going to be a performer at a high level, you have to cultivate the ability to relax on cue. You don't want to be totally relaxed. What you're after is the optimal arousal level—focused but not anxious." He was not sure that Cathy could attain this state.

Endicott did not verbalize his doubts to Cathy, who was concentrating on her workouts on the Potomac. The way the Potomac pack worked out—with every practice a series of races—was ideal for dissipating the tension of race day. Cathy knew that the guys pushed her harder than she would be pushed in most races and that she was holding her own in practice.

The wildwater events were first at the week-long world championships. In individual wildwater, Cathy finished thirteenth, not impressive but third-fastest among the American women, good enough for a place in the team event. Leslie Klein and Carol Fisher were her partners. They had been disappointed with their own performances in the individual wildwater race, finishing eighth and fourth, respectively. Going into the team event, the American trio was expected to finish fourth, behind the British, the French and the West Germans.

A wildwater race is an endurance event, similar to a cross-country ski race. Racers must fight constantly to keep their boats away from rocks and out of the shallows that will slow them down. The battle is to maintain concentration despite fatigue. Racers start at fixed intervals and try for the best time down the river. Their boats are narrow and pointy, with v-shaped hulls designed to track the fastest line down the river. In team wildwater, the time is from the first boat's start to the last boat's crossing the finish line. The objective is to get the slowest paddler to go as fast as she possibly can. Cathy Hearn was the slowest wildwater paddler on her team. That meant she would be the first boat across the starting line. Then Carol Fisher would pass her and lead her down the river. Leslie Klein would paddle behind her, exhorting her to go faster, and would sprint past her at the finish. The team had chosen Carol to lead because she was fast, she knew the best lines down the river and she could keep an even pace. Cathy's job was to mirror everything Carol did, staying close and riding her wake on flat water and plunging into each rapid after her. Leslie, in the rear, had the speed to catch up if she made a mistake and had the energy to scream at Cathy all the way down the river.

The race began as planned. Cathy started, then Carol sprinted past her and led her down the river. Every fifteen seconds, Carol would look back to make sure Cathy was still with her. She was. She picked up on Carol's lines perfectly and picked up on her speed, too. Leslie was behind her, pressuring her to paddle by yelling, "Go. Go. Go." She was also coaching her—"relax your hands"—and encouraging her—"you're really strong." But mostly, she was screaming, "Go. Go. Go." Carol crossed the finish line. Then Leslie sprinted past Cathy to cross. And finally, Cathy, giving everything she had left, plowed across the line. Leslie and Carol were pleased with their time. Cathy was too tired to care when they told her she had taken an incredible thirty-five seconds off her time from her previous run down the river in the individual wildwater event.

The American team was one of the first of the better teams to race. So the three women waited at the finish line and timed their competition coming down. Carol and Leslie both were hopeful that they would beat the British and get a bronze medal. When the British team came down the river, Carol's watch showed that the Americans had been faster. Unofficial as her reading of the time was, the difference between the two teams was still significant enough for the Americans to know they had gotten the bronze. Leslie and Carol smiled. Cathy was too tired to show any emotion. Then the French team, which was favored to win the silver medal, came down the river. Carol's watch showed that the times were close, but the Americans were slightly faster. "We got the silver," Leslie said, shaking Cathy, who still was trying to recover from her effort. Finally, the West German team came down the river. This was the last team and the gold medal favorite. As Carol clocked the finish, she knew the race was incredibly close but probably the West Germans'. She and Leslie looked at each other and, without saying anything, knew they had raced a great race, probably the race of their lives. They could be proud of their silver medal. They looked away from each other and back at the finish line. There they saw the West German coach standing and shaking his head. That's when they realized that they—the darkhorse Americans—had won the gold. The margin, it turned out, was less than a second in a twenty-minute race. They whooped and celebrated and encouraged Cathy to join in. And, tired as she was, she began whooping along with her teammates.

Leslie: "The whole race was a credit to Cathy and the teamwork. We created a situation that allowed her to push herself that hard. She was the one that had to improve from thirteenth place."

Cathy: "The gold medal was fantastic for my self-confidence and relaxation. It psyched me up for the slalom. But I was really tired, tired enough so I couldn't get too anxious about the slalom."

Slalom is a completely different kind of event from downriver. Bill Endicott compares running a slalom course to doing a series of 100-yard dashes. The race takes two to three minutes, during which time the paddler has to negotiate twenty or twenty-five gates, which are wooden poles suspended from wires above a half-mile plunge of water. The gates are set so that the paddler must pass through some of them downriver and some of them upriver. In 1979, each gate consisted of a red pole and a green pole; the paddler had to keep the green pole on her right. The score for a run is the actual time of the run, plus penalty points. Touching a gate with the boat or the body cost ten seconds in 1979. Missing a gate added fifty seconds to the score. The boat is a thirteen-and-a-half-foot-long kayak that is made of fiberglass and kevlar (the same material used in bulletproof vests), flat on the bottom and lower at its flat ends than in the middle so that the paddler can slip the back deck underneath the outside pole as she sneaks through a gate. A neoprene spray skirt stretched over the cockpit keeps the water out of the boat. The paddler sprints in the straightaways, but may slow way down to make difficult turns. The start and stop nature of the slalom puts a high demand on an athlete's lactic acid system.

A paddler is allowed one practice run once the course is set and then two real runs, the slower of which is thrown out. Cathy had three days after her wildwater race to get ready for the slalom. She ran the rapids every day, trying to guess where the gates would be set. Her practice runs felt terrible, but when she watched herself on video, she looked fine. She concentrated on the image that the video gave her to boost her confidence.

On her first run, almost from the moment her boat passed through the electronic eye on the starting gate, Cathy was distracted. She felt sloppy all the way down the course. She *was* sloppy on gate 22, where she took a twenty-second penalty for hitting both poles. After all the other paddlers' first runs, she was in fourth place.

She spoke to Jay Evans, a 1972 Olympic coach and former whitewater paddler who had coached some of her workouts at Hampshire College, about the troublesome gate 22. He suggested an approach: Go through gate 21 and "paddle like heck" without even looking at gate 22. Paddlers who looked ahead at the gate were being swept down low and having trouble getting through without penalties. She consulted with Bill Endicott, who advised her to concentrate on having a clean second run, rather than going for speed. She was naturally so fast, he told her, that she didn't have to think about speed. Think clean, he said.

Cathy went to her car, one of the few places where she could get away from other paddlers and spectators, and tried to put herself in the frame of mind that she needed for her second run. She played a Rolling Stones tape and let her mind drift. Then she read some of her training log and realized all the work she had put toward this day. She began to focus on how well she paddled and how confident she could be. "I knew I could do every move at least as well as any other woman in the world. And I also knew that in the past I had beaten myself, and I wasn't about to let that happen again."

Before her second run, Cathy warmed up thoroughly and did a couple of sprints "hard enough to hurt." After easy paddling for a few minutes, she sat still in her kayak and visualized the course and the fast, clean run she would have. Then she headed for the starting gate. All during the run, she was calm, concentrating on paddling well, not allowing herself to look ahead to the finish or think about how great it would be to win.

She was more cautious than usual. But she was moving well. She hit gate 12 with her paddle, but didn't let that penalty get to her. She knew she could afford it. And she was right. She swept through gate 22, squeaky clean.

Cathy Hearn won the gold medal in women's whitewater slalom. She was the first American woman to win a gold medal in an individual world championship event. Her margin over Liz Sharman of Great Britain was slight, but it was the difference between silver and gold. Linda Harrison won the bronze. The next day Cathy and Linda teamed up with Becky Judd to win the world team slalom title. When the Jonquière championships were over, Cathy Hearn had three gold medals. She was only the second woman in the world to accomplish such a feat. (The first was Ludmila Polesna of Czechoslovakia in 1969. Most likely, because of increasing specialization among athletes in the sport, Cathy will be the last triple gold winner at a world championship.) She had led the entire American team to its first title in the thirty-year history of the world championships. Her training buddies from the Potomac River had done their share, capturing all three medals in slalom canoe: Jon Lugbill got the gold, Davey Hearn the silver, and Bob Robison the bronze.

Cathy was ecstatic. When she and Leslie Klein and Carol Fisher went to get their gold medals for the wildwater team event, they turned cartwheels all the way to the awards stand.

◆ ◆ ◆

In October of 1986, Cathy Hearn cemented her alliance with paddling by marrying Jacob Alexander Haller, known as Lecky. Cathy and Lecky had met on the paddling circuit, where he and his brother Fritz were C2 world champions in 1983. In Lecky, Cathy found a partner who was just as serious about having fun paddling as she was and who expected her to continue in the sport. (Leslie Klein, Carol Fisher and Ann Turner were her attendants at the wedding. Cathy's father, as he walked down the aisle with her, whispered: "When are you going to let go of my arm and start the cartwheels?")

On the home front, Cathy and Lecky are equal partners. They take turns cooking, and they take turns working to support their paddling. He works as a lacrosse, wrestling and football coach at a private school near Lime Rock, Connecticut, where they live in a house that was a forge during the Revolutionary War. It is a cheerfully rustic place with rough-hewn beams and worn planked flooring. The living room has a vaulted ceiling two stories high, and the tall walls are draped with Cathy's and Lecky's medals and with photographs of them paddling. The most prominent decoration is a large chart of the upcoming racing season. At Christmas, Cathy and Lecky use their medals to decorate the tree, which droops under all the weight. When she moved into the renovated forge, Cathy experienced "a quantum leap in luxury." For three-and-a-half years, she had lived in a cabin on an island in the Potomac River where the only access was by boat. The only running water was the river going by, and there was no electricity. A tiny wood-burning stove supplied what heat there was. Now, she and Lecky have a furnace, electricity, indoor plumbing and too many other amenities to list. They can drive right up to their front door. They consider themselves about as lucky as two people can be.

Cathy Hearn's decision to make competitive whitewater paddling a career was not one that she made lightly nor one for which she has gotten much encouragement from the world at large. After her triple gold in 1979, many people advised her to retire from the sport. They told her she had accomplished everything she could. The way her fellow paddlers responded to her performance also made her wonder about her place in paddling. Some of them had not joined in the acclaim for her; instead, they were dumbfounded and edgy around her, acting as if they considered her three gold medals a fluke. She was not prepared for that kind of attitude nor for how visibly upset one paddler was at losing to her. Cathy's mother remembers riding home with her after the world championships and feeling helpless to alleviate Cathy's sadness after what should have been the greatest week of her life. They stopped at Hampshire College, where Cathy saw her paddling buddies Angus Morrison and Ann Turner, who helped to cheer her up. Angus and Ann had not been at Jonquière, where everyone's nerves were stretched after a week of competition—they weren't jealous that she had won nor burned out from the super-charged world championships atmosphere. Ann, in fact, was packing to go to the flatwater world championships and took Cathy's spectacular success as encouragement for her own efforts.

After Jonquière, Cathy began to realize that winning was not the point of competing. "You don't do this stuff to win. That's such a small thing. It's one moment. Half the people hate you, and the other half think you're a total goddess. Neither one of these is something I like."

Cathy's three gold medals made her a mini-celebrity outside the paddling community. A film entitled *Fast and Clean*, about her and Jon Lugbill, was shown on public television. ABC's *American Sportsman* took her and three other kayakers to the jungles of southern Mexico to paddle the previously unnavigated Rio Jatate, a stretch of continuous white water in a deep canyon. She consulted with advertising firms who wanted to push the image of the success-oriented woman. Whitewater paddlers do not normally get this kind of attention; when Cathy did, she lost some of the sense of community that comes from the outsider mentality that many paddlers have. Slalom racers consider themselves outsiders because their sport is one that few other people know about or understand, that most people would consider too dangerous to try and that offers little in the way of material rewards.

The community of slalom racers is close-knit and knows no national boundaries. Even though people race under different flags, they see each other as part of the same small, intense, unique community. They often train together, compare technique and equipment and discuss the way the water moves. The international cooperation among athletes also is due in part to the nature of the sport. Whitewater races are against the clock; racers are on the course by themselves and not going head-to-head the way they do in other sports. This eliminates some of the psychological warfare that characterizes other kinds of athletic events and that works against camaraderie. Competitors also practice together; they have to because of safety considerations. A rapidly moving river can be dangerous. "There's a lot of interdependence when you're on the water," Cathy says. "It's a matter of safety and survival." She got her first real lesson in this in 1977 at her first world championships. In a practice run, she broke both blades off her paddle and then lost control of her boat and flipped. Some British paddlers helped right her, but the boat had taken on too much water. She had to abandon her kayak and swim. Some German paddlers helped her to shore and then rescued her boat.

To feel cut off from this small, close community that had been her entire life was hard on Cathy. But she persevered, sticking with competitive paddling and trying to understand where she fit in the sport. She felt she was still in the early stages of her quest for excellence and was still inventing technique and experimenting with equipment. She was getting stronger, and she was learning to control her mind. Above all, she was having fun on the water. Why should she quit?

In the years between the 1979 world championships and marrying Lecky in 1986, Cathy had not come close to repeating her astounding performance at Jonquière. In fact in 1986, she had just won her first national championship in K1W. In an interview after her winning run, the television announcer asked if she wasn't a bit old—twenty-eight—to be racing. Cathy said she had to admit that if someone had asked her a few years before what she would be doing at twenty-eight, she would have bet on being retired from racing and having a couple of kids. "But," she said, "I'm not retired. I don't have kids. And I'm better than I've ever been."

In 1988, when the International Olympic Committee announced that whitewater slalom would be an event in the 1992 Olympics, Cathy knew that she would remain in the sport for at least four more years. "I've been training for the 1992 Olympics my whole career," she says. She will be thirty-four when and if she makes the 1992 Olympic team and goes to Barcelona. She will have been paddling competitively for almost twenty years.

It is unlikely that Cathy Hearn will ever get out of paddling, which is a vocation that allows her to express everything she believes in—the pursuit of excellence, international goodwill and respect for nature. "I've learned a lot from paddling. I've learned about being independent and being strong, and not just physically strong. I've learned about challenging myself. I've learned a lot about friendship and relationships with other people. Anything we can do to gain respect for the world and the people who live in it is the best thing we can do with our lives."

Since 1986, she and Lecky have been part of a group of paddlers that was started by Jamie McEwan when he and his wife, the artist Sandra Boynton, moved to the Berkshires. Jamie founded the Housatonic Area Canoe and Kayak Squad (HACKS) and began encouraging people to move to the area to train with him. In return, he gave them places to live and facilities for training and for building boats. "It helps me out to have people train around here," Jamie says. "The ideal situation is to help yourself and help everyone else." He and Sandra Boynton own several buildings along the Housatonic River that serve as boathouses, living quarters and equipment sheds for paddlers and canoe builders. They also own the house where Cathy and Lecky live. They are helping Billy, the youngest Hearn, set up a paddle manufacturing business. Billy got into the sport, too, and for three years—in 1987, 1988 and 1991—all three of the Hearn children were on the national team.

Jamie, who inspired Cathy Hearn to make paddling her life and now helps her sustain that devotion, has tried to retire from the sport twice, once in 1973 right after his bronze medal at the Olympics and once after making the U.S. flatwater team in 1977. He came back again in 1984 and was concentrating on paddling the C1 until the fall of 1986, when he got into a C2 with Lecky. He has been training and racing with Lecky ever since, and their goal is to paddle their C2 in the 1992 Olympics in Barcelona.

Cathy, Jamie and Lecky are the core of the Housatonic River group, which has become one of the U.S. Canoe and Kayak Team's Centers of Excellence. These centers—six of them around the country—are development programs for paddling set up with surplus money from the 1984 Olympics. The part of the Housatonic River where national team hopefuls paddle is a picturesque stream, with a set of reliable rapids just below the reservoir that Northwest Utilities has built to generate power. With the permission of the power company, the paddlers have hung gates over these rapids. The flow of water that the power company releases every day below the reservoir keeps the rapids moving so that the paddlers can be on the river no matter how frigid the Connecticut winter.

Between 1986 and the fall of 1991, Cathy spent most of each winter training on the Housatonic and reveling in contradicting experts who told her she would not be able to train effectively for slalom in below-freezing weather. "It's pretty neat to have it be so cold around you that your sweat is freezing as it rolls down your eyeballs," she said, as she went to the river twice a day every day, no matter how cold and miserable the weather was. After her morning workout, she would pull on the clothes that had been drying on the heating ducts and head back outside where the temperature was just a few degrees above zero. In 1989 after training all winter on the Housatonic, she turned in silver- and bronze-medal performances at the world championships. In 1990, after another winter on the Housatonic, she was first at the pre-world championships.

In 1991, Cathy had, in her terms, a "lousy season," placing

nineteenth in K1W at the world championships and seventh at
the pre-Olympics in Spain. But her disappointing performance
had nothing to do with the sub-freezing temperatures in which
she trained during the previous winter. Instead, the simple fact
was that she had tried to do too much in the 1991 racing season. She had overtrained and traveled to too many races.
"Overtraining is something we all periodically do, even though
we should know better," she says. And then she quickly finds
the positive aspect of her 1991 season. "It was better to overtrain in '91 than in '92. And I got a tremendous amount of racing experience."

After the 1991 season, Cathy did not return home to Lime
Rock, Connecticut, for a long winter of training. Instead, she
went to the south of France, to a village called Saint Pe, where
Jamie McEwan had found what he considered the perfect pre-
Olympic training site. Jamie and Lecky both wanted to be near
the Olympic course, which is about 200 kilometers across the
Pyrenees from Saint Pe. Cathy had mixed feelings about moving to France. She did not like leaving her home and "going
from a minimally secure life to a less secure life." She would
miss training with the group that gathers every winter on the
Housatonic. She had been the leader of that group, making up
the workout schedules and giving her expertise to the less experienced paddlers. Working with those paddlers had helped keep
her motivated. Debbie Bailey, for instance, who began training
on the Housatonic in the fall of 1989, reminded Cathy of her
younger self. "Deb is incredibly hardy. She's got total spirit and
she's tough. She's got one set of clothes, and they're wet all the
time. All she wants to know is what the next workout is. She
gives me new motivation."

Cathy can understand wanting to be as prepared as possible
for the 1992 Olympics and, thus, moving to be closer to the
Olympic course. Being in the Olympics is the ultimate for the
amateur athlete. Having waited twenty years for her one shot at
the Olympics, she wants to do everything she can to make the

team. But sometimes she is unsettled by the intrusion of the Olympics into her sport.

One of the attractions of whitewater slalom racing for Cathy has been the opportunity to figure out for herself what works to make a boat go fast. Whitewater paddling has not had an army of sports physiologists, psychologists, trainers and coaches quantifying every move an athlete can make on a race course. Cathy has been one of the pioneers at finding the fastest route through a set of gates on a spill of water. She is still inventing techniques and discovering the best training methods for the sport as she goes. She and other elite paddlers experiment to find the right combination of weight training, endurance work and speed work.

When whitewater slalom was announced as an Olympic event for 1992, a battalion of trainers, researchers and designers was suddenly interested in the athletes. Cathy was excited at the prospect of learning more about what physiological elements the sport requires and what designs and materials work best in equipment. But when the experts take over, she says, the athletes lose control. Suddenly, the training schedule she developed through trial and error is under the scrutiny of a committee. She is inclined to think that she knows best since she has learned to listen to her body and knows when to push and how hard. Aside from a concussion that she suffered during a race in 1980 (and raced nevertheless), she has had only two serious injuries, both of them tears to the same rotator cuff in her shoulder. The first one occurred in August of 1988, and the second in March of 1989. At the 1989 world championships, she won a bronze medal in the individual K1W and a silver in the team slalom, despite being unable to paddle at full speed.

Cathy is grateful for all the years when no one cared about whitewater paddlers. "It's fortunate that we weren't real organized at the beginning. We weren't limited by people saying what we couldn't do."

As a potential 1992 Olympian, Cathy is eligible for money

from the Olympic Committee. The basic grant is $2,500. Additional money is based on performance and need. If, at the end of a season, she is ranked in the top five in the world, which she usually is, she gets a total of $10,000 for the next season. Getting more money just to paddle means that she doesn't have to scrounge up outside work to support herself. She has been a waitress, a gymnastics coach and, for three years, worked for Sandra Boynton, doing layout and production. The extra money from the Olympic Committee, she says, has strings attached. "Having more money available to athletes is a mixed blessing. All of a sudden you have this whole administrative structure. The athletes are merchandised. There's a lot of interest from outside people in how we train and whether we're winning medals. It becomes a business, and we're the product. We're essentially owned by our governing body. Our athletes have always been responsible for what we do and how we do it. That's what makes us so successful. We perform well internationally and have done it getting no money from anybody. One of my best years, I camped for a whole season in Europe."

On the other hand, she says she realizes that she would be unable to train and compete at a world-class level without the funding that she receives from her sport's governing body. Olympic status automatically increases interest in a sport worldwide. Every country that sends a team to the Olympics begins to put more effort and money into the newly ordained sport.

Another issue for Cathy in her sport's gaining Olympic status is sponsorship. The sport's national governing body, the U.S. Canoe and Kayak Team, solicits sponsors and has the contractual right to sell half of the advertising that the athletes wear on their boats and their bodies. The first sponsor that the governing body signed was Champion Paper. Cathy, who donates space on her boat to advertising for Greenpeace and to American Rivers, was shocked. "I had some problems with having a paper maker as a sponsor. A paper company—anybody that's got a brain can figure out that a paper company is not that great an image. People say to us, 'They [Champion] pollute the river near my home.'" Cathy was one of a group of athletes who protested the choice of Champion and who refused to wear the sponsor's name on their helmets. "We all wanted individual okays of what went on our helmets. Whatever's on my helmet, that's my face and it's got something written across it. It's much more personal than something on my boat. I don't think they own my head."

The athletes compromised in the sponsorship battle by agreeing to wear plain white helmets, with no sponsor name, and to accept Champion as sponsor. Cathy has since turned her attention to working with Champion on what she calls the "somewhat unique challenge of melding a paper company with a semi-wilderness outdoor sport." She says she appreciates Champion's sponsorship of the entire U.S. Canoe and Kayak program, including a series of slalom races around the U.S. begun in 1990. Those races award prize money to help athletes with training and racing expenses.

Before the fall of 1988, when the sport received Olympic status for 1992, Cathy did not have to face such issues as the ethics of taking money from a paper company. "Before, we used to live in this little paradise. We didn't have any money, but we were happy." She and Lecky had a network of friends all over the world. They traveled to warm places, like Chile, for part of the winter to help set up paddling programs. They got by on very little money by living simply and spending all their time doing what they loved. A basic life has great appeal for Cathy. She remembers going to trade shows with Sandra Boynton, where buyers were shopping for the next season's linen designs. She liked to speculate about what would happen if suddenly they were all reduced to having to live off the land. "For them [the buyers] subsistence living meant 'Am I out of mousse? Is my blow-dryer working? Is the takeout place open?' One of my things is not to get too far from what we used to be. The human

animal didn't always have running water and microwaves."
Paddling gives her the contact with the basic elements that she
craves.

Having a whitewater slalom event included in the 1992
Olympics should help Cathy stay in paddling after she retires
from competition. Because of the increased exposure for the
sport and the increased funding available, there will be more
coaching opportunities. Cathy has done some coaching of the
junior team, and she would like to do more. She refuses to say,
however, when she will retire. "I tell people I'll always be paddling."

Most people who work as hard as Cathy Hearn does and are
at the top of their profession, as she is, make more than
$10,000 a year and are congratulated for their success, not
asked when they are going to start living real lives. She is constantly being asked if she isn't too old to be doing what she is
doing: "There is so much pressure on us to be getting on with
our real lives. We're not making money at this, so we're completely denying the American way. But I don't think money is
where it's at at all. Money is one of the least important things in
life. Respect for the world and the people who live in it are the
two most important things. We need to have respect for everybody no matter where they're from or what they do. We need a
willingness to put ourselves in their position and make ourselves a little bit vulnerable."

Cathy also gets questions about when she is going to have
children. Before her sport was made an Olympic event, she debated about having children. She had Carol Fisher as an example of a competitor who has managed to combine racing with
having children. Fisher has two children, a son who was born in
1985 and a daughter in 1988. When she was pregnant with her
daughter, Carol was also doing her residency in orthopedic surgery. Carol's friends like to tell the story of how she took four
weeks' vacation from her residency in 1988—two to have a
baby, one to go to national team trials and one to go to the

world championships. They consider her a wonder woman, a title she shuns. "The only way I'm different is that I do what I think I want to do, even though people tell me I'm not supposed to do that. I think, 'Why not? At least I can try.' Bill Endicott, the most respected of all whitewater coaches, said I couldn't be a good international paddler and go to medical school. It's not that he doesn't have a lot of good ideas; but you don't always have to listen to what they say. Like my adviser at medical school. He said, 'You can't be a surgeon and have children.' I'm looking at him, and he's a surgeon and has two children."

Carol Fisher, Cathy decided, was unique in her capacity for doing it all. Cathy Hearn, on the other hand, would postpone having children until she had done everything she could to fulfill a twenty-year-old dream—winning a medal at the Olympics. "I often ask myself if I'm being selfish, continuing my paddling. I've decided that no, I'm not. What I do is pretty valuable for other women to see. We have not been encouraged to realize our potential in any field. If I can either inspire or teach somebody to realize her potential and push her potential, then I should do it."

In this attitude, Cathy has the full support of her parents and her brothers. Her brother Davey is still racing and hopes to be on the 1992 Olympic team. Her brother Billy would like to make the team, too. "I think they're all very successful," says their father, Carter Hearn. "They really like the training and the lifestyle. They have friends all over the world. They get to do a lot of interesting travel and to work with other paddlers. They're not making big money at it, but they're surviving."

"I understand perfectly why they do this," says their mother, Mary Alice Hearn. "There is something so wonderful about getting in those little boats and going down that beautiful water. When they get into a boat, it's kind of a balance of body, mind and spirit. It's oneness with the boat, oneness with the water, oneness with nature." She marvels at the way Cathy has pursued her passion. "Cathy is a special person. I'm really in awe of her. And I've learned a whole lot from her." When Mary Alice Hearn's life took an unexpected turn and she and Carter, whom she had known since they were in the first grade together, were divorced in 1983, she took inspiration from her daughter's approach to life. "We can look at things from so many different perspectives. Cathy is great at looking at the positive. She helped me to see that there are different ways of looking at things and you might as well look with the attitude, 'What can I learn from this?'"

When the 1992 Olympic Games are over, whether Cathy Hearn's name is among the medalists or even the finalists in the women's whitewater slalom event is beside the point. She has made major contributions to the sport, and it, in return, has given her a framework for her life. For nearly twenty years, Cathy has lived for those moments like a night in early March when she is on the Housatonic River, in the rapids just below the reservoir, for her evening workout. Her paddling clothes are barely dry from her morning workout, which was a leapfrog race down miles of river with Swiss national champion Heinz Roethenmund and Debbie Bailey. In leapfrogging, one paddler goes all out until she is too tired to continue, then another paddler passes her and sets the pace. All the participants try to stay in the pack and ride the wake so they can overtake the flagging leader in turn. Cathy and her friends had leapfrogged for an hour that morning. Now they are all back on the river to practice on the gates. The moon is rising over the river, illuminating bare tree branches on its ascent. The paddlers' footprints down to the river are visible in the snow. The temperature is ten degrees. All the athletes paddle hard for about an hour, going repeatedly through each gate, reading the river, which is never the same, striving for the fastest, most efficient way down. Then the mood lightens, and they start to play. Suddenly, as she scoots through a gate in her flat-bottomed kayak, Cathy Hearn lets out a whoop. She shouts that she is inventing a cool new move. She paddles once to get out of an eddy. Then by body movement alone she rides the river through the next two gates. Ice is forming on her jacket and her helmet from the spray. She paddles back up river to try the new move again. She couldn't be having more fun.

Lloyd Fons

Valerie Fons has accomplished incredible feats as a paddler: first woman to paddle around the Baja Peninsula, half of the first women's team to make the qualifying time in the 240-mile Au Sable River Marathon, holder of the speed record for paddling the length of the Mississippi River and first and only woman to canoe 21,000 miles from the Arctic to Cape Horn. In this photo taken by her father Lloyd Fons, she is paddling through the surf in the Gulf of Mexico.

Verlen Kruger

In this photo, taken by her paddling partner Verlen Kruger, Valerie is with two native Brazilians by the Rio Negro. The two men, who lived on the riverbank, greeted Valerie and Verlen and invited them to camp there. The men were fascinated by the contrast between their canoes and paddles and Valerie's and Verlen's.

Valerie Fons

~

O NE NIGHT in the twenty-fifth month of her 21,000-mile canoe trip from the top to the bottom of the earth, Valerie Fons
realized that she could no longer remember her home, her
friends or her family. The sweet white cottage on the banks of
the Grand River in Michigan refused to appear magically in her
mind the way it had every previous night of the most arduous
journey of her life. She lay in her tent and tried to visualize the
pair of swans that had built their nest near her cottage and en-
chanted her with their grace. She could no longer get the shape
of their bodies right nor the shade of brown of the river running
underneath them. She searched her memory for the group of
friends at her church who had baked a cake and wished her god-
speed. She strained to see her parents, Lloyd and Venita Fons,
whose kind faces had reassured her every other night of this trip
from the Arctic to Cape Horn. She could not remember her two
younger sisters, Lynnette and Lisa, who had no notion of why
she would want to spend month after month paddling away
from everything she knew, but who cheered her on nevertheless. Also lost was the face of her dear older brother, John, who
had caught some of her passion for traveling the waterways and
had been part of her land crew on two previous canoe adventures. As she lay in the dark, yearning for the faces of those she
loved, other faces intruded, faces of people she had encountered
on her journey. When she tried to bring the white cottage into

focus, its walls disintegrated under the pressure of a rushing river or the heave of the ocean. All that she knew, all that her memory contained, was the trip she had embarked on two years earlier. Its momentum had replaced any other idea of time. Its scenery had obliterated the tall pines and leafy maples of home. Its people had become the only ones available to love. She had lost her past and her identity and had become the journey. Nothing in her life was attached. Nothing was secure. She was terrified.

Beside Valerie in the tent that night was Verlen Kruger, the man she had married two years and two months earlier. He had offered this trip as a honeymoon. If he felt the same sense of disconnection and panic, he was not admitting to it. He did not talk much, and he certainly never complained. Verlen lived to push beyond barriers. Having already made a 28,000-mile canoe trip around North America, spending more than three years paddling, he was convinced that physical barriers did not exist. Any limitations, he thought, came from a person's state of mind. Consequently, he kept his mind clear of negative thoughts. If he felt fear, he used it as a stimulus. What scared him attracted and challenged him, and he headed right for it.

Valerie knew that talking to Verlen about her fears would not soothe her. So she talked to herself. And she prayed. Her faith had helped sustain her each day of this trip. But her faith did not have a face, and she wanted that human connection. In the morning, she lifted the stern hatch of her canoe and looked at the collage of familiar sights she had pasted there: photos of the swans on the Grand River, the church group's sendoff, a young friend. She repeated the sayings she had taped to the hatch: her own Eleventh Commandment, "Thou shalt not give up," and "All things are possible with God." She took out the waterproof box that she called her treasure chest and studied the pictures of her family, trying to force their features back into her memory.

Realizing that she had nine months left on her journey—

that is, if all went well and they made Cape Horn as scheduled—she thought about how to get through to the end. Her faith certainly would be her primary support. But she longed for a tangible supplement to it, something to comfort her the way burying her face in the fur of her big old Newfoundland dog had during another difficult time in her life. She needed to see her faith made flesh.

And then she began to remember the women she had met on her journey. The times she had felt closest to home were the times she had spent with them. She saw very clearly the face of the woman in Canada who had invited her to sit at home with her as she wove by candlelight. The candle flame reflected in the window had reminded Valerie of all the warmly lighted houses she had passed by while paddling. The woman's weaving had soothed her, and the conversation had cheered her. She was homesick for that woman's life, for the domestic choice that she had abandoned.

Valerie remembered a sixty-seven-year-old park warden named Peggy whom she had met in the Bahamas. Peggy skippered a tugboat named Moby and had a dog she called Powerful. Peggy knew everything that went on in the 120 square miles of park territory that she patrolled.

Valerie remembered the black women singing in a church in the Caribbean. These were big women, tight in their dresses, clapping their hands and making sure their rich voices carried to Jesus. "Don't move that mountain," they were singing. Valerie carried their song with her as she climbed into her canoe to begin that day's portion of her long journey. Dipping her paddle into the water, she started to sing along with those women in the Caribbean church choir. "Don't move that mountain that I have to climb." Her voice got louder and steadier, taking assurance from her memory of their strong voices. "Just give me the strength and power so that I can climb it." She sang that song all the way to Cape Horn.

✦ ✦ ✦

Valerie Fons has accomplished incredible feats in her canoe. She was the first woman to paddle all the way around the Baja Peninsula. She was part of the first women's team to make the qualifying time in the grueling Au Sable River Marathon. She holds the speed record for paddling the length of the Mississippi. She paddled from the Arctic to Cape Horn, arriving only one day off schedule. From the time she discovered canoeing in 1981 until the end of that decade, she put more than 30,000 miles on her paddle. "I don't have a lot of ability to hold back," says this slender, dark-haired, bespectacled paddler.

Her family was startled by the intense interest she developed in canoeing when she was thirty years old and living in Seattle, Washington. Nothing in her childhood had predicted this turn in her life. "Canoeing came as a surprise to all of us," says her mother, Venita Fons, who lives in Houston. "We never did much boating as a family. We were not campers." The Fons family has spent some time trying to analyze Valerie, who is the oldest girl and the second oldest child, born on Valentine's Day in 1951. They all agree that she was the one kid who ran ahead whenever the family went anywhere together. "She would always dash right out to the edge," her brother John remembers. "Then she would wait for the rest of us to catch up," her father Lloyd adds. They all talk about Valerie's predisposition toward action. "She doesn't sit around and think about things too long," says her mother. And they remark on her talent for organizing events. "We used to say she can get the show on the road," says Venita.

John, who is the sibling closest to her in temperament and spirit, characterizes her as "compassionately curious" about everything around her and says she has always liked to make connections with people.

"But we don't know what possessed her, really," Venita says, pausing before she ventures a guess about why her daughter spends so much time exploring places and states of mind in a canoe: "All of my dad's people were Norwegians. Well, maybe she's got a little Viking in her."

Valerie became interested in canoeing in 1981 when she decided to enter the annual Ski to Sea Race in Washington state. This event is a relay race from Mount Baker in the Cascades to Puget Sound and involves a team of two skiers, a runner, a bicyclist, two canoeists and a sailor. Valerie called the Seattle Canoe Club to find a partner for the race, and she started training, paddling every night after work. "At the end of the Ski to Sea Race, I was absolutely hooked. I liked canoeing because it is very fair: My effort translated equals motion. Canoeing became for me the place where life was. And I let it take over my life."

She joined the Seattle Canoe Club and began to enter races. At the time she was recently divorced. She lived with her two Newfoundland dogs in a 4,000-square-foot house in Woodinville, a town within commuting distance of Seattle. She had learned to hang sheetrock and lay tile to fix the house the way she wanted it. Her income came from her job as a technical assistant to a geologist. She did map work and calculations. "As soon as I could put that work away every day, I went training every night."

Valerie Fons was on her way to becoming an excellent canoe racer on the flat waters of small lakes when Verlen Kruger paddled into Seattle in 1982. He was in the midst of a three-and-a-half-year, 28,000-mile journey around North America that he called the Ultimate Canoe Challenge. He was fifty-nine years old, married to a woman named Jenny back home in Lansing, Michigan, and the father of nine grown children. He looked like a north woodsman, or a jolly, gentle Ernest Hemingway. He was short and barrel-chested with white hair and a white beard. His cheeks were always rosy. His paddling partner was Steve Landick, who was also one of his sons-in-law. They were a loose team, at times paddling 1,000 miles apart. But they arrived in Seattle together and were guests of the Seattle Canoe Club.

Valerie was intrigued by the adventure that the two men were on, and she spent as much time as she could talking to them. She was still training for races and was fit. Her hands had calluses, and her slender frame was getting some muscle on it. She was slightly taller than Verlen, whom she studied with her calm, penetrating stare. She noticed that Verlen's symbol for his trip was a monarch butterfly; he had a large decal of one under a layer of fiberglass on his canoe. Valerie fingered the butterfly pendant that her mother had given her and that she always wore around her neck.

One day Valerie paddled with Verlen, Steve and a group from the canoe club onto Puget Sound. This was her first time on open water. "When I got on the big water, feeling the swells, it was like breathing. I began to see the vision that this guy had of traveling on the big water and living there." She asked if she could go with him on part of his trip. He said no. He had made a commitment to his partner Steve that theirs would be a two-person trip.

Verlen and Valerie continued to talk. They found they shared a deep Christian faith and a joy in being alive. Verlen was a born explorer who could not resist finding out what was around the next bend. He had not discovered canoeing until he was forty. He took short trips first, then he started entering canoe marathons. Finally, he retired from his work as a plumber and set out to paddle the waterways of his home continent. Valerie thought she could learn something from Verlen, something about adventure and embracing the entire world as home. She sensed his strength and stability and saw the glimmer of her own dream in the technicolor dream he was living. The idea of being out on the big water and feeling at home there attracted her. "The Ultimate Canoe Challenge was an entity. It had such force and momentum." When Verlen and Steve left Seattle to continue their journey, Valerie's spirit went with them. When she wasn't training in her canoe, she was writing letters to Verlen's various mail drops. Later, after he and Valerie had completed a trip around the Baja Peninsula, Verlen would say, "It seemed like circumstances kept intervening that seemed to put us together."

The first intervening circumstance occurred when Verlen and Steve were paddling off the coast of Oregon. Verlen capsized and lost his canoe. He returned to Seattle to wait for his spare boat to be sent from Michigan and to re-outfit himself for continuing on the trip. Valerie and other Seattle Canoe Club members helped him. When his spare boat arrived, Valerie drove it and him to Oregon, to the place where he had capsized. The day they arrived, a fisherman brought in Verlen's original boat, the one he thought he had lost. Valerie put it on top of her car and took it back to Seattle to store it in her garage. Consequently, she had one of the seventeen-foot kevlar canoes that Verlen had designed for the Ultimate Canoe Challenge.

The second intervening circumstance came when Verlen and Steve reached Long Beach, California. There Steve received word that his infant daughter had died. He left the Ultimate Canoe Challenge to go home to his wife. Verlen decided to continue. He asked Valerie if she would like to paddle with him on the Los Angeles to Yuma, Arizona, leg of the Ultimate Canoe Challenge. This meant paddling 2,411 miles on the Pacific Ocean and the Sea of Cortez around the Baja Peninsula. Despite her lack of any experience that would prepare her to make such a journey, she immediately said yes. She put an ad in the paper that said: "Please love my home. I'm going to the ocean," and found renters right away. She found people to take her dogs; she stored her furniture in the basement. She quit her job, sold her car, packed her gear and found sponsors to finance her trip. Three weeks from the day she said yes, she was in Long Beach ready to go.

Her family was startled. Her parents had not heard anything from her that prepared them for this sudden departure. They knew she had taken up canoeing, but that was all they knew. Her brother John recalls: "When she called me and sprang this surprise, I think for the first time in my life I felt real dread. I felt that I might be hearing Valerie's voice for the last time. She spoke so glowingly of Verlen and his concern for her safety. I said, 'If he is so concerned, how can he conscience taking you along on such a trip?'"

Verlen did not have a chance to respond to John's question just then. He was oblivious to the concerns of Valerie's family. "To me her greatest qualification to do the trip was desire. I would rather have someone who knew nothing but what she wanted. Valerie was willing to drop everything. She did drop everything."

After three weeks of being consumed by all the preparations necessary to put her old life in storage and embark on the new adventure she craved, Valerie was suddenly struck by the monumental nature of her undertaking. She and Verlen were paddling away from Long Beach, out into the endless Pacific, when the nausea started. "It was only when I got out there on the water that I kind of flipped out. I threw up and wondered what I had done. I am susceptible to seasickness. But they say seasickness is tied to emotion. The hectic stuff was over. Now it came just to paddling. Now it looked big and empty. I saw 2,400 and some miles and it looked like a brick wall. I just kind of hit the wall." Verlen rafted their two canoes together and did all the paddling as Valerie got weaker and weaker. He told her the seasickness would not last, that she would recover and get stronger. She didn't believe him. He kept paddling. "I didn't for a minute believe that she wanted to quit," he says. "Besides, there was no place to quit there." Finally, Verlen paddled the two canoes into shore at San Diego. Valerie could feel the solid, reliable earth underneath her once again. A family had even offered the paddlers shelter. When the host showed Valerie to her room, and Valerie saw that she was being offered a waterbed, she collapsed on the floor, sobbing and laughing.

Valerie recovered her strength in San Diego, and began to believe again that she could paddle around the Baja. Slowly, she adjusted to life in a small canoe on the big ocean. In good weather, she and Verlen would paddle as long as they could, sometimes fifty hours without a rest break. In bad weather, like

the hurricane that beached twenty-seven sailboats, the two paddlers survived on faith and determination. From the beginning
of the trip, as soon as Valerie was physically strong enough, she
and Verlen alternated days acting as captain. Valerie grew into
that role, planning the route for the day, keeping the team
moving. When they were going north up the Sea of Cortez and
Verlen began to have doubts that they would make the deadline
he had set for them, Valerie started issuing the pep talks. This
change in their relationship from mentor-pupil to equal partners exhilarated Valerie. The high point of the three-and-a-half
month trip for her was "coming into my own and taking responsibility for my boat and going on." When they were near
the end of the trip, their charted waterway disappeared into
knee-deep mud. They had to drag their loaded canoes for miles.
They were both exhausted but determined to keep moving.
They would take turns sleeping. Valerie says: "The last portion
of the trip I was pulling Verlen and he was asleep. I didn't wake
him up. I just kept pulling."

From the moment she got into her first canoe back in Seattle, Valerie had begun to redefine her ideas about how she
should live her life. The process of training for a race and seeing
herself get stronger and gain athletic proficiency was a profound
revelation. Never before had she realized such a return on investment. Whatever she put into paddling, she got back out.
The notion of seeing how much she could put in began to take
over her life. And when she took that show on the road, testing
her limits on the wilderness of the ocean, she became a different
person. Before her Baja trip, her vision of what was beautiful in
the world was sitting on a mountaintop and contemplating the
view. After the Baja, sitting and looking lost their allure. What
mattered was striving to develop potential. She would never return to the old life she had put in storage, and she would not go
back to live in the big house outside Seattle that had been her
center for so many years.

The particular intervening circumstance that persuaded her

not to go back to her house after the Baja trip was the death of her Newfoundland, Angus. She and Verlen were a week from the end of their journey together when she learned that Angus had died. "My whole future changed. My link to Seattle was gone. I was just going to rush back and pick up my dog. I had a real bond with that dog. When I got a divorce, we had a BMW and a Jeep. When I first left the house, I took the BMW. Then I turned around and got the Jeep and the dog. The dog was heart rather than status. The Jeep was utilitarian rather than status. All through the divorce, I would just bury my head in the dog and cry in his fur. When he died, that was the turning point for me."

She went to her parents' home in Houston to rest for a couple of weeks and to recover from her Baja adventure. She visited with people she had known when she was growing up. Lucy Collins, who had been the youth director at the Methodist Church Valerie attended as a teenager, remembers a "glow" about Valerie that she had not noticed before the Baja trip. Lucy: "I think she grew spiritually from the trip. She felt closer to God and closer to the world itself. When you come face to face with God, you know more about yourself. I think there were times on the Baja trip when the only thing she could face was God. I think she recognized some divinity, some God-likeness in herself." According to Lucy Collins, Valerie had been different from other teenagers. She had a unique perspective on the world. "She was extremely courageous in everything she did, always wanting to try new things. Yet she was solid as a rock. Her faith was as strong as anyone's. Some of her prayers led me to believe she was almost a religious genius. She knew how to get in touch with the eternal. She had an affinity with creation. I used to think she got up every morning saying, 'Thank you, God, for the world and for letting me be me.'"

Valerie went from Houston to a farmhouse in Iowa next door to her brother John and his family. While she lived there, she wrote a book about her Baja experience. (The book, *Keep It*

Moving, was published by the Mountaineers Press.) John was thankful to have Valerie back safely from her adventure and was intrigued by the change that adventure seemed to have made in her. "Valerie is in love with life. Her consuming reality is she knows she is alive. She marvels at it. She wants to do big and wonderful things that she can hold up and say, 'My God, I'm alive.' When she started paddling, a wonderful thing happened between her and the world she lived in. It was a coming out party for Valerie, for her love of being alive. Paddling gave her a way to connect with the whole world."

◆ ◆ ◆

John Fons wanted to get involved in the experiences that were making his sister Valerie feel so alive. He volunteered to help out on her next adventure, the Au Sable River Marathon, an annual 240-mile canoe race through northern Michigan held in July. Almost as soon as she completed the Baja trip, Valerie was on the telephone, trying to find a partner for the Au Sable. She had been thinking about competing in the marathon before going to Baja. On the trip, Verlen talked about the race, which he had finished eleven times. He told her that a third of the teams entering the Au Sable do not finish because of exhaustion or damage to their canoes. The race begins at night and ends, for the fastest team, fifteen hours or so later. The river rushes around islands and twists through forests. It is full of fallen logs and weeds. There are six dams around which the racers must portage. The idea of it thrilled Valerie. "It was attempting the impossible. It was big. I love things that are big."

Verlen said he would take a break from his Ultimate Canoe Challenge to act as a bankrunner along with John. Valerie's sister Lynnette, who works as a lawyer in Houston, said she would be a bankrunner, too. All that was left for Valerie was to find a partner. In February of 1983, Valerie phoned Anne Kobylenski in Condon, Montana, and asked her to be her partner. Valerie did not know much about Anne except that she had been recommended by other canoeists. She had six years of racing experience, in addition to her background as a distance swimmer in college. She turned Valerie down at first, but Valerie persisted and in April went to Montana to train with Anne.

The race begins in Grayling, Michigan, where the Au Sable is a pretty little trout stream. The teams of paddlers carry their canoes and run to the river. Some teams do not survive the elbowing and jostling of putting in. Anne and Valerie were the second women's team in the history of the marathon. They were well-suited as paddling partners. Valerie paddled in the bow, where she could supply the power she had developed on her Baja adventure. Anne was in the stern with the compass and proved to be an able navigator. Their plan was to rely on map and compass to find their way along the quirky river. They lacked the familiarity with the river that many of the other teams had; winning teams on the Au Sable are usually Michigan natives, some of them third-generation river runners. Valerie was bursting with optimism and enthusiasm for the adventure. Anne was quiet and realistic, expecting to finish the race in about twenty hours, a respectable time but not among the fastest teams. Anne admitted that on one ten-hour training run Valerie's singing had driven her crazy. Valerie did not seem offended, nor did she try to contain her high spirits.

Verlen, John and Lynnette drove along the bank, connecting with the paddlers every couple of hours and tossing them soft foods and warm liquids in tubes. Anne and Valerie had a good start, surviving the crush without damage. They quickly settled into their planned sixty-stroke-a-minute race pace, which they hoped to hold for the duration of the race. They paddled steadily through the night, around corners, through debris. They ran around dams. Spectators on bridges shone lights into the boats below. As if the darkness were not enough of a navigational challenge, a thick fog moved in. Anne and Valerie relied on the compass and counted their strokes to determine where they were on the river; they knew from previous runs how many strokes had taken them how far. The added pressure of not being able to see made the two women concentrate even harder. "I was extremely high," Valerie says. "I have never been so intense in my life as I was on that race."

In the morning, as the sun came up, the two women saw a sign that a stranger had strung on a bridge: "Val and Anne. Yes you can." Valerie was inspired. Anne was beginning to hallucinate. She told Valerie there were mice on the river and in the boat. Valerie told her to keep paddling. "I had no thought at all but getting there fast," Valerie says. "I asked Jesus and all my friends to help paddle."

Seeing the two women come out of the night, exhausted but paddling steadily toward the finish line, thrilled John Fons. "I had never seen people work that hard. It was just soul-wrenching to see them work like that. It was absolutely inspirational. I had never seen anything like it."

Valerie and Anne finished the race in sixteen hours and fifty minutes and placed tenth. "It was really a good piece of work," Valerie says. "Everything was right."

After the Au Sable, she rested for a week. Then she paddled 1,500 miles with Verlen through the Boundary Waters, covering twenty-five miles a day in what she called "sweet touring." She was staying in shape for her next major canoeing test. This one would involve Verlen again, after he finished his Ultimate Canoe Challenge in December. Verlen had mentioned something to her on the Baja trip that intrigued her even more than the Au Sable marathon. It was bigger, thus more promising.

◆ ◆ ◆

In 1984, the published record for paddling the length of the Mississippi—2,348 miles from Lake Itaska in Minnesota to the Gulf of Mexico—was forty-two days. In distance, the trip down the Mississippi was only slightly shorter than the trip that Valerie and Verlen had made around the Baja Peninsula. But their paddle around the Baja had taken a leisurely three-and-a-half months. They hoped to make the Mississippi passage in thirty days. Their plan was to work with the current as much as they could and to paddle one eighteen-foot-long canoe twenty-four hours a day—twelve hours together and six hours each of paddling solo. Sleep shifts in the canoe would be three hours long, with each partner getting two per day. If they averaged slightly more than seventy-eight miles a day, they would break the record with time to spare. The motto for the trip was: "With equal effort."

Valerie was living in central Iowa when she began training for the Mississippi paddle. Since winter had frozen all canoeable waterways, she was jumping rope in the basement and trudging through snow to the mailbox to send off detailed strategy reports to sponsors. She had persuaded Eddie Bauer, the outdoor clothing retailer, to be the major sponsor. When she joined Verlen at the end of his Ultimate Canoe Challenge in December of 1983, she handed him a contract from Eddie Bauer. He had hoped that his mention of his desire to race down the Mississippi might plant a seed in Valerie's mind. On the Baja trip, he had told her he would like to do the race with a woman "to prove that it's not age or gender that makes a difference." He could see that she liked the idea, and he was tickled that she had organized the entire trip before he could even envision the end of his 28,000-mile journey.

After welcoming Verlen home, Valerie returned to Iowa to continue training. She was agitated and restless, wanting to be in a canoe but unable because of the frigid weather. Her sister-in-law, Marianne Fons, who writes books and teaches classes on quilting, suggested that they start making a quilt about the upcoming Mississippi trip to help take Valerie's mind off her frustration. Valerie had done some quilting when she lived in Washington. In fact, she had once worked on a quilt for a year and was so pleased with the result that she decided to enter it in the Western Washington State Fair. However, she considered driving it to the fair too casual a method of transporting all the effort that the quilt represented. So she took two days to walk the quilt the fifty miles between her house and the fairgrounds. For her Mississippi quilt, Valerie, with help from her sister-in-law, selected traditional quilt block patterns and started to sew. She immediately felt peaceful and strong. With each stitch, she focused on the race and the determination necessary to beat the current record.

John and Marianne Fons had agreed to act as the land support crew for the Eddie Bauer Mississippi River Challenge. This meant they would drive a van along the Mississippi and tow an extra canoe. They would cook for the racing team and supply fresh flashlight batteries to get the pair through each night.

Verlen designed the seventy-pound kevlar canoe for the trip. He equipped it with foot pedals so that one person could paddle and steer while the other slept. He rigged a canopy for protection from the weather and installed two small chamber pots. Both he and Valerie would wear headlamps when they were traveling at night.

On April 27, 1984, they started what they hoped would be their record-breaking trip. A small crowd assembled to see the unlikely pair off. Verlen had been quoted in *People* magazine as saying that if a woman and a senior citizen could paddle down the Mississippi faster than young fellows from the British Royal Air Force, a lot of people would have to change their image of peak performers. "You expect record setters to be big, sturdy athletes," he said. "But there's more to being best than age, size and strength. There's spirit, guts and determination." At the firing of several black powder muskets, Verlen and Valerie started paddling on what was, in Minnesota, a small, friendly creek, so narrow in places that it was diverted through culverts. They had to make a number of portages at the beginning— around beaver dams, foot trails and walkways. By the second day Valerie's hands were so swollen she could hardly paddle; by day ten they were twice their normal size. She was also suffering from the usual paddler's complaints—butt raspberries, bleeding tailbone and back pain. "If I had acknowledged how bad I felt, I might have stopped."

They had one last encounter with winter in Minnesota. A blizzard, complete with a wind chill of fifteen below, hit them in Minneapolis. When Verlen's sleeping shift ended at two a.m., he had to crack the ice off his canopy to emerge and regain his seat for paddling. In Iowa, head winds gusting to eighty-five miles per hour kept them off the water for six hours. Back on the river, they were carried along for the rest of the trip in the rush of the high spring waters. Their best day was below Memphis when a dramatic current in the rising river carried them 162.4 miles in twenty-four hours. During the journey, they tried to stay in the current as much as possible, using the river as their ally and partner in their record-breaking effort. But being in the current also put them in the middle of the main shipping route. They always had to be alert for tugs and barges and other boat traffic, as well as for locks and dams. For the last 300 miles of the trip, they both had to stay awake because traffic on the river was so heavy. At night it seemed that every moving light was coming right for them. Valerie, who paddled in the bow during the whole trip, began to hallucinate when they were three days from their destination. "For the last ninety miles at night, I felt like my mind was going to blow apart. I felt like I was losing control, but I didn't let up. I kept paddling." When they reached the Mile Zero navigation marker some ninety-five miles south of New Orleans in the Gulf of Mexico, Valerie reached out and hugged that post as if it were the dearest thing in the world to her. They had made the journey in twenty-three days, ten hours and twenty minutes, breaking the British Royal Air Force record by nineteen days.

The Mississippi trip left Valerie far more depleted physically than the Au Sable marathon had. "I was a changed body. My zip was gone." She went back to Iowa to recuperate. She worried that she had done permanent damage to her bladder by ignoring its demands in order to keep paddling. Verlen, on the other hand, seemed to come off the Mississippi even stronger.

The Mississippi trip had been a departure for him in one way—it was only the second time he had shared a canoe on one of his serious adventures. (In 1970, he had paddled across Canada with a partner.) To break the Mississippi record, two people paddling the same canoe seemed to be the most efficient approach. He had no hesitation about sharing a canoe with Valerie since he knew they were so similar in their goals and determination and confidence in each other. In fact, Verlen was beginning to be sure about wanting to share his entire life with Valerie, a thought that had flickered in his mind soon after they met in Seattle. The thought came more frequently and stayed longer as circumstances intervened to put the two of them together. As Verlen puts it: "We didn't fight the circumstances."

✦ ✦ ✦

In November, after the Mississippi trip, Verlen drove to Iowa to visit Valerie. He told her he was divorcing his wife, and he asked her to marry him and paddle with him from the Arctic to Cape Horn. Valerie hesitated at the proposal. She loved Verlen's vision of the world and the way he embraced life. But she considered their differences too great to overcome in a marriage. First of all, he was twenty-eight years older than she was, two weeks younger than her father and older than her mother. He had nine children and dozens of grandchildren. She thought she wanted to have children of her own, but Verlen, having had a vasectomy, was finished with reproducing. Their backgrounds were completely different. He was the son of sharecroppers and had never gone to high school. He served in the Air Force during and after World War II and belonged to the National Rifle Association. Valerie grew up in a comfortable middle-class home. Her father was an oil executive. She had gone to college for a year, protested the war in Vietnam, edited an underground newspaper and attended Students for a Democratic Society meetings. Verlen thought material possessions were a burden.

Valerie was starting to miss all the furniture and knickknacks that she had in storage.

Valerie finally responded to Verlen's proposal by refusing marriage but offering to help him organize his trip, though she doubted that she herself would go along. When her mother heard that she was involved in planning a trip for Verlen, she predicted that Valerie would go. "We knew that anything Val started, she would finish." Venita Fons was right. As Valerie began imagining the trip from the Arctic to Cape Horn and writing proposals to potential sponsors, more and more she saw herself as one of the paddlers. The route itself thrilled her. It was big, more than 21,000 miles long, beginning at the mouth of the Mackenzie River in Canada's Northwest Territories, going along the Great Lakes, then south through the U.S. on the Wabash and Ohio rivers and the Tennessee-Tombigbee Waterway. Intercoastal waterways and the Gulf of Mexico would carry the travelers to Miami, and 2,400 miles of the Caribbean Sea would put them in Trinidad. From there they would paddle the Orinoco River through Venezuela into Brazil to the headwaters of the Negro River and through the equatorial jungle to the city of Manaus on the Amazon. They would travel to the mouth of Madeira River, which would lead them to the Paraguay River and to the Parana, which would take them into Buenos Aires, Argentina. After paddling for 3,800 miles along Argentina's coast, they would turn west for Punta Arenas, Chile, and push on from there to Cape Horn.

The purpose of the trip would be more than a test of the paddlers' endurance and survival skills. They wanted to contribute to environmental research by collecting water samples and testing for acid rain all along their route. They wanted to promote international friendship by visiting homes and schools wherever they went. They planned to learn conversational Spanish. Verlen would design all the equipment for the trip.

When Canadian Hunter Exploration Limited, an oil company in Canada, sent the first sponsorship check, Valerie admitted

1. *Mackenzie River mouth*
2. *Au Train, Michigan*
3. *Fort Wayne, Indiana*
4. *Mobile, Alabama*
5. *Miami, Florida*
6. *Trinidad*
7. *Manaus, Brazil*
8. *Buenos Aires, Argentina*
9. *Cape Horn, Chile*

that she was going on the trip. "I wanted to go on the trip. I would do anything to go. It began to be so beautiful. It was beautifully organized, with wonderful purposes. It was an opportunity to grow. I knew I would grow and change." She knew, too, that she would marry Verlen. And, on April 3, 1986, two months before the departure date of the trip, Valerie and Verlen were married.

The General Motors Research Lab and Valerie's father, through his company, Lloyd Fons Exploration, Inc., signed on as corporate sponsors. The Michigan governor appointed Verlen and Valerie citizen ambassadors for the state, and the Michigan Sesquicentennial Commission gave them money. Michigan State University's Institute of Water Research contracted with them to collect water quality data. More than a score of companies contributed products, ranging from food to cameras to thermal sleeping pads.

On June 8, 1986, Verlen and Valerie put their canoes into the Mackenzie River where it flows into the Arctic Ocean and began the trip to Cape Horn. For this trip, they had separate boats and separate mottos. Valerie's motto was "Love one another." Verlen's was "All things are possible." Valerie's brother John was not so enthusiastic about this adventure. In fact, he had advised them against going because he knew they had not found enough sponsorship to meet their budget of $70,000. "I told Valerie she was ill-advised to go on a shoestring." John Fons was also worried about the dangers of the trip—violent storms in open water, weather extremes, sharks, poisonous snakes and insects, uncharted territory, drug traffickers. "The two-continent trip reintroduced dread. We worried about her. We knew she could die or be killed."

Valerie's parents, to whom she mailed rolls of film that she shot along the way, were initially thrilled to be able to watch the trip progress through her pictures. They would have the film developed and put the slides in the projector. "It was sort of exciting," Lloyd Fons says. "Then I began to realize how dangerous it was. Then I didn't like it that much. First, I saw shots of their tent after it had been knocked down by a bear with them in it. Then there were a few snaps of huge mounds of ice breaking off and crashing into the Mackenzie River just after they had paddled by. Then there was the upset mama moose that charged their canoes."

The paddlers were taking water samples, marveling at the scenery, talking to strangers about their adventures and feeling totally alive. Valerie had her own maps, her own compass and her own purposes. She collected a momento from each place she stopped—fabric for a quilt she hoped to make when she returned, place-name stickers that she plastered all over her canoe, leaves, rocks, bones. She put a small pine tree on the bow of the canoe at Christmas time, and people left gifts under it during the night. Decorating the canoe gave her a sense of security and control over her environment. "The canoe was my home. If I was decorating, that meant I was in charge."

Valerie also had a typewriter with her in the canoe. She and Verlen both wrote dispatches from the trip. They sent their news home to be printed in a newsletter that went to friends and sponsors. Valerie phoned radio station WJR in Detroit with reports on the journey whenever she had the chance. When she and Verlen found a red-tailed hawk with its foot caught in a trap on the banks of the Wabash River in Indiana, they freed it. They reported that their hearts had soared as it circled slowly above them.

The two paddlers dressed alike so that people would recognize them as a team—and also so they wouldn't have to think much about what to put on in the morning. They wore matching pants, shirts, parkas, hats, mittens, boots, everything alike. By the time they reached Miami, Valerie hadn't worn a dress for almost a year. The day they arrived, she marched into Nieman Marcus and opened a charge account. She bought a pink-flowered rayon dress and wore it paddling.

In Miami, Verlen went to see a doctor to get vaccinations

for South American travel and found that his heart was beating irregularly. The doctor took Valerie aside and told her that Verlen should never paddle for more than twenty minutes at a time. He told her that Verlen could die at any moment. Valerie knew that they were about to paddle across the Caribbean at the beginning of hurricane season, and that they would have to race from island to island. On one of the crossings, they would have ninety miles of open sea in front of them—not exactly what the doctor ordered. Verlen called the doctor a quack and got into his canoe to begin the first crossing. Valerie followed. They paddled for fifty hours straight, making their first landfall in the Caribbean exhausted but alive.

In December of 1987, Valerie and Verlen reached South America, having safely raced from island to island in the Caribbean. Their biggest problem now was getting the money to continue. All they had left when they got to South America was $900. When they were in Trinidad, Valerie had sent a letter to Alex Tilly of Tilly Endurables, Inc., a clothing manufacturer. She had thanked him for the hats he had contributed to the trip and given him a progress report. In South America, she heard from him that his company would be sending the paddling team a weekly stipend for the duration of the trip. Valerie was astonished that a person whom she and Verlen had never met would be so generous. She called him and asked what she and Verlen could do for him. "Just come back alive," he said.

For the South American portion of the trip, Verlen had designed a canopy to protect the paddlers against the sun and netting to keep insects from getting at them. Nothing he had read, however, had suggested that he and Valerie might be dive-bombed by hundreds of iguanas. When the trees along the Paraguay River in Brazil started raining iguanas, Valerie and Verlen were startled and horrified. They tried to shield themselves from the falling reptilian bodies. But there were too many. They started paddling as fast as they could, hoping to get clear of the hail of lizards. Finally, the storm ended. Later,

Valerie and Verlen learned that iguanas dive when they feel threatened. When the canoes intruded into their habitat, they had taken the only escape route they knew. Understanding why the iguanas had hurled themselves at her did not make the memory any less traumatic for Valerie.

In Paraguay, Valerie and Verlen were swept along by the greatest flood of the century. They stayed in their canoes for seventeen days because there was no place to get out. Families were living on their rooftops, along with their chickens and dogs. The two paddlers rafted their canoes together to form a catamaran. Their bedroom was the catamaran deck. Water pythons, some of them twenty feet long, would slither up onto the deck to take a break from swimming.

The greatest danger in South America came not from insects or reptiles, but from people engaged in illegal pursuits. Drug traffickers and people hunting snakes and alligators for their skins worked at night on the rivers. One night as Valerie and Verlen were paddling close to shore looking for a spot to anchor, a shotgun shell whizzed by right over their heads.

Most of the people they encountered, however, were friendly. A group of men along one river bank applauded as Valerie and Verlen successfully navigated a powerful current. Others joined them for segments of their journey and invited them into their homes for food and rest. Occasionally, the two paddlers would visit a school and talk about their adventure.

As Valerie and Verlen progressed toward Cape Horn, each day was an adventure. Yet the physical and mental challenges of the trip were wearing Valerie down. In the summer of 1988, more than two years since they had put their canoes into the Mackenzie River, Valerie got word that her father had suffered a pulmonary embolism and was in the hospital in Houston. She immediately flew to visit him. "When Valerie came into the room to see Lloyd," Venita Fons says, "a friend who was visiting, too, said, 'She looks more tired than you do, Lloyd.' She did seem pretty well spent." Valerie was thin and drawn. The hospital staff expressed concern over her condition. A doctor suggested some tests for her. After she had her blood taken for the tests, Valerie broke down. "All of a sudden, I couldn't walk or talk. I had pushed too hard. I just held on to my mom. She was really scared. I was scared. Then it passed. Like a wave, it passed."

Valerie insisted she was all right and strong enough to resume her epic journey. Her parents did not try to persuade her to give it up. Venita recalls: "We didn't say much. There was no turning back."

Valerie was in Houston for about a week, long enough to see her father leave the hospital to recuperate at home. Then she returned to Verlen and the two-continent canoe trip. Their plan was to paddle from the Parana River into the Atlantic Ocean, north of Buenos Aires, and then hug the Argentina coast as far south as they could before weaving through the South American archipelago to the cape. To make the transition from the river into the ocean, they would have to paddle through a seething swirl of surf and current. They hooked their canoes together in preparation for this effort and then went into a restaurant to have something to eat. As they were sitting in the restaurant, Valerie saw a bird fly in and then panic. As it tried to get back out, the bird crashed into a window. It died. "I don't know that I believe in omens. But when I was paddling [on the ocean, trying to get through the surf], I said, 'Hey, that's our window.' The surf was just like that closed window. The bird was just the same as I was." The surf was too powerful for the two small canoes, linked with poles. The churning water broke the poles. Valerie's canoe flipped and came down on top of her head. "I remember tumbling and then being up out of the water. I swam awhile and walked the rest of the way to shore. The townspeople waded out into the surf and started helping us gather our equipment."

Valerie was in a daze after her accident. Her head felt cold. Within two days, it had swelled so that she could not get her glasses on. The night of the crash, as she was lying in bed, she felt fluid oozing from her nose. She asked for ten days' rest before she and Verlen went on. While Valerie was resting, Verlen worked with some of the men in town to modify the way the canoes were linked so that they could handle the pounding they had to take to make the transition through the surf. He still wanted to paddle from the Parana into the Atlantic and then go right down the coast. When the modifications were complete, Valerie climbed into her canoe and he climbed into his. They both paddled furiously, but they could not get through the surf. Finally, they left town in a truck and went inland to travel on rivers for awhile longer. The paddling still was not easy. They encountered winds with more force than they had ever seen. In gusts of up to a hundred miles per hour, Valerie kept paddling, singing the hymn, *How Great Thou Art*, to remind herself of her faith in a god who was bigger than the present danger.

Three months after she had injured her head, Valerie and Verlen reached Punta Arenas, Chile. They were eating in a restaurant when Verlen casually mentioned that he had been having trouble with one eye for quite some time. In fact, he began losing sight in it when they were on the Amazon, more than six months earlier. Valerie became alarmed and insisted that he go to a doctor. Grudgingly, he went. The Chilean doctor told him that his eye could begin hemorrhaging at any moment and advised him to go back to the States for treatment. At Valerie's insistence, he caught a plane bound for Houston.

Alone in Punta Arenas, Valerie made friends with members of the Chilean Navy, who one day invited her to go on a boat ride to Antarctica. She was excited about being on a boat that she didn't have to paddle and seeing a place that wasn't on her itinerary. Her enthusiasm lasted until the boat got into the Drake Passage and she began to feel seasick. When she went to her bunk to lie down, she felt fluid coming out of her nose. She called the ship's doctor, who looked at her and then ordered the

crew to turn the boat around and return to port in Punta Arenas. There, Valerie had a series of neurological exams. "I wasn't
doing too good. I think it was more mental than anything else.
I was just stretched to the break. I was nauseated and dehydrat-
ed. I was just kind of a basket case." She flew to Houston. Her
father remembers going to the airport to pick her up and watching every other passenger get off the plane before Valerie was
wheeled out by a flight attendant. "I didn't know whether to
take her right to the hospital or home. She looked pretty bad."

Verlen was still in Houston and stayed there until he heard
the results of Valerie's CAT scan. His eye problem had not been
the emergency that the Chilean doctor thought, so he was ready
to resume the trip. At one point several months earlier, Verlen
had offered to end the trip. "I could see her lack of enthusiasm,"
he says. Valerie had insisted then that she wanted to keep paddling. In Houston, her doctor told her she had paddled far
enough. "I was shaking and crying. He said I was going to need
professional help if I didn't quit." Her father told her she did
not have to finish the trip, that she had accomplished enough.
When her CAT scan showed no serious head injury, Verlen returned to Chile. He told her that he planned to finish the trip,
and she had to decide what she wanted to do. He would accept
whatever decision she made. Valerie stayed with her parents for
a couple of weeks, resting. Her mother knew she had made the
decision to return to the trip the day she asked to go to a fabric
store to buy quilting supplies. "Verlen was going to go on
without me. I guess my competition rose up. There was no way
I could live life having quit. Even if I had one thimble full of
strength, I could not quit. I hate to quit."

When she returned to the trip, she knew she would have to
stay focused and use every bit of her strength and faith to get to
Cape Horn. She began working on a quilt, concentrating on
each stitch. She prayed. She found a puppy that made her think
of home. The puppy was on Cape Ross, thirty-seven miles from
Cape Horn where the Chilean Navy operated a small weather

station. She and Verlen were windbound there for four days. The men who ran the weather station told Valerie she was the first woman on the island. They took her to a Quonset hut and showed her a litter of puppies all piled together sleeping. She called out "Cabo" (Spanish for cape) and picked up the one pup who lifted his nose out of his littermates' fur. "At the time I was just hanging on for the finish. This dog made me think about home and family. He symbolized life beyond Cape Horn. I craved the warmth and security of his little environment. After seeing pumas and whales, here was this little animal, something that I could touch." She kept the puppy with her, cuddling it the whole time, until the wind subsided and she had to get moving again.

Cape Horn is a place where oceans collide and weather fronts move in several times in a day. Valerie and Verlen were prepared to spend weeks getting there from Cape Ross. Valerie was trying to keep herself together, but with the hardest part of the journey facing them at the end of thirty-three months of paddling, she faltered. "My physical and emotional state was pretty marginal at that time. We were seasoned, but I wouldn't say strong. You can't keep a level of strength for thirty-three months."

The day the wind stopped blowing on Cape Ross and Valerie and Verlen began paddling for Cape Horn, Valerie felt a difference in the atmosphere. The calm was almost eerie. They paddled, marveled at the rugged beauty of the landscape, and then paddled some more. They reached Cape Horn in one day, arriving March 1, 1989. "It was like there was a hand on the weather," Valerie says.

✦ ✦ ✦

Valerie and Verlen returned to the white cottage on the banks of the Grand River in Lansing, Michigan, on April 3, 1989, three years to the day after they had been married. Valerie stored her thirty-seven leather-bound journals from the trip in the old ice box in the basement. Her intent was to protect them from fire. The journals were the most important thing in her life after the trip. They were filled with drawings, pressed plants, postcards and her words. They would be the basis for the book she planned to write. She would sit out in her writing shed—an old trailer fifty feet from the house—and look out onto the lazy brown river flowing by while she remembered wilder water and the challenges of surviving it.

She did not recover from her two-continent adventure right away. For months, she would wake up in the middle of the night feeling as if she couldn't breathe. She craved ordinary experiences like taking baths and talking on the telephone and relied on them to bring her back to normal life. The punishment to which she subjected her body left some permanent damage to her bladder and joints.

After a few months of recuperating at home, Valerie began to feel better. She planted flowers all around the house. She went to Washington State in September of 1989 and retrieved the furniture that she had put in storage in 1982 when she went on her first big canoeing adventure to the Baja Peninsula. Valerie also began to work on a quilt that would tell the story of her canoe expedition. She made a presentation to the Capital City Quilt Guild and discovered that many of its members were eager to help with her project. The group began meeting once a week and eventually blocked out three quilts using the fabric Valerie had collected in the twenty-four countries through which she traveled. As she spent those Thursday evenings, sewing, talking and laughing with the women of the quilt guild, Valerie felt herself beginning to heal from the trauma of her arduous journey.

Eventually, Valerie began to feel the urge to organize another big project. "I feel more on solid ground organizing. Out there [on the water] I didn't have the control that I have here. But I do love it out there. You're not in control, but that's good for you." She turned her organizational talents to a project that was literally in her backyard. She conceived an event that she called Grand River Expedition '90. It was designed to get the people of Michigan acquainted with the Grand River's history and ecology. Valerie organized festivals, a baseline study of water quality, school programs and lectures.

Valerie thinks of herself primarily as an explorer, and her definition of the explorer's role places an emphasis on sharing with others what she has discovered. "Explorers shed light on the area where they are. Exploring is reaching out. It certainly is not thrill-seeking. The adventure part is really just some of the fallout. As I'm becoming a more responsible explorer, I know that exploring is being able to use and share what you've learned. Sharing is the blessing of the adventurer. I'm not highly motivated by doing it for myself alone."

She shares what she has discovered through her writing and through lectures. She is particularly interested in reaching women with her message of finding courage and following dreams. On the two-continent trip, she took both inspiration and comfort from women. "Women were always supplying for me what was essential." When she needed a role model, she thought about Mina Benson Hubbard, who in 1905 paddled across Labrador, an uncharted region on maps of North America. "I remembered Mrs. Hubbard when I was being eaten by bugs. If she could do it, I could do it." She also thought about Dorothy Moulter, who was allowed to continue living in the Boundary Waters after the area was declared a wilderness. Valerie interviewed her when she and Verlen passed by her cabin on their way to Cape Horn. "When I was on a portage, I thought of Dorothy. She became my hero. Verlen's heroes were Daniel Boone and Davy Crockett. What books did I have? None. Women need these role models, these examples."

She found strength in the faces of the women she encountered on her journey, and an immediate rapport that eased her heart. "Women seemed to give me a softness and an understanding. They provided me with something I was really missing. I'd sit down with a woman for five minutes and she knew exactly what I was talking about. Continually, I saw women's love and their strength. It was different from the strength of Verlen. There was comfort in it."

As Valerie used the story of her trip from the Arctic to Cape Horn to encourage others to reach for their dreams, she began to realize she had dreams of her own that she was neglecting. On her epic journey, she had seen glimmers of these dreams. When she returned home, they grew stronger. Verlen was unable to support Valerie's vision of what shape her life should take. Having spent most of her paddling career alongside Verlen's canoe, helping him prove that his dreams were possible, she was stunned that he could not do the same for her. After much soul searching, she faced the pain of leaving Verlen. That act took more courage than she had needed to summon in all of her experiences on the oceans and rivers of the western hemisphere. "But I feel more whole about things," she says. "I have more peace."

Applying to seminaries now and thus chasing one of her dreams, Valerie continues to lecture. When she tells people to reach for their dreams, she has even more conviction that no one has to settle for less than she can be. She also knows exactly what it feels like to face tremendous fear and to push past it. "Fear is a door, not a wall. Once you choose courage, you begin practicing it. Then it's all the easier to choose courage again. Overcoming fear is the thing I know about. Some songs you can sing because that's where your voice fits."

In 1988, seven women paddled the length of the Back River—630 miles to the Arctic Ocean through the last great wilderness in North America. The Back presented the women with many challenges, which stretched them further than they had imagined possible when they set out to see what they could accomplish together as women. From left, members of the expedition are: Michele Buchmann, Ellie Horsnell, Barb Francis, Deb Sussex, Kristen Gilbertson, Nanci Olesen, Mary Linders.

The Back River Seven

Day One—June 26, 1988

THE DAY WAS WARM and sunny in the part of the Northwest Territories that the seven women had chosen for the start of their adventure. When the float plane dropped them and their gear at Muskox Lake, they celebrated with champagne. Finally, after nearly two years of planning and preparation, they were only minutes away from putting their three canoes into the wild waters of the Back River to ride 630 miles to the Arctic Ocean. They raised their glasses and cheered the fact that they had no more items to cross off on all the lists they had made. When they had drained the last of the champagne, they put the two empty bottles on the float plane back to Yellowknife. They would not be seeing any more champagne for the next sixty days. They might not see any other human beings in the vast wilderness that surrounded them, the last great wilderness on the North American continent.

These seven women, who were going to attempt to paddle the length of the Back, one of the wildest rivers in this remote region, were confident of their abilities. But people they encountered as they traveled from Minneapolis, their trip-planning headquarters, to Yellowknife, where they caught the float plane, had been amazed that they would take on the Back without men. The river has more than eighty sets of rapids and waterfalls. It passes through isolated territory, where grizzlies and wolves are more common than people. Until 1948, the only map of the Back River was one made in 1834 by the British explorer whose name the river bears. George Back had taken a crew of nine men down the river as part of the general European penetration of the tundra. He was a captain in the British Navy and a veteran of Arctic land expeditions. He had a thirty-foot dory built for the trip. The boat, which weighed two tons, had to be lowered on ropes over waterfalls and down rapids. Back fought the river all the way to the sea. He wrote about its "fearful velocity" and described it as "a succession of falls and cascades and whatever else is horrible." His crew was always "in the most imminent danger of perishing" during the thirty-one days that it took to reach the Arctic Ocean.

In 1855, another European crew rode the length of the Back. After that, there was no record of white men on the river for more than one hundred years. In 1963, four men made the expedition and found "little beauty here on this vast expanse of sterile tundra."

The written record of trips on the Back River is sparse—Back's account, which was published in 1836, and a few magazine articles from the 1960s and 1970s. It is the least traveled of all the great North American rivers. Those men who have attempted the Back and written about their journeys have gone into the wilderness with the idea of prevailing over obstacles thrown in their path. The seven women had a different approach to the river and their days in the wilderness. They were all in love with the north and the tundra. Where Back had been terrified by the desolation and vastness of the treeless landscape, the women loved the feeling of limitless space. Where their male predecessors described bleakness and barren hills, the women saw teeming life—mosses, lichens, grasses, sedges and millions of tiny flowers. They knelt on the land and put their faces close to the soil so that they could appreciate all the complex forms of life that Mother Tundra, as they called her, nurtured.

The seven women—all in their twenties—did not all know

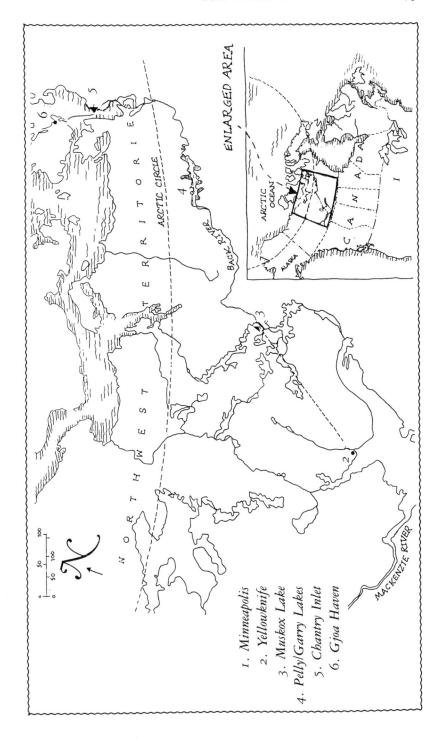

ENLARGED AREA

ARCTIC OCEAN

ALASKA

CANADA

ARCTIC CIRCLE

NORTHWEST TERRITORIES

BACK RIVER

MACKENZIE RIVER

1. Minneapolis
2. Yellowknife
3. Muskox Lake
4. Pelly/Garry Lakes
5. Chantry Inlet
6. Gjoa Haven

each other before the proposed trip united them, but they all had experience of the northern wilderness. Four of them—Nanci Olesen, Barb Francis, Mary Linders and Deb Sussex—had been together on a fifty-five-day trip down the Hood River in the Northwest Territories in 1984. Five of them—Barb, Mary, Deb, Ellie Horsnell and Michele Buchmann—had the common experience of summers at Camp Widjiwagan, a canoe camp in Ely, Minnesota, at the southern edge of the Boundary Waters Wilderness Area. Every year that a camper returns to Camp Widjiwagan, she is eligible to go on a longer canoe trip and one that is farther north. Ellie had spent thirty-one days on the Albany River in Ontario during one of her summers at camp. Barb had made her first extended northern river trip—forty days on the Hanbury-Thelon river system with four other campers and a twenty-three-year-old counselor—when she was eighteen. When she returned, she enthralled Deb, who had been her friend since they both were twelve, with her description of the wilderness. She talked about the intensity of the northern landscape and the rhythm of days in the wilderness. It was possible to strip life of all its niggling details in the back country and to live each moment as an adventure. Deb knew immediately what she was talking about; she knew, too, that she wanted to live as much of her life as possible in that kind of intensity.

Kristen Gilbertson was the only one in the group who had no white water paddling experience and no extended outdoor adventures. The longest camping trip she had been on was ten days. But she was a dog musher who was about to marry Nanci Olesen's brother and live with him on a homestead along the shores of Great Slave Lake in the Northwest Territories. She had just spent six months there, working with the dogs, making trails through the country around the cabin. She was drawn to the north, and she had always wanted to do a trip with women. When Nanci proposed that she come along on the Back River trip, she hesitated because of her lack of paddling experience. If the Back was as turbulent as she had heard, she wondered how she would fare as a white water novice. Nanci had assured her that she would not have to run any rapids if she did not want to.

When Kristen decided to go on the trip, Nanci took her to Nina Koch for white water lessons. Nina had been on the Hood River trip and had planned to be part of the Back River group, too. As the trip approached, however, she had to give up her plans to go. She and her husband could not agree on her leaving their small child alone with him for three months.

Nina was a good paddling teacher. She saw right away that Kristen was putting pressure on herself to master every nuance of white water technique all at once. Kristen's determination was holding her back. Nina insisted that she slow down, step back and go over just those moves that she knew. Gradually, Nina added pieces of technique. Kristen began to progress. By the time that she stood by her canoe at Muskox Lake, Kristen felt that she was ready for the paddling challenge that the Back River promised. And she knew that she had made the right decision in deciding to go on this trip. Her experience with Nina had given her a preview of what she hoped to get out of the trip. She had wanted a wilderness experience with women because she knew that she could be fully involved in learning and testing her skills. Her attitude about learning was different in the company of women—she was more enthusiastic and confident because she didn't expect what she learned to be taken away from her, the way it sometimes was when men were the teachers.

All of the women on the trip were interested in seeing what they could do as women in the wilderness. Michele, who had been on both all-female and mixed trips, felt that the all-female trips were "more real." She disliked the sexual politicking that went on in mixed groups. "I didn't want to deal with any of that power struggle stuff," she says. "I wanted to know what a group of women could do together, what the dynamics would be. I wanted to be with women working on ourselves."

They were all eager to escape gender roles, to define their own roles according to their emotional and physical capabilities. None of the women wanted to be stuck acting in any one way; they all wanted to be free to change as the demands of the river, the group and their moods changed. They wanted to be able to be as strong or as scared as they felt like being. They also wanted to be able to take off their shirts on a hot day without thinking about it.

The comfort of being with women away from men and machines was a compelling element of the trip to everyone in the group. They envisioned long, deep talks around the campfire and time to develop emotional ties that would sustain them when they returned to their everyday lives.

To prepare for the trip, the women had spoken with everyone they could find who had any familiarity with the river. Ellie's brother had paddled the Back in 1984. Male friends from Camp Widjiwagan had also done the trip and shared what they knew about the rapids and the best portages. Nanci's house in Minneapolis became the trip headquarters. Nanci, who worked as an actor, loved planning for wilderness trips, particularly the sense of anticipation and the focused activity. She was thrilled when the donated gear from various sponsors began accumulating in her basement office. Woolrich donated clothing. Buck donated knives. Marmot gave the women a discount on their sleeping bags, and Sierra Design gave them a discount on tents. Everyone going on the trip got to Minneapolis as soon as she could to participate in the planning; those who couldn't be there physically were there in spirit and were constantly checking in by phone. Barb moved in with her parents and worked for her father as a night janitor a year before the trip. Kristen worked with her when she arrived in Minneapolis two months before the departure date. Michele took a job planting trees in British Columbia to earn money for the trip. The estimated cost was $1,500 per person, with most of that money going toward transportation—gasoline for the truck trip up and back between Minneapolis and Yellowknife, the float plane trip from Yellowknife to Muskox Lake and then the boat pickup at the end of the trip and the plane rides home.

Nanci was in charge of the transportation arrangements. The women had decided to allot sixty days for getting down the river, with five days' grace. This seemed a reasonable amount of time in the light of others' experience. Their goal was King Island, a speck of land in Chantrey Inlet in the Arctic Ocean. Nanci wanted to be sure that someone would be at King Island to pick them up. She had talked to a group of men who had paddled the Back in 1986 and then hitched a ride on an Inuit fishing boat across forty miles of open water to the village of Gjoa Haven once they were off the river. The men had suggested that the women do the same—just get to King Island and flag down a boat. Nanci did not want to be so casual about getting to Gjoa Haven. She got a commitment from an Inuit fisherman to be at King Island when the women arrived and to ferry them across the Arctic to the village. She packed a two-way radio so they could contact the fisherman when they were certain about their arrival on the island.

The women debated over taking a gun along on the trip. The main reason to carry a gun, they had been told, was for protection from grizzlies. None of them knew how to shoot a gun, however, and they finally agreed that it would be more dangerous to have one than to be without one. They did carry an air horn, figuring the noise might scare off a curious bear. They also carried a flare gun to attract attention to themselves in case they needed help, though they knew the likelihood of someone's seeing their distress signal was not great. They were venturing into an unpopulated area, and there were no settlements on the tundra between Muskox Lake and Chantrey Inlet. The women could spend sixty days watching the land change from rolling chocolate-brown muskegs to flat ridges of stone to sandy eskers without spotting another human being. They had great respect for the river and its power, and they planned to be cautious about running rapids. All of the men they had talked to, and all of the accounts they had read mentioned the challenge of the white water. No expedition that they knew of had gotten down the Back River without dumping at least once.

Other expeditions had arranged for food drops so that they wouldn't lose all their provisions if they lost a canoe. The women decided that they would carry all their food with them. They planned to eat well. They had nine huge packs filled with food, most of which Mary had grown. She spent the summer of 1987 tending a third of an acre at her home in Madison, Wisconsin. She grew assorted vegetables, including beets, zucchini, eggplant, beans and tomatoes, which she harvested and dried for the expedition. She was motivated by the memory of unmemorable meals on past outings and the expense of purchasing dried food. "I couldn't face sixty days of the same gruel," she says. The women planned to grow their own bean and alfalfa sprouts on the trail and to bake bread and bagels from scratch. Kristen, who had worked as a baker, decided that she would start some sourdough early in the trip and use it throughout.

The all-women Back River expedition was thoroughly organized and planned to the last detail that anyone could imagine. When the women arrived by truck in Yellowknife and registered their route with the Royal Canadian Mounted Police, they were all confident that they knew exactly where they were going. They were sure they would get there, and they were thrilled by the prospect of heading off into the wilderness together. As Deb put it: "I feel a strong sense of pride when I'm traveling with a group of women. Now we're allowing ourselves to do these great things together. We take big leaps and go on big adventures."

Part of the planning for the trip included deciding how decisions would be made once the expedition was underway. The women agreed to run daily operations using a technique that the earlier Hood River group had tried. Each woman would take a regular turn as leader of the day. She would wear a rust-and-white sash and carry the expedition's one watch. Her first daily duty would be to make coffee and start breakfast. She would get everyone up in the morning, and she would set a time to camp at night. She was not to act as a dictator; but, rather, her job was to be sure that everyone's opinion was heard. She was responsible for knowing where everyone was and how everyone was feeling.

The Hood River group had adopted the leader-of-the-day technique after a near-disaster on day thirty of that expedition. The women had reached a place in the river where the water cascaded into a huge lake. They had to make a choice between portaging around the whole series of rapids or portaging to a pool where they would paddle in very fast water and then portage again. They chose the two-part portage. When the first canoe began to ferry across the pool, which was at the base of a cascade, the paddlers lost control and nearly capsized. Fortunately, they did not lose the canoe or get swept downstream into the deep gorge below. They escaped their predicament safely, but they were shaken, as was the rest of the group. Immediately, the women gathered to try to reconstruct the events that had led to the incident. They soon discovered that six people had taken one person's word for what was ahead and how to negotiate the river. At the time they made the decision to try to navigate the pool, no one realized that only one person had looked at the route. Somehow, they had the sense that everyone agreed on what to do. In reality, there had been several people who had disagreed with the decision but who had not expressed their opinions. Finally, they spoke up. Communication in the group had broken down, they said; there was generally not enough discussion before decisions were made. Certain people just took on leadership and made assumptions for the whole group.

To make sure that everyone's opinion was heard for the remainder of the expedition, the Hood River women borrowed a technique called "facilitator of the day" from the National Outdoor Leadership School (NOLS), where Deb had been a student and would later become an instructor. The technique, as the women practiced it, was so successful that those who returned to the north country for the Back River trip wanted to use it again. Their companions agreed.

The leader of the day was to be particularly careful that everyone's opinion was heard about whether to shoot white water. At each set of rapids, the whole group would stop to scout the route. Each woman would describe in turn the path she would pick. Then the leader would keep the discussion going until she was sure everyone was thinking the same things and reading the water in the same way.

Serving as leader of the day was bound to be stressful. So the leader had the option of taking the next day off, of taking the position known as "duffer." With three canoes, only six women could paddle, which meant that someone had to "duff" every day. If the most recently retired leader did not choose to be the duffer, the position was up for grabs. The women also decided that they would change paddling partners and tent mates every day to keep everyone in the group mixing together.

Exploring the far reaches of human interaction was just as important to the group as exploring the Arctic wilderness. As they prepared to put their canoes into the Back River for the first time, all of the women anticipated making great discoveries. They were eager to embrace the tundra and all its creatures. They wanted to push all the limits they knew, to feel their bodies grow stronger, their emotions run deeper and their spirits expand under the vast Arctic sky. They wanted to experience life in its most basic form and learn all they could from their sister travelers. Mary, who liked nothing better than to work hard, get her hands dirty and live outside, tried to comprehend all that lay ahead of them: "There's the lighting, the landscape, the spaciousness, the animals, the white water. Being there so long and being there with your small group—you learn so much and you grow so much in that time." The Back River journey promised much to the seven women who had prepared so long. It delivered significantly more.

Day Thirty-five—July 30, 1988

The day was bright and warm on Garry Lake, where the Back River spills out to meet the horizon in every direction.

The seven women were about 300 miles from their destination in the Arctic Ocean. For once, the paddling seemed nearly effortless. The water was calm, and the sun was energizing. The night before had been one of the most wondrous of the trip. All of the women had watched a spectacular moonrise together. Barb described it in her journal: "She was awesome, an astounding sight, light pink and orange, larger than life against a deep dark blue sky. We took a closer look with binoculars and could clearly see her cratered terrain. She was in rare form like I have never witnessed before. And to the northwest the sky was lit by the setting sun traveling just below the horizon. Toward the northern shore, three yellow-billed loons sang and called to each other, creating an amazing, glorious moment. All three boats were still in the calm water—each of us taking the magic of the moment in. A moment I don't ever want to let go, a memory to hold and cherish and refer to when I need to be reminded of the simple wonders of this world, and the beauty that no words could ever truly describe. I can hold those feelings and sights close to me forever and for that I am thankful. I love the Arctic. I love Mother Tundra. No wonder I keep coming back. There is no other place like this. I am fortunate to experience her beauty and challenges. Take the good with the bad. Isn't that what life is all about?"

Barb's reference to taking the good with the bad seemed optimistic in light of what Mother Tundra had thrown the group's way during the first thirty-four days of the Back River expedition. As Michele put it, the journey had not always been sunshine and happy paddling. In fact, the sun had been a fickle, feeble companion, and the paddling had been a struggle when it was not impossible. Mother Tundra had not been the nurturing, caring teacher that the women had imagined. She had not been all mystery and magic. In fact, she had been a raging windbag who sent the women scurrying for their pathetic little tents on most days. She howled and stormed and drove the women to scream back at her. Michele was shocked to find herself getting angry at Mother Tundra. "But there were days when I felt she was just laughing at us."

Mother Tundra laughed in gales, most of them sweeping in from the northwest, losing none of their force across the treeless plain. The powerful winds kicked up waves that were easily capable of swamping the three small canoes. Some days, when the waves seemed slightly less malevolent, the women put their canoes in the water and headed for the strong current. And they sat in the middle of the river, making no progress. The winds pushed against the current to keep the women paddling in place. After countless times of being forced off the river by the wind, the paddlers cried in rage and frustration. They wanted a break, just one day of decent weather. Sometimes they would get a break—the wind would disappear for five minutes. But then it would whoosh in again, from exactly the opposite direction, blowing just as hard.

The women's heads buzzed and echoed with the sound of the wind. They huddled in their sleeping bags while the wind battered their tents. They tried to read or write in their journals. They made bracelets and necklaces out of the beads Deb had brought along; Deb did beadwork on everyone's clothing. They drew pictures and maps. Mary got out her plant press and preserved some of the Arctic wildflowers she had found. They napped. Ellie visualized being at home in her bed with her electric blanket on. Everyone got impatient and edgy.

One of the lowest points of the first thirty-four days of the expedition was an afternoon when they had to stop paddling because of the wind, the rain and the cold. The only place they could go was a grassy beach that had recently been a refuge for hundreds of geese. "We were all really off, in our moods, not communicating very well," Michele says. "We were all thinking we wanted to be anywhere else in the world rather than goose shit beach."

Mother Tundra had not been completely unkind to the seven women on the first half of their expedition down the Back River. She had teased them with just enough of her wonders that they wanted more and were frustrated on the days when they could not even get out of their tents to explore. Barb loved to walk around, finding what she called "little Arctic treasures—beautiful rocks and bones." For Deb, some of the best days passed when she found native artifacts. With each bone or tool that she saw, she thought about the native people who had the land to themselves for so many thousands of years. She imagined how intense their lives must have been in the delicate and harsh tundra, and she longed for the simplicity of such lives. She wondered what threads held their culture together and how the people coped in the vast howling emptiness. Her own culture did not seem rich enough in myth and mystery to sustain human identity in such an inhuman place.

One evening Ellie found a human skull. It was sitting on a sandy beach surrounded by thousands of caribou tracks. The women were amazed that it had not been smashed. Ellie held the skull for a long time. It was paper thin and broken at the nose. She wondered about the person who had preceded her to this place, and she noticed the contrast she felt between discovering animal bones and human bones. As she held this skull, she felt the tug of spirits.

Finding the skull evoked the need for a ritual among the other women. The next morning, they built a cairn in a tent ring (a circle of stones) and set the skull in the center. They thought about the people who had lived on the land where they now stood. Mary had brought books about the native cultures, and Ellie borrowed one to read about burial customs. She read that the people of the tundra could not bury their dead because the ground was frozen. When somebody died, they moved camp.

Rituals of all kinds marked the women's passage down the Back River to the Arctic Ocean. They observed the typical celebrations, like Ellie's twenty-fourth birthday, which occurred on the trip. (She was the youngest paddler; Nanci, at twenty-nine, was the oldest.) They also created their own observances, like the Day of the Muskox to fete their glimpses of that improbable creature of the tundra; they drew names and exchanged gifts, sang songs and watched a puppet show that Nanci presented. They often had group hugs, in which they stood in a circle, arms entwined, and thought about the people back home who supported their adventure and about their own proud, strong spirits.

The biggest thrill for the women was finding themselves in the midst of the caribou migration. They had seen signs of caribou—tracks and bones—and they had also seen individual animals. But one day, they went around a bend in the river and suddenly the usual barrenness of the tundra was gone. The landscape was moving. A great mass of caribou was marching across the horizon, with no beginning and no end. The women were awestruck. Kristen made a circle of her hands and counted the caribou she held. Then she moved that circle across the herd until she estimated that there were thousands of the animals. Nanci was in tears, and Barb, who could not bear the intensity of the moment, whispered to her, "Don't they look like maggots on a big apple?"

The women beached their canoes and got out. They raised their arms over their heads, trying to imitate antlers, and they sneaked up on the herd. They got close enough to feel a part of the migration. The animals, so intent on their journey, seemed not to notice that seven women were running along at the edge of the herd. Eventually, the women went back to their canoes. Their route on the river kept them with the caribou for several days. Each time they put their canoes into the water, they parted masses of caribou hair. They paddled for miles in caribou hair. It looked like ice.

By day thirty-five, all the women had more confidence in their white water skills. No one had dumped despite the challenges that the combination of wind and water presented. At the beginning of the trip, the group was conservative about which rapids to run. But their lack of progress because of the wind made them push harder when they had a chance to get on the water. They became bolder about which rapids to run. Michele marveled as she watched her companions' skills increase. "It always amazed me—I'd look at these women and realize, 'We're competent!'"

Deb, who was one of the more experienced white water paddlers on the trip, loved the rush of running white water. The Back River offered rapids two miles long, with waves up to seven feet high. Deb couldn't have been happier. "There's few things in life that give me that type of thrill," she says. "It's hard to describe the high but it's really something, especially when you're really hanging it out there so far away from help. I know that, when I get to the bottom, if I come out of it upright, I'm going to feel really good."

Kristen, who was the least experienced paddler on the trip, discovered that she loved everything about running white water. She loved the rushes. She loved working with a partner, scouting the rapids and deciding how to maneuver through them. "It is immediate gratification. The problem is set in front of you and you deal with it right away. You see immediate results."

The goal of the group was to accommodate the various levels of white water experience. If two paddlers wanted to shoot a rapid that seemed too much for the rest of the women, the two could take all three boats through it while the rest walked around. Everyone agreed not to take unnecessary chances. And they all tried to remember how powerful the river was. As Mary says, "The Back River is one of the best places for making sure that you never say 'I've got it.' One of the keys to success in white water is not getting too confident."

Mary felt her own skills increasing. She was growing into bigger challenges. "There's a thrill that pushes you, a big thrill," she says. "It's the thrill of taking a risk and succeeding. It's not a blind risk because you have your skill level. Your body and your timing and your partner and your canoe do all the right things at the right time. When it works, you feel it. It's a big ride. It's like you're on a ride at the fair, only you're at the controls."

Communication was key to negotiating the rapids safely. But the group's consensus-centered communication process, while it was aiding success on the river, was frustrating and wearying for everyone involved. Ellie found herself longing for an outside authority: "There were a lot of days when I personally wished that somebody other than the seven of us would come in and say, 'This is the decision. Do it.'" Whoever was leader of the day felt the pressure of making sure the group lived up to its goal of consensus when no one seemed to want to cooperate. The leader had to try to tune in to everyone's feelings and drag into the discussions those who were, for one reason or another, fed up with constant communications. According to Deb: "Some days it was a pain in the butt to be the leader. Because of chemistry we weren't gelling. Or there were difficult weather calls. Or white water calls. Or energy was low. You definitely felt like there was a lot of pressure, definitely felt like you were on stage. It's difficult being a leader in a group of peers. It's demanding when you're out in the wilderness dealing with group safety and group happiness."

Deb herself was moody much of the trip. "I was at a difficult time in my life personally. There were days when I had a hard time communicating with people, days when I felt like I couldn't talk because I was too upset about other things in my life, hard stuff from before the trip that I had a hard time letting go of. It was upsetting me a lot of the time, keeping me from feeling happy or normal."

The group's process did not allow hidden feelings. It demanded honesty from everyone. Moreover, all of the women had experience in working with groups and group dynamics. "It was like having seven psychiatrists on trail," Mary says.

The group's commitment to have everything out in the open caused stress but may have kept the expedition from blowing up. No one's frustrations, with either the weather or the group process or her own self-examination, were allowed to build. Communication was the rule all day every day. Each woman found her own challenge in working through this process. Deb tried to open herself up to and to be open to everyone in the group. "I ended up being able to express myself well to certain people in the group, but some I didn't feel comfortable with," she says. Michele worked on being honest with herself and the rest of the people on the trip. "I didn't always feel the necessity of putting on a happy face," she says. "On a trip like that, there needs to be some clean honesty. That's not easy all the time; it takes a toll."

Michele felt that the paddling and the group process took her to her limits physically and emotionally most days. Yet she was impressed with the way she and her companions were dealing with problems. Spending so much time trying to reach a consensus was exciting to her. It was frustrating, too, but she was proud of the group for sticking with the plan. Her expectations about getting beyond the limitations of gender roles with a group of women were being fulfilled. On past trips in mixed groups, she had seen women take the mothering role and men take the hunter role. She hated that. "Those roles would sort of slip into place and were difficult to get out of." On the Back River, everyone was, in turn, nurturing, strong, timid, aggressive, pacifying, pouting. There was a constant flow and exchange of roles.

The main conflict of the trip came over whether to push to reach King Island, the goal they had originally set, or to alter the goal. After ten days or so on the river, the women realized that at their current pace, they would not finish according to the timetable they had established. They had the first of many discussions about how to proceed. Some in the group wanted to be in the wilderness according to their own internal clocks and not have any time standards imposed; for them, just being out in the wilderness for sixty days was the point, not how far they got. Others wanted to do whatever it took to reach King Island as originally planned. Sometimes it seemed that the more the women debated which course of action to take, the harder the winds blew. Mother Tundra was not going to make the decision any easier. Those who wanted to push for King Island finally relented and said that getting to Chantrey Inlet, the nearest finger of the Arctic Ocean, would be enough. Those who wanted to end the trip after sixty days no matter where they were talked about being flown out.

Ellie was the only one who had a schedule; she had taken a three-month leave of absence from her job and had to be back in Seattle by a certain date. She was definitely in the fly-out-after-sixty-days camp. "I'm lazier than the others," she claims. "I wanted to enjoy it. I didn't want to break my body just to say we got to Chantrey Inlet."

Kristen was in the Chantrey-Inlet-or-bust camp. She urged the group to be creative and to push. She became a cheerleader and came up with creative ways of getting more mileage out of everyone. One calm afternoon, when she could see that everyone was tired, she suggested that they switch partners every hour. This gave them an additional five or six hours on the river. "I like to finish things that I start," she says. "It was really important to put my all into it and see if we couldn't finish."

After much discussion, everyone agreed to do what she could to get to Chantrey Inlet. Michele was surprised that what she considered a macho attitude would win the day. "The trip became real goal-oriented for me," she said. "We lost sight of the process and became goal-oriented. I was disappointed by it, although I bought into it as much as anyone else. It's really hard to fight against that sort of energy. It became a constant drive to finish the trip."

Besides the physical challenge of pushing their bodies to the limit every day, the decision to go for Chantrey Inlet required the sacrifice of time to explore, to walk, to write, to wander about alone. It added pressure to an already pressure-packed trip.

The women constantly had to reevaluate where they were and how hard they had to push to reach Chantrey Inlet on time. The winds seemed most days to be pushing back as hard as the women pushed forward. Each day the women would sit in a circle and recommit themselves to their goal. Everyone would speak her piece. Kristen often thought that the amount of time they spent talking at each juncture was one of the biggest reasons they were so far behind schedule. But she listened to everyone in turn after she did her bit to rally the group to push to the end.

By day thirty-five, Mother Tundra seemed to have bent to the women's will to make their goal. She sent such sunshine and calm water that the women paddled for fifteen miles in one day. Had they been able to do that every day, their destination would be less than a hundred miles away instead of the 300 that it was. Deb took a break from paddling to fish, and she caught two big trout. Everyone talked about how good those fish would taste for dinner. They also looked forward to preparing their usual gourmet meal in favorable conditions instead of having to fight the wind. Their plan was to find a place to camp, to cook a great dinner and to sleep soundly under the stars.

Everyone was feeling so good that when a great sand cliff came into view, the idea to stop and leap from the top of it was irresistible. They beached the canoes and scrambled to the top of the esker. The feeling of running along the top and then leaping, sure of a soft landing in the sand below, was delicious. Soon Deb and Barb, old friends from junior high days, were having a contest to see who could leap the farthest. They ran as fast as they could, tucked their legs under and flew. Each jump was farther. Barb was determined to win the contest and on her final jump felt herself rocketing toward victory. Unfortunately, when she landed, she tumbled face-first down the esker. She knew right away that she had done some serious damage to her leg. The pain shot up from her ankle to her knee. She started screaming and crying. Her first thought was that she would have to be airlifted out and that the trip would be ruined. She then thought about how selfish she was, putting the whole group in jeopardy because she had wanted to jump higher.

Her companions were most concerned about doing what they could to minimize the damage she had caused to her leg. They had just paddled past a snowfield, so two of them ran back to get the makings for an ice pack. Since they were all trained in first aid, they knew exactly what to do. They set up camp and got Barb calmed down and her leg elevated and iced. All reassured her that they were not angry with her. She protested that she had let them down. They told her not to be so hard on herself. They discussed their predicament. Could they keep going with an injured paddler? They decided that if Barb thought she could continue, the rest of them could pick up her share of the work. They had a duffer's seat in one canoe that she could claim as long as she needed to. She would have to let herself be taken care of and resist the urge to do more than her injured leg would allow. Barb agreed to continue, knowing that her inability to contribute would be the biggest challenge yet of the trip for her. Mother Tundra apparently meant for her to learn even more about taking the good with the bad.

Day Sixty-four—August 28, 1988

The day was gray, cold and windy on King Island in Chantrey Inlet. The seven women, confidently calling themselves the Back River Upright Expedition since they had completed the white water portion of their trip without once dumping, had reached their original destination on the day of the original plan—day sixty. Their journey, however, was not over on that day. Mother Tundra insisted that they extend their stay; she sent in another big wind, which made travel impossible for the small boat that was to pick the women up. Now, four days past the time when they planned to be on their way home, the seven stranded paddlers were hungry and edgy.

Reaching their destination had not been easy. Barb had suffered from her inability to be fully useful to the group. She had struggled to learn to live with her injury and the limits it imposed on her. When the group arrived at a portage, six of them would take off with gear and Barb would stay back and organize the next load. Then she would start hobbling across, empty-handed. At the end of the portage, she packed the gear into the canoes and got the canoes into the water. That was all she could do. She hated not being a pack animal like the others. "Portaging is a lot of the hard work, a lot of the sweat and the aches and pains," she says. "After a portage, they would stop and talk and laugh. I felt really left out." She got as many of her frustrations out as she could by writing in her journal. She also talked to Nanci about what she was feeling. Her leg was healing, and by the time the group reached King Island, she was able to carry her own pack.

Barb's injury was not the only medical emergency of the trip. About five days after Barb hurt her leg, the women began to notice that Michele was not looking right. The whites of her eyes had a yellow cast to them. She admitted that she had been feeling tired and nauseated for about a week. Because she had not wanted to let the group down, she had pushed herself. She felt that her strength was nearly gone. Watching the others eat their gourmet meals sickened her. The women looked up Michele's symptoms, which also included brown urine, in their first aid book. They fit the description for hepatitis. Kristen was familiar with the disease; her mother has chronic hepatitis, so she knew how serious it could be. She also knew that the disease is highly contagious.

Michele was concerned about long-term damage to her liver and about infecting the group. She separated her dishes from everyone else's, marking her own plate, spoon and water bottle.

After several group discussions, during which the women spent much time pondering what to do if Michele had to be flown out, whether she would go alone or everyone would accompany her, they decided to try to get through to Kristen's father, a doctor in North Dakota. To reach him, they radioed

Dave Olesen at his Great Slave Lake homestead. They described Michele's symptoms to Dave and told him to ask Dr. Gilbertson whether she needed to be evacuated. After several North Dakota-Great Slave Lake-Back River relays, they were satisfied that Michele could safely stay on the trip. Dr. Gilbertson said there was nothing to do to treat Michele and that she sounded as if she were on the mend. He suggested that she lighten her workload and watch for any worsening of symptoms. He predicted she would be better in a week.

In fact, Michele seemed to improve as soon as the message relaying was over, almost as if she had been relieved of a burden. Just having a name to attach to her exhaustion and nausea was comforting. She took four days off, letting the others paddle. Then her appetite came back and she began to regain her strength. She recovered quickly. She was glad she had kept pushing during the worst times and that she was still on the Back River. "There were numerous times I wanted to leave the trip; I thought what the hell am I doing here," she says. "But those thoughts were pretty fleeting."

The women were spending every moment that the weather and their own endurance allowed on the river. They were all caught up in the drive to reach Chantrey Inlet on schedule. They had planned their food to cover sixty-five days in the wilderness, but they had been taking from that extra five days' supply to supplement some of their meals; they were working so hard that they were ravenous. Each night when they looked at the map to estimate how much farther they had to go, the realization grew that there was no way to ride the river to Chantrey Inlet by day sixty. But the map seemed to indicate a shortcut, a fork of the Back River that ran north instead of east with the main channel. They knew of no one who had taken this fork; they knew nothing about it except what they saw on the map, but they decided to follow it to the Arctic Ocean.

Part way to the ocean, the fork disappeared into the tundra, forcing the women to portage. Fortunately, this task was made easier by a series of tiny lakes that stretched to the ocean. After a full day of lake-hopping, they arrived on Chantrey Inlet, a southern bay of the Arctic.

The day that the Back River Upright Expedition reached the ocean, Mother Tundra held her breath. The sun radiated heat. The seven women began to relax, knowing that they were going to get to King Island, which was only fifteen or twenty miles away, and that they would soon be home. They had accomplished something that would sustain them for all the rest of their lives. Michele says: "When we finally did reach the ocean, I felt a lot of love for where I was and a lot of love for the group. I felt we had reached our goal. I felt really good about having completed something so incredible."

The women decided to let up a bit to enjoy their introduction to the ocean and the break in the weather. Some took walks. Others paddled to see the sights. Michele, Nanci and Kristen decided to paddle close to a sandy beach and look for wolf prints. They found some and began to giggle with excitement. Then they looked up and saw a wolf standing on an escarpment looking down at them. According to Michele, "She was the queen there. We didn't present any threat. There was no fear. She trotted along, then threw her head over her shoulder and looked at us one last time. All three of us just burst into tears. It was so powerful to see this creature. I didn't feel in that awful position of having a creature be afraid of us humans. She just proudly walked away."

The good weather did not hold; nevertheless, the expedition landed on King Island on day sixty. Everyone was elated. Everyone was also ready to leave the Arctic, to return to her individual life. They had radioed for the Inuit fishing boat to come from Gjoa Haven, the village across forty miles of ocean to the north, to pick them up. They placed bets on when Saul and Ben, the fishermen, would arrive. This was on August 24th. Mary was the least optimistic and predicted that their water taxi would pick them up at 11 a.m. on the 25th.

Mother Tundra, however, was not finished with the group. Another of her winds made the forty miles of open water between Gjoa Haven and King Island impassable for the fishing boat. The women were on the radio to Gjoa Haven every three hours to see whether conditions there had changed enough for the fishermen to start across the water. The report was always the same: blowing in Gjoa Haven. The women joked bitterly that no matter what the weather was doing anywhere else, they could count on blowing in Gjoa Haven.

Mary's pessimistic pick-up time passed. The wind kept blowing. Barb and Mary prepared the last of the gourmet dinners—egg rolls. They were hunched over in the dark, trying to block the wind enough to make egg roll batter. The next morning, Deb was scheduled to prepare their last big breakfast—sourdough pancakes. The women had been talking about eating these sourdough pancakes for a long time. When the pancakes were gone, tea and soup would be the only provisions left. In the windy dawn, Deb accidentally put salt in the pancake batter instead of sugar. She desperately tried to salvage the batter by mixing in Koolaid. It was hopeless. She woke the six others to a breakfast of tea and soup.

The wind kept blowing, giving the women no peace, whipping their edginess into a froth. After several days of this, everyone was losing weight and energy. The constant wind made exploration impossible. The island was tiny; crossing it on foot took ten minutes. There the women were again hunkered down in their little tents, listening to them flap in the wind. They would make the effort to gather three times a day for tea and soup. They would sing and tell stories and then return to their separate tents to knit, write, read, talk and wait.

Kristen took a walk one day looking for food. She returned to camp holding a ptarmigan's carcass in the palm of her hand. She had stoned the bird, cleaned it and skinned it out. "Look, you guys, dinner," she said. They made a ptarmigan stew.

Because they had the radio, the paddlers were in contact

with the Royal Canadian Mounted Police. The Mounties arranged for a food drop after the women had been stranded on the island for several days. They made giant cheeseburgers and ate half of what the Mounties had dropped right away. Some in the group were sick the next day.

Seeing the Mounties fly over with food increased the pressure that some of the women were exerting to radio for a plane to pick up the whole group. Ellie, who had a job to get back to, was all for flying out and had lost patience with the group process. She was kicking and screaming about being stranded. "I wasn't going to do anything to make it more pleasant," she says.

As the women were arguing over what to do and trying to find ways to cope with being windbound on the Arctic and calling to Gjoa Haven for a wind report every three hours, an Inuit man, who was camped nearby on Chantrey Inlet, heard their radio messages. He decided to visit the women on their tiny island and to take his whole family along. His name was Mark Tootiak. Nevee, his wife, was with him, as were their three daughters, Anna, Belinda and Christine, and their son Jason. Also in the group were Christine's infant son, Kyle, and Arjan, the baby's father. The family lived in Gjoa Haven and was out for two weeks of gathering caribou caches for the winter.

The Tootiaks arrived on King Island on day sixty-four of the women's expedition. They set up two big white tents and immediately offered flour, tobacco and tea to the seven stranded women. The two groups talked and played cards. The women fussed over the children, braiding their hair and going for walks with them.

The Tootiaks' progress was also stymied by the winds, but they didn't seem concerned. They certainly were not frustrated. Instead, they calmly accepted their current circumstances. Michele was struck by the contrast between them and her own group. "I felt like this disgusting middle-class white woman who had the money to call in a plane to get herself out of this predicament. I felt uncomfortable with all the possibilities I had. I compared myself with the Inuit family. They just didn't have that kind of choice. This was their land, their home. There we were, big white women coming in and barging in on their territory because we wanted this magical experience. And there we were flipping out and frustrated because we couldn't leave on time."

All the women in the Back River expedition were aware of the Tootiaks' incredible patience. They tried to adopt their accepting ways, telling themselves that they could not change the fact that there was no food or that some would be late for work or that their families did not know where they were. They tried to find joy in the present moment.

Soon after the Tootiaks arrived, the same day, in fact, they organized a caribou hunt. The women had seen one lone caribou on the island. At dusk on day sixty-four, everyone—the whole Tootiak family and the seven members of the Back River Upright Expedition—set out to find that animal and to kill it for food.

Belinda Tootiak, who was ten, spotted the caribou. It looked young; it was probably a yearling. The whole human pack moved in on the animal. Mark handed thirteen-year-old Jason the gun. Jason fired, and the caribou fell to its knees. When it struggled to its feet and started to limp away, Jason fired again. Mark approached the stricken beast and plunged his knife into its head.

"My heart dropped to hear the sound of a big rifle," Deb says. "At the same time I was completely fascinated by what we were doing. We really needed food. But what a primeval thing the hunt is. Even though I'm a vegetarian by and large, I believe in eating meat like that—where you can work and hunt it. Where you appreciate the fact that this animal has given its life for you. I believe it has done that. The caribou was meant for us."

After the group carried the animal back to camp and began

skinning it, the women asked if they could have the heart. Kristen knew that the heart and the tongue were good, and the Tootiaks didn't appear interested in those parts. The women watched hungrily as the Tootiaks finished dressing the animal. They were disappointed when the family said goodnight. They had thought the caribou feast would happen right away. They had their own separate feast, however. They retreated to their campfire and cooked and ate the young caribou's heart.

Day Seventy-two—September 5, 1988

The quality of the weather was finally irrelevant. The seven members of the Back River Upright Expedition were aboard a Coast Guard icebreaker, a vessel that appeared in that part of Chantrey Inlet once every three years. Its timing was perfect— the expedition members had been windbound for twelve days. They were picked up by helicopter and taken aboard. They were now on their way to Gjoa Haven and, from there, home.

Six days earlier, they had thought they were heading home. They were on King Island with the Tootiak family, picnicking on caribou, singing and laughing in the afternoon sun when Ben and Saul arrived in the fishing boat to pick them up. They packed their gear, and the Tootiaks did, too. The two parties hadn't been on the waters of the inlet for very long, however, before another big wind blew in. They raced for an abandoned Inuit hunting camp, where they stayed in a large platform tent and slept on caribou and muskox furs. They were stranded there for another four days. After one more short move, they were yet again stopped by high winds. One night in a particularly ferocious wind, the Tootiaks lost one of their boats and all the caribou meat and clothing that was in it. The wooden boat had been beached, but the waves blew in and smashed it to bits. The women were horrified that the family had lost so much of its food for the winter, but the Tootiaks showed no anger, frustration or worry. They shrugged off the loss. That's just the way it was.

When the Coast Guard icebreaker steamed into view, the women all knew that their Arctic adventure was finally over. They were scooped up and put aboard what appeared to be a luxury liner, offering showers, clean clothes, cold beer, fresh fruit and anything else they wanted. Even as they began to shed the smells of the wilderness and replenish their bodies with food and rest, they began to miss the Back River. They all had been changed by their experience. The time with the Tootiaks had taught them profound lessons about their own impatience and desire to control events. "It left a lasting mark," Nanci says. "I understood something that I hadn't before. I understood that I really couldn't do anything about it, that some things were just beyond my control."

"I learned that my patience has its limits," Barb says. "I did get pretty frustrated. But there's nothing to do about the weather. You just have to deal with it. I've carried that with me. You're powerless. All you can do is put up shelter, put on hot water, make hot drinks and try to be as comfortable with it as you can."

Each member of the Back River Upright Expedition carried her own version of the trip in her heart and would take sustenance from the experience in the years to come. Each one was going back to a life that she now saw in a different way, with more clarity and objectivity.

Nanci had spent a lot of time on the trip thinking about motherhood and whether having a baby would restrict her freedom to do the things she loved. She looked at her friend Nina Koch, who had been on the Hood River trip in 1984 and had dropped out of the Back River trip because of the demands of motherhood. She concluded that she could have a child and depend on her husband to share equally in child-rearing, leaving room for her own pursuits.

Ellie, who was already a week late getting back to her job, had learned that tardiness was a small price to pay for the experience she had had in the Arctic.

Mary, who knew before she went on the trip that she had to concentrate on what was going on in her surroundings so that she would not go stir crazy inside her own mind, was already thinking about the next expedition and how she would do it differently. The next time, she thought, she would take small motors, a two-burner Coleman stove and wall tents that a woman could stand in should she happen to be stuck in one spot for days at a time. She would take a fishing net to scoop up fish when lures weren't working. And she would probably take a gun to shoot animals for food.

Barb came away feeling like the most competent person in the world. "When you come off a trip like that, your confidence level is so high—like I'm capable of doing anything I want."

Michele knew that being stranded at the end of the trip had changed her whole way of looking at life. "I look back and know that there's only now, really. Being stranded at the end made me learn how to just be there now and take everything in every moment and be amazed by everything that is happening and not be constantly steps ahead of myself and concerned about what is going to happen next."

For Deb, the trip had been an epic experience. The last two weeks had presented a challenge unlike any other she had faced in the wilderness. On previous trips she had enjoyed the fact that each day was different and required pulling new tricks out of her hat. "But on the Back at the end, the hat was nearly empty. Our destiny was more out of control than I'd ever felt." She also learned from her traveling companions that she could be herself, even if that meant being upset and moody. "Communication is something that doesn't come easy for me. I've had to learn good ways of expressing myself. That requires taking risks, and it can hurt. The trip required a lot of that. It was a unique group. We were pretty intimate with each other and very open and revealing of our strengths and weaknesses. You don't often do that in every day life. The Back River was one of the best things I've ever done in my life, despite how hard it was. I love all those women very much and have a great deal of respect for every one of them. We did a great job of pulling together and sticking together as a group despite great rifts. We tried hard to respect each other. We cared about each other. We tried not to let goals and hang-ups get in the way."

Kristen, the newcomer to extended river trips, got more from the experience than she had imagined she would. She felt different about herself at the end—confident, happy and whole, like she was on top of the world. She had learned to be bolder about expressing her feelings. "Before, if something was bothering me, I never could find the right words to be angry or to express myself. I found I had to do that on the trip." She had formed a bond with the other women on the trip that she felt would last her lifetime. "It was a big, big deal," she says.

The journey down the Back River was a milestone for all the members of the expedition. As the women returned to their everyday lives, they took an extra dimension with them. No matter what happened, they could think of themselves in the vast Arctic, riding big water, running with thousands of caribou, calling with the loons at moonrise, staring into the yellow eyes of a she-wolf, laughing with an Inuit family and, above all, feeling their hearts open to everyone and everything around them.

About the Author

Linda Lewis is a writer and editor who "got the religion of rowing at age forty." She has worked as a journalist for the *Rochester Times-Union* and the *Seattle Post-Intelligencer* and is a former book sales representative. She lives in Seattle.

Selected Titles from Seal Press

UNCOMMON WATERS: *Women Write About Fishing* edited by Holly Morris. $14.95, 1-878067-10-9 This wonderful anthology captures the bracing adventure and meditative moments of fishing in the words of thirty-four women anglers—from finessing trout and salmon in the Pacific Northwest to chasing bass and catfish in the Deep South.

HARD-HATTED WOMEN: *Stories of Struggle and Success in the Trades* edited by Molly Martin. $12.95, 0-931188-66-0 Women employed in nontraditional work—ironworkers, carpenters, firefighters and more—vividly describe their daily experiences on the job.

GETTING THE REAL STORY: *Nellie Bly & Ida B. Wells* by Sue Davidson. $8.95, 1-878067-16-8 Written in a simplified format that engages the interest of adults learning to read as well as young adult readers, these inspiring stories follow the lives of two women, each born in the 1860s, each overcoming sex and race barriers to become pioneering journalists.

CLOSER TO HOME: *Bisexuality and Feminism* edited by Elizabeth Reba Weise. $14.95, 1-878067-17-6 This dynamic collection gives voice to a bold new movement of women who are demanding recognition for the truth of their lives—for their attraction, desire and love for both sexes.

GETTING FREE: *You Can End Abuse and Take Back Your Life* by Ginny NiCarthy. $12.95 0-931188-37-7 The most important self-help book in the movement to end domestic violence, *Getting Free* offers support, practical help and inspiration.

ANOTHER AMERICA by Barbara Kingsolver. $10.95, 1-787067-09-5 (paper), $14.95, 1-878067-15-X (cloth) A beautiful collection of poetry exploring themes of courage and resistance by the author of *The Bean Trees* and *Animal Dreams*.

Seal Press, founded in 1976 to provide a forum for women writers and feminist issues, has many other books of fiction, non-fiction and poetry. You may order directly from us at 3131 Western Avenue, Suite 410, Seattle, WA 98121 (add 15% of total book order for shipping and handling). Write to us for a free catalog or if you would like to be on our mailing list.